Lily Brett was born in Germany and came to Melbourne with her parents in 1948. Her first book, *The Auschwitz Poems*, won the 1987 Victorian Premier's Award for poetry, and both her fiction and poetry have won other major prizes, including the 1995 NSW Premier's Award for fiction for *Just Like That*. Lily Brett is married to the Australian painter David Rankin. They have three children and currently live in New York.

Also by Lily Brett

FICTION

Things Could Be Worse
What God Wants
Just Like That

POETRY

The Auschwitz Poems
Poland and Other Poems
After the War
Unintended Consequences
In Her Strapless Dresses
Mud in My Tears

In
full
view

—essays by—

Lily Brett

PICADOR
Pan Macmillan Australia

First published 1997 in Macmillan by Pan Macmillan Australia Pty Limited
First published 1998 in Picador by Pan Macmillan Australia Pty Limited
St Martins Tower, 31 Market Street, Sydney

National Library of Australia
Cataloguing-in-Publication data:
Brett, Lily, 1946– .
In full view.

ISBN 0 330 36086 8.

1. Brett, Lily, 1946– . 2. Authors, Australian – 20th
century – Biography. I. Title.

A824.3

Typeset in 11/15 pt Bembo by Midland Typesetters
Printed in Australia by McPherson's Printing Group

for Gypsy G.L.
on her twenty-first birthday

I wanted to resurrect the thread
that stitched us head to head
heart to heart

CONTENTS

AGEING

AGEING, I THOUGHT, WAS SOMETHING that happened to older people.

Soon after I moved to New York, I went to a concert by the pianist Daniel Barenboim at the Lincoln Center. I was very excited. I'd been playing his recording of Beethoven's *La Pathetique* in my Peugeot everywhere I drove in Melbourne. It was the first piece of music I had grown to love. It was the only piece of music I listened to.

Listening to music was new to me. For a lot of my life, I couldn't bear to listen to any music. I needed silence. Every time I took the cassette out of its box, I looked at Daniel Barenboim, dark, brooding and handsome, on the cover.

Daniel Barenboim came onto the stage to deafening applause. I wasn't the only one who was excited about seeing him. The audience clapped and clapped. I sat there numb. Daniel Barenboim was stocky and grey. When the applause died down, I turned to my husband and said in a shaky whisper, 'I thought he was dark.'

'We were all dark, once,' my husband said.

I think I thought ageing was something that happened to other people. And, in a way, it does. We are not who we used to be. I look at photographs of myself at twenty. My hair is ironed straight. I have thick black eyeliner above and below my eyes. I am wearing a long, psychedelic-patterned dress and bells around my ankles and wrists.

Who was I? What was I thinking? I must have thought I looked great. I remember feeling pleased with my diamante-lined false eyelashes. I remember my father crying when he looked at me. I had painted small, black hearts across my cheekbones. 'What happened to my daughter?' he said. 'Where is my daughter?'

Where was I? I don't know. I was buried under a mountain of pancake make-up, blusher, mascara and lashes. I was also buried under pounds of fat. Fat covered me like a comfortable blanket, except it wasn't very comfortable. It coated me and protected me. I felt encased and safe. Safe from whom? From what? It would take me decades to work that out.

And who was I in another photograph? I am smiling

in a hospital bed. I am dressed in a white lace Victorian nightgown. My hair is parted in the middle. I am holding my newborn son. I am a picture of serenity. Who was I? I was twenty-two. And all the mess was covered up, as it can be when you're twenty-two, by fearlessness, by innocence, by good skin, good hair and the right shade of lipstick.

My son is twenty-seven now. He's one of the great joys in my life. Why did I have him? Why did I have an IUD removed and set out to get pregnant at twenty-one? I had no idea why, then. For years afterwards, I wondered why I so adamantly wanted to have a child. I was a child myself.

I think it had something to do with sabotage. The sabotage of myself. I had a successful career. I was a rock journalist. I'd travelled the world interviewing rock stars: Jimi Hendrix, the Who, the Mamas and Papas, Janis Joplin, Sonny and Cher, the Doors. Everybody who was anybody in the rock world. In Australia I was also on television and radio. I think the success was too much for me. I couldn't wait to give it all up. Of course, I didn't know I was doing that.

I was so thrilled to give birth to a boy. I was ecstatic. I couldn't believe my luck. I thought our family didn't have boys. I thought they lost boys. My mother lost a son, in the Lodz ghetto. She lost four brothers in Auschwitz, and she aborted a small boy, in shame, in Melbourne after the war.

In Guys Hospital, in London, I couldn't sleep. I

3

stayed up for two days and two nights looking, with amazement, at my beautiful boy. Several days later I was even more amazed. I realised I had to take him home with me. I hadn't thought further than giving birth to the baby I wanted. I certainly hadn't thought of taking him home. What was I thinking?

I wasn't thinking about my mother. Now, I think part of the reason I had my son was my mother. I wanted to give her the sons she'd lost. I wanted to give her some of her family back. I wanted to give her the grandchildren she never dreamt she'd live to see when she was lying, near-naked, ablaze with typhoid on the frozen ground at Stuthof, where she was sent after Auschwitz.

My baby boy made a big difference to my mother. She fell in love with him. And he fell in love with her. When she introduced him to people, she said, 'My son.' Sometimes, when I was there, she corrected herself: 'My grandson,' she would say.

Ten years ago, when she lay dying of cancer at sixty-four, she wanted him at her side. And he wanted to be there. Did I know about the fierce love that would grow between my mother and my son? The love that would fill gaps and dreams. I don't know.

I didn't know much then. I didn't know why I got married, the first time around. I married someone I'd met when I was nineteen. He was tall and blond. He was as Aryan as you could get. Later, when his blond hair darkened, I bleached it right back.

The second time I married, I was thirty-four. And I knew why I was getting married. I was crazy about him. I was crazy about a man who was a stranger. I fell in love with him minutes after I met him. What did I know? I knew something. I'm still crazy about him.

Recently, my younger daughter asked me how I could have fallen in love with someone I hardly knew. It was a hard question. I stumbled around, talking about what we unconsciously perceive and understand about each other. But she wasn't satisfied. And she was right. I didn't have an answer. I don't have an answer to many things. I thought I would. I thought age brought answers. It does. But not all the answers.

I have some answers. And so I should – I've spent half my adult life in analysis. Anyone who's read my books will know the head count. Three analysts. Many years. It has been a crucial part of my life. One that both separated me from others and gave me a greater insight into other lives, as well as my own. For most of those years, I knew no one in analysis. When I began, my mother wept and said I was casting shame over the whole family. My father said he'd heard shocking things about my analyst.

I dedicated my first book of fiction to my second analyst. I named a child after my first, and my next book will be dedicated to my last analyst. Analysis saved me. It saved me from being the least I could be. It wasn't easy. I've travelled to analysis sessions early in the morning, four times a week, in different parts of the world. In hot weather, in below-freezing temperatures, in snow-storms and in pouring rain. I've walked, driven and bussed. I've cried gallons of tears. I've wept everywhere it's possible to weep. On the bus, in the car, on the streets.

But I made it. The better part of me emerged. The part of me that feels entitled to have a life. To live without paying a price. And I'm grateful. I'm surprised at how much gratitude I feel. I feel grateful for things I didn't notice or understand in the past. A new sense of perspective came with the gratitude.

Last year, in an acceptance speech for an award, I said that my novel *Just Like That* was a celebration of love:

A celebration of the lives of my mother and father who survived Auschwitz. And a celebration of the fact that my mother and my father, who lost everyone they loved in Auschwitz, did not lose the ability to love.

My mother and father survived five years in the Lodz ghetto before being transported to Auschwitz, where they were separated from each other, but not separated from their love for each other. It took them six months after the war to find each other, and they are a rare statistic – two Jewish people who were married to each other before the war, each surviving. I was very lucky to grow up in the middle of that love.

I wrote this speech very soon after being told I had won the award. I knew, and quite surprised myself by how sure I was, that it was my parents' ability to love that saved not only them, after the war, but me. It took me years to see how lucky I was to experience that love. I spent decades dwelling on what was missing. I spent decades wishing we weren't surrounded by the dead, by past and future Nazis, by anguish and absence.

I'm also surprised at how lucky I feel. Feeling lucky has always felt dangerous. So I've preoccupied myself with what's wrong. Once I start thinking about what's wrong, I can shuck off the discomfort that feeling lucky brings.

But I do feel lucky. Lucky to be married to the man I'm married to. Lucky to have my children. Lucky to have lived long enough to see my children grown up. When they were younger, I dreaded dying before they'd done enough growing. I kept detailed diaries of their childhoods, and of my feelings for them, in case I wasn't around to remind them of their past. It wasn't that I was ill. I never even caught colds, but I did catch the notion of death accompanying love. And that was true for my parents. Everyone they were related to died; everyone they loved died.

I allowed myself to feel lucky so rarely that the moments stand out. When my son was small, he said to his best friend, within earshot of his best friend's mother, 'My mother is much nicer than your mother.' I was told this by the mother. When I stopped laughing, I felt very lucky to have a kid who thought that.

I feel lucky to have written the books I've written.

I didn't finish high school. I threw my education away. It was only one of the valuable things I discarded. I was in the A-form at University High School, a school for bright kids, when, seemingly out of the blue, I couldn't understand anything any teacher said. I was sixteen.

I spent the next three years trying to pass the final year of high school. I couldn't read any of the textbooks. Nothing I read made sense. Words and paragraphs swam around the page. One year I would pass French, Economics and English, the next year I would fail all three and pass something else. Another year, I gave up and went to the movies when some of the exams were on. I never managed to pass the requisite number of the right subjects in the one year.

In retrospect, I realised I was having a nervous breakdown of sorts. Nobody was troubled by it at the time. My parents were bothered, and very puzzled, but they had greater concerns about me. I was too fat. I had to lose weight. So the failing and flailing of a bright young girl went largely unnoticed. No teacher commented on it. In fact the Economics teacher said, after I failed Economics the first time around, that he would rather I didn't come back to his class. He said I was a disruption in the classroom.

I was shocked and hurt. I thought I was good at economics. I used to be, before my decline. How I was a disruption wasn't clear to me. I guess it must have been my chatting. I was always chatting.

In school photographs I look bright and cheerful.

Over the years, when I've met people I went to University High School with, they tell me they remember me always cheerful, always laughing. What was I laughing about? Why was I looking so cheerful when I was so clearly in trouble?

I stopped trying to study and got a job as a journalist. Boy was I lucky to land that job. At the job interview, no one asked me if I could write. They wanted to know if I had a car. I said yes, a pink Valiant. I got the job. Soon I was writing page after page of the newspaper, every week. And I hardly saw my car again.

Feeling lucky still has an edge to it. I don't want to push my luck. So, I filter and dilute my days with odd complaints and aches, and let the heady giddiness of feeling lucky seep in in bits and pieces.

I'm forty-nine now, and I can feel lucky. Physically, I've changed too. I'm older and lighter. I weigh less than I did when I was twelve, but I was a bit of a hefty twelve-year-old. I've been regaining my body, which was lost to me for years.

I have uncomfortable memories. Me, at nineteen, a rock journalist at the Monterey Pop festival in California. I'm wearing a nylon orange and yellow spotted dress. The dress is loose, designed to flow around and over my hips. It has short sleeves that are obviously too tight. They weren't too tight when I'd last worn the dress, and when I put it on I was shocked and depressed by the fact that the sleeves were strangling my flesh. I'm interviewing Eric Burdon and trying to suck my breath in, as though holding my breath will lessen the width of my arms. It's hot and I feel awful.

The same year, another scene. I'm interviewing Sonny and Cher in their house in Los Angeles. Cher is wearing barely anything. She's all shoulders and midriff and legs. She admires my purple false eyelashes. She asks me where I got them. I can't answer. I'm too distracted by my chafed thighs, red and sore from perpetually brushing against each other.

I had succeeded in making my body ugly and almost obsolete. It seemed my brain was the only part of me I used, and I could have done a better job with that. I thought fast and spoke with reasonable speed, but everything else about me was slow. I walked slowly. I never played sport. I didn't dance. When I look at photographs of myself, I want to cry. I look awful. I never looked at my body. After the shower, if I passed a mirror, I'd look the other way. I never touched my body. I thought I was lucky if someone else thought I felt nice.

I created this havoc with myself because of a complicated confluence of history and family. Death camps, starvation, greed, a beautiful mother who'd lost everything except her looks. It was a heady brew. I took my regular, symmetrical, attractive features, and I huffed and puffed until I'd distorted myself and resembled somebody else. And in that other person, I was free to feel peaceful.

Feeling free is not easy for me, still. 'Freedom was never something you let yourself get away with for very long,' my first analyst wrote to me, fifteen years ago.

'You're much freer now,' says my younger daughter, who is home from college for the weekend, looking over my shoulder as I type. 'You can dance, too,' she says. 'You never used to dance.' She's right. I can dance. 'You can get out on the dance floor and have a wonderful time,' she says. I smile at her. 'You're much calmer, too,' she says. 'It's easier to tell you when I don't like something. I don't think the world will fall apart or anything.'

I understand exactly what she's saying. She's always been a good kid. Too good. I used to worry that she felt she had to be good. That I had too many demons to deal with without her adding to the distress. Last year I bought her a T-shirt. It read, 'No More Ms Nice Person'.

The former Ms Nice Person looks at the title of this piece. 'I think you've gotten older *and* younger,' she says. 'I think you take more risks than you used to. You're more curious, more confident.'

This is my baby who's talking. The child who, despite the fact that she's 5'8" and in her final year of college, I can't stop feeling is still my small girl.

'Yes,' she looks at me and says, 'you're not so scared of things. You've worked through a lot of sad things. You've worked through the pain of your mother's death, and you've got a great friendship with Grampa. And you've had the power and strength to finish a very intensive analysis.'

I've stopped writing and am just staring at her. How can she sum up my life like this? 'You growing has helped me to grow up,' she says.

Grown up. I feel grown up. Now, I can rock and roll to Little Richard, turning and whirling and laughing, and feel very grown up. I have the freedom to be silly, to jump, to ride a bicycle, to not *think* about what anyone thinks.

This freedom, this ability to feel my body, to be excited by my body, started in very small ways, over a decade ago. It progressed very slowly, more slowly than my analysis, with which it was inextricably woven.

I began by walking. One block, two blocks, three blocks. It was a foreign experience. I was like my father. He drove the car to the milk bar, seven houses away.

Our family wasn't big on movement. Movement of the mouth, maybe, but not sport, exercise. Where would that get you? Certainly not into law school, where my parents hoped I was headed.

At Lee Street Primary School in Carlton, someone suggested I go to gym classes. I was eight years old and chubby. I went once. A woman told me to swing from a rope. Everyone before me, one by one, had swung from this rope. I couldn't. I couldn't lift my legs off the ground.

I never went back to the gym. I couldn't see why I should. How was swinging from a rope going to help me? Would it help me avoid the sex that went on in the lane after school? I didn't think so. In the afternoons,

I walked as fast as I could past whichever poor girl was being fucked in the lane by one of the bigger boys in the school. My heart pounded. I held my breath and hoped I was invisible.

It was bad enough being masturbated by one of those big boys at the school assembly in the morning. As we sat cross-legged on the floor, listening to a teacher speak, many of us girls had boys' hands down our pants. I've often wondered why nobody noticed.

But it wasn't an age of notice or concern or thought, in many ways. We had kids of all ages in our class. The older kids were there because they couldn't speak English. I remember being frightened by the huge patches of blood that would appear on the back of Ada's dress from time to time. I thought she was dying.

I spent a lot of my time at Lee Street pretending that I wasn't scared. I was counter-phobic. Years later, all the fears would surface, and I would become phobic. A fear of the streets was one of my phobias. Now I walk the streets of Manhattan every day.

I power-walk across the Westside Highway to the path along the Hudson River. I pump my arms and walk as fast as I can. Five miles a day. It takes me an hour and fifteen minutes. I love it. Some mornings I don't want to stop. I want to walk and walk. When Samuel L. Jackson said in *Pulp Fiction*, 'I want to walk the earth,' I knew exactly what he meant.

There is a whole life on the Hudson River. There are ducks and birds. There are tugs and barges and boats and yachts. One morning the QE2 sailed up in front of me out of nowhere. There it was, in the pink, early-morning light, as big as a city block, and so close.

There is always traffic on the river. There are police launches and ferries, and sometimes there are fishermen. The Statue of Liberty is always there, and always a moving sight. The air smells of salt, and I breathe in as much of it as I can.

I've made friends on this river path. An elderly Chinese couple wave to me, with a broad and enthusiastic wave, every day. They jog in heatwaves and in blizzards. I adore them. It's a sweet, and sometimes strange, community of exercisers. There are joggers, runners, power-walkers, strollers. A young woman I see most days passed me her card in mid-run last week, and suggested we meet for coffee. I said yes, and then felt nervous. I've nodded to her daily for over a year, but don't know her at all. Will we have anything in common over a cafe table? At least I know she drinks coffee. She probably won't have a piece of cake with her coffee. They look a pretty healthy lot, these runners.

Something healthy I've been doing for myself is eating well. It's such a simple phrase, *eating well*, but it's taken me so long to put it into effect. I've always eaten strangely. I've been on a diet for most of my life. I've been trying, with varying degrees of desperation, to lose weight since I was ten. My school books were filled with calculations. I would give myself six months to lose two stone. I'd look at the calculations. Two stone in six months. That would be roughly a pound a week. Easy. In fact, too easy – I needn't start the diet for another month.

The calculations would continue. Two stone in five months. Still no need to rush into it. Two stone in three months. Still possible. Two stone in one month. I could fast. Two stone in two weeks. Impossible. I'd have to give up. I did these calculations over and over again. I can calculate pounds per stone, and divide that by weeks, faster than anyone I know.

All my notebooks were filled with figures, and I was still fat. Maybe I could be somebody else? I wished I could swap myself for somebody else. Somebody old, somebody infirm, somebody ugly, it didn't matter as long as it was somebody slim.

How could I have wanted that? I was so pretty. Huge brown eyes, thick, curly hair. What was wrong with me? The same thing that is wrong with lots of women. I know very few women who aren't preoccupied with their weight. Thin women, average-sized women, overweight women.

My elder daughter, who's worked on and off, part-time, as a waitress, says she rejoices when she sees women who eat heartily and who enjoy their food and their appetite.

I'm always stunned by how complicated the matter of food and their own body-size is to women. Women who would be revolted by one excess pound on their own bodies happily date fat men, and find them attractive.

I'm also a bit stunned by the change in my own eating. From the girl who once thought she'd cure herself of an addiction to Mars Bars by eating as many as she liked – I ate twenty-five in one day, and the feeling that I never wanted to see another Mars Bar lasted two days – I've turned into a person who eats three well-balanced meals a day. I was over forty when I began to change my eating habits. I can't believe that I prefer chicken and vegetables to chocolate. But I do. If this is sounding all too good to be true, it isn't. I sweated for this. Analysis isn't cheap or easy.

I sweat in other ways, now. Two years ago, at forty-seven, I took up weight-lifting. No one in my family had ever lifted anything heavier than a large cheesecake. Physical strength was not something that our family dwelt on, although my parents were very impressed by the fact that I could swim. I learnt to swim at high school. Every time my mother or father saw me swim, they would say to each other in amazement, and with some pride, 'Look at how she swims.'

I thought I was a pretty good swimmer, too. I was swimming in the Olympic-sized pool at the Beverly Hilton Hotel in Los Angeles a few years ago. I was doing my third lap when I heard a man at the edge of the pool say to his young daughter, 'Look at her style, look at her style.' I felt very proud. The little girl looked at me. 'Not her,' the father said. 'The woman in the other lane.' I swam the rest of that lap trying not to come up for air.

I don't know what prompted me to want to lift weights. My need seemed to come right out of the blue. But I've spent enough hours on analysts' couches to know that nothing comes out of the blue.

I overwhelmed myself by going out and buying some weight-lifting equipment. I asked the man in the store what I needed to begin with. The store sent someone to set the equipment up for me. I found myself a trainer.

At first I had no chance of bench pressing. I was too scared to lie on the bench. It seemed too narrow. I was sure I'd fall off. I didn't. Now I squat with one hundred and fifty pounds and can do partial dead-lifts with one hundred and eighty pounds. These are heavy weights. I discovered, years after I came into it, that I have a strong body.

In the beginning, I was mesmerised by my new muscles. I rushed to the bathroom mirror several times a day, rolled up my sleeves and flexed my biceps. I couldn't believe they were still there.

Weight-lifting has changed the shape of my body. It took me quite a while to get used to the change. I used to wake up, in fright, in the middle of the night. I'd have bumped into myself and not recognised who I was. I'd touched myself and felt a strange body. A body that was a different size, a different texture, a different density.

I love weight-lifting. When I began I wanted every-one I met to lift weights. I stopped talking about it, to

anyone who'd listen, when I heard the strident, evan-
gelical tone in my voice. A Jewish-Polish, born-again,
middle-aged iron pumper. Who'd have believed it?

I lift weights three times a week and I always love
it, even when I'm very tired and I've had a dismal day.
Four reps into a bench press, I feel much better, and the
world looks much better.

It's so easy. You do it three times a week, and that's
it. It works. It's not like learning to play the piano. You
don't have to practise in between work-outs. Lifting
weights also increases bone density, which, for women,
decreases more sharply in menopause.

I prepared for menopause as I've prepared for most
things in my life: I read about it. Half a dozen books. I
read them years before I needed to, and I was convinced
I was undergoing an early menopause. Did my moods
fluctuate, the books asked. Of course they did. Did I cry
more? I cried for half of our first year in New York.
Did I feel irritable more easily? Less patient? Have headaches? Yes, yes, yes.

A woman who lives upstairs in our building was
menopausal. She told me it was the worst time in her
life. She's a warm, intelligent woman and I like her a
lot. One day I met her coming down the staircase. She
was sobbing. I asked her if there was anything wrong –
a stupid question. 'I was driving my car down Mac-
Dougal Street,' she said to me, 'and I came to a police
barricade and I drove through it. I knew it was a police

barricade,' she wept, 'but I just had to get to the post office.'

'I can understand a need to get to the post office,' I said. It didn't cheer her up. She kept weeping all the way down the stairs. 'At least I'm doing better than she is,' I said to my husband.

'I'm managing my menopause really well,' I said to my elder daughter. And I was. I was swallowing buckets of Evening Primrose oil and glasses of motherwort, chaste tree and fresh Valerian root drops, in water, to counter pre-menstrual and pre-menopausal stress, insomnia and restlessness.

My doctor called to give me the results of the hormone level tests I'd had to determine what stage of menopause I was at. 'Ms Brett,' he said. 'We've got the results. You haven't even begun menopause.'

'No wonder I've been managing it so well,' I said, when I recovered my composure. He didn't laugh.

My husband couldn't stop laughing. I didn't think it was that funny. I'd been battling the irritability, the lack of patience, the headaches, the mood fluctuations. I'd given up tea and coffee.

The next morning I woke up feeling peeved. All that struggle and I wasn't even menopausal. What would the real thing be like? 'I think we're in for a rugged few years,' I said to my husband.

I threw out the Evening Primrose oil and the motherwort, chaste tree and fresh Valerian root. I bought two pounds of freshly ground Colombian coffee, and packets of Earl Grey, English Breakfast and Orange Pekoe tea.

That was a few years ago. Now I'm well and truly menopausal. Verified by blood tests. Jewish women, I read, statistically experience the worst menopausal symptoms. At least in America. I was gearing myself up to fit right in with those statistics. But something happened. I think it was a combination of all those years of analysis – menopause, the change of life, wasn't going to bring me any new revelations, regrets or disturbances, not after examining every detail of every revelation and disturbance – and the walking, the weight-lifting and the eating well.

What happened was an asymptomatic menopause. Yes, no symptoms. 'Do you think I'll get some symptoms?' I asked my gynaecologist.

'Not if you haven't had any up to now,' she said. 'You're well and truly on your way through it.'

Asymptomatic menopause, weight loss, dancing, biceps and triceps. Happy endings, in my own life, make me nervous. I feel the need to say that this is not the perfect life. I feel the need to dredge up difficulties. I'm as imperfect as I ever was, in many ways. And not all the damage can be fixed up. I can't get rid of the scars of self-mutilation. One of them runs wildly down my stomach, the result of an unnecessary emergency appendectomy. I was only ten and wanted to cut all the excitement out of me.

I carry traces of the welts that dotted my teenage legs, red and inflamed, when I was too young to understand how distressed I was. The welts used to itch and itch. And I would scratch and scratch. I've made myself sad thinking about this. Sadness is always a good antidote for too much happiness, for me.

Some things don't change. No matter how much you think you've changed. No matter how much clarity, wisdom, or maturity you may feel you've achieved. I can feel the same hurt I felt as a teenager, at a friendship not turning out to be what I imagined it was.

Friendship, deep friendship – a subject that has pre-occupied me for most of my life – has, in a strange way, eluded me. I still have the occasional fantasy of the best friend. The friend who shares everything with me. The friend with whom I'm completely connected. Connected to each other, to each other's partners, to each other's children, to each other's pasts.

Maybe what I'm longing for is the passionate, unbridled friendship of more youthful years. Those years when you don't wait until you feel good, or look good, or an opportune and not inconvenient moment to call and see each other. Maybe I long for the unguarded, more truthful, less competitive friendship of the young.

I've tried to put my version of a deep friendship into effect a couple of times in the past few years, but of course it hasn't worked. The women involved had no idea what they were in for.

My husband doesn't understand my need for friends. He's never wanted a best friend. I am his best friend. He points out that we have lots of friends. Maybe I don't understand my need, either. Despite the thousands of hours I've spent lying on analysts' couches, there's much that I don't understand, and possibly much that I haven't faced.

The city of New York forces me to face others and myself in a way that no other place I've been to does. When I first moved here, I wept each time I passed a homeless person. I looked at the homeless and I saw myself. I looked at the men, and an occasional woman, sleeping in doorways and on park benches, and saw pictures of Jews dying in the streets, in the Lodz ghetto.

I cooked huge vats of soup for City Harvest, an organisation that picks up food and delivers it to the homeless. I cooked lentil soup with large chunks of beef. I put pork into the split-pea soup. I thickened the soups with a roux and seasoned them carefully.

The first time I did this, I waited for someone to call me up and tell me how delicious the soups were. I felt let down when no one called. And then I felt foolish. What did I think I was doing? Cooking for a dinner party?

Just before the pick-up, I'd stopped myself from writing a list of ingredients on each of the hundred and fifty containers of soups. It dawned on me, at the last minute, that this was not a group of people who'd be scanning labels for the percentage of fat or fibre in their food. My husband saw the labels I'd started writing. He looked sad. 'I don't think this will be the allergic-to-wheat, lactose-intolerant, additive-averse, vegetarian crowd,' he said. I laughed. 'I must be crazy,' I said.

There are crazy people on the streets of New York. On every street, it seems some days. They talk, mainly to themselves. A young man who was around a lot last summer, carried a yellow plastic toy telephone with him. He shouted into this telephone as he walked the streets of Soho. At first I was frightened of him, frightened by his intensity, and unnerved by the yellow plastic telephone cord that trailed behind him.

One day he followed me for four blocks. I don't think he really followed me. I think we were both just going in the same direction. His shouting drowned out my thoughts. I listened to him. Business strategies were flying into the yellow handset, which he had gripped firmly to his ear. He made intricate social arrangements and argued about politics and love. I admired his eloquence, and felt grateful for my sanity.

Like everyone else living in New York, I have to face the racial inequalities and the racial tension. It may feel uncomfortable to face this, but it's healthier than being able to pretend that it doesn't exist. New York is not like Los Angeles, where you can go from the valet parking in your apartment building to the valet parking at the supermarket or the restaurant. In New York you have to inhale the carbon monoxide, and it's good for you.

The weather in New York City is as volatile as the population. Oppressive heat, bitter cold. There's no way to avoid it. You have to walk in New York. To the subway, to the bus stop, to find a taxi. And the weather changes are so dramatic. I've often been frightened by changes in weather. Before I moved here, news of impending heavy rain unnerved me. As though nature was about to unleash a catastrophe. Catastrophes were on my mind a lot, then. I seemed to spend a lot of time either averting or inviting one.

I've had to adjust to snowstorms and arctic temperatures, stifling heat and one hundred per cent humidity. Last week this adjustment was severely tested. The weather forecast said a storm warning watch was in effect. A lot of snow was expected. This forecast soon changed to a blizzard alert.

I hear the words *warning*, *watch*, *alert*, with more drama than the meteorologist intended. I have to remind myself that this is not the war, just the weather.

And what weather it was. It snowed and snowed. Big, fat, wild, spinning snowflakes thickening the air. You couldn't see where you were. It kept snowing all day and all night. I stood at our windows for hours, watching the performance.

By the next day, the snowstorm is called the Blizzard of '96, and it's the largest snowfall in New York since 1947. It is still snowing. I've braved the snow to go to the store for supplies, a couple of times. I feel it *is* the war.

'We've got enough food in the house to eat well for a month,' my husband says. I go out again, to buy toilet paper. So did lots of other New Yorkers. Supermarkets and smaller stores were depleted of most of their perishable items, and their toilet paper, within hours of the forecast.

The State of New York is declared to be in a state of emergency. I'm strangely calm about this. Well, it *is* my area of expertise. I've been directing and dissecting emergencies, in my head, for years. I go out to buy some more toilet paper. I step into knee-deep snow. When I come back, I count the rolls of toilet paper on my shelves. Fifty-four.

Later in the day, the snow eases. I tell my husband that I want to walk. My need to walk is very strong. It seems to have replaced my need for Mars Bars, chocolate, chatting on the phone, cooking too much and shopping.

I know I won't be able to do my five miles, but Mayor Giuliani has said that snow ploughs are already out, clearing some of the main streets. My husband says he'll come with me.

We walk, very slowly. The streets are deserted. It is so quiet. A lone skier glides down the middle of West Broadway. We get to the Hudson River. The river looks extraordinary. Large, round, flat slabs of ice are nudging each other, covering the surface of the Hudson like a cracked jigsaw puzzle. The ice forms the same shapes as the congealed fat on top of chilled chicken soup. I'm mesmerised.

We walk back through Tribeca. No one is out. I feel bold. An adventurer at one with the elements. I plunge my legs into the snow with pride. I'm not scared.

A woman and a young girl come out of a building. It's still snowing and I have a large cap on. I see them out of the corner of my eye. I look up and notice that they are mother and daughter, and that they're wearing matching fur hats.

The woman calls out, 'Hello.' It's a loud and enthusiastic greeting. The hello of a fellow traveller. The hello of those of us who are not cowed by some snow. 'Hello,' I call back. The woman laughs with pleasure. She has a radiant laugh. She really is not scared of this snow. Then I recognize the blonde hair and the big smile. It's Bette Midler. I smile at her again. Us Jewish girls are tougher than you think.

Well, Daniel Barenboim is grey. But I'm always going to be dark. I decided that when I was forty, and the first few grey hairs began to show. Daniel Barenboim obviously didn't make the same decision.

MY DAUGHTER

'ALMS FOR THE UNSURE,' the transvestite standing on the corner of West Broadway says when I pass her. I laugh. That's very funny. I'm one of the unsure, too, I want to say to her. Different details, but the same doubt. Instead, I smile and give her a dollar. She looks gorgeous. I've seen her before, and she always looks gorgeous.

Her make-up is subtle but complete. Eyeliner, eyelashes, eyeshadow, foundation, blusher, powder, lipstick and lipliner. She is wearing a low-cut purple tulle dress. She has flawless milky-white skin. Her breasts sit up over the neckline. They look as though the lift they have is their own, and not underpinned by a Wonderbra. I think of my own breasts, and then think better of pursuing that thought. They don't stand up to her breasts.

It is nine a.m. on a Saturday morning. Soho is still very quiet. I cross the road. A young black man rides by on a bicycle. Something looks odd; odder than the regular oddities. I look twice. He is wearing a kilt. A beautifully tailored, red orange and green tartan kilt. He has got the whole outfit on: A black sporran, long socks, a waistcoat, white shirt, a fitted jacket.

It is hard not to smile. Who is he? Why would a young African-American man be cycling around lower Manhattan in a kilt? I'll probably never know.

I walk along Spring Street. I'm meeting my elder daughter for breakfast. This is the daughter I didn't give birth to, the daughter I inherited when I married her father. She was eight when we first met. She is twenty-five now.

I stop to buy some coffee beans for her. She loves good coffee and, like her father, has a very high tolerance level for caffeine. Outside Auggie's, the coffee shop on Thompson Street, a woman in her fifties is talking to herself and grimacing. She's annoyed at what she's saying. She's disagreeing with herself. I look away. People who've lost their minds bother me. They frighten me. Sometimes I feel separated from them by only a thin thread.

I don't know why I identify with the unhinged. I hinge my life together quite tightly. I get up at the same time every morning. I walk five miles. I work. I have lunch, often the same lunch. At night I prepare my vitamins for the next day. This is all in an effort to ward off chaos. What sort of chaos? The sort of chaos that could leave you arguing with yourself in the street? Whose chaos? My mother's chaos? At seventeen, the chaos that was to encase my mother for the next decade arrived and encompassed all the Jews of Lodz, Poland.

Part of my mother always remained the bewildered seventeen-year-old girl she was when her family was given two days notice to leave their home and move into what would become known as the Lodz Ghetto. They would share their two rooms in this slum area of Lodz with ten people. The Germans allocated 5.8 Jews per broken-down room. Ahead of my mother was an unrecognisable universe. Nothing was predictable, everything was uncertain. And what she was to experience was unimaginable.

I have spent much of my life creating order, in order to avoid the unpredictable. I don't like surprises. I used to imagine that if the clothes hanging in my closet all faced the same direction, and my towels and sheets were folded in perfect squares, there would be harmony in the universe.

Order was a disorder of sorts for me. This year I've taken great pride in my untidy linen closet and my wayward coat hangers. I've let my desk become messy and I no longer straighten the papers on other people's desks. I still make lists, as though if I list things they won't evaporate, won't shift. I often make a list of my lists. Armed with a good list, I feel a certain serenity.

I look at the woman who is arguing with herself. She doesn't look serene. I buy two pounds of coffee and a Bodum coffee maker.

My daughter has moved recently into a new apartment. For the three and a half years before that, she lived with the Jewish, African-American lead singer of a thrash band. It was a long three and a half years. We tried to like him, but it was hard. He had so much potential. And he was in such a mess.

While he sang with his thrash band, whenever they managed to get a job, he thrashed around endless possibilities, fantasies and prospects. He switched his dreams, plans and ambitions with alarming regularity. While waiting for his big break, he switched channels on the TV set he always seemed to be watching, and he ate. He was a big boy when my daughter met him, and he grew bigger and bigger.

He'd had a tough and difficult childhood. My daughter used to weep as she told me constantly emerging details of his terrible childhood. He didn't work for most of the time they were together and he took drugs. She waitressed long hours to support them both.

This daughter, this beautiful, six-foot-tall, slender doe-eyed daughter with a burning social conscience and a robust sense of humour, has had a history of awful boyfriends. Her first boyfriend was the pits and they got worse. 'You know how she brings home stray and injured dogs and birds,' I said to her father. 'Well, I think she's looking for similar qualities in boys.'

When she was going out with that first boyfriend, I tried to keep my mouth shut. I knew that one antagonistic word from me and they would be jammed together forever. I practised looking serene. I didn't practise hard enough. 'He's a jerk,' I said to her, when she told me he was coming over. That was in their first week together.

He's a jerk. The words had just flown out of my mouth. I know about words flying out of your mouth. My mother tried hard to hold in the words that were flying around her head. But they flew out. Frightening words. Words about children. Children with holes in their cheeks. Words about babies. Babies who were used as footballs. It took me years to find the name of the disease that caused holes in the cheeks of children in the ghetto. I want to discard the memories of some of my mother's words. I speed up.

My daughter won't be late. She's always punctual. The first time I met her, she was a shy, thin, large-eyed small girl. She looked at me and said: 'Do you know about my mother?'

'Do you mean that she's very sick?' I asked.

'Yes,' she said.

'Yes,' I said.

She put her hand in mine. Her mother was dying. From then on she held my hand whenever we were together. I took her out with my son and daughter. My son was almost ten. They got on instantly. They sat in the back of the car and talked and talked. They were both serious kids. Two small solemn faces talking and talking. They never stopped talking. Except briefly when I explained to my son that I was leaving his father for the man who is now my husband. The father of this elder daughter of mine. My son liked him a lot. 'He can stay,' he said. 'But she's got to go.' My son's distress about the split in his world came out as anger at his new friend.

My younger daughter, my biological daughter, was only four. For the two girls, it was love at first sight. And it still is. I felt lucky to have my new daughter. I'd wanted more children. We each beamed when people commented on our similarity. She held my hand in the street, in planes, in cafes. I never used the word step-child. I wasn't sure which step it referred to. Was the step a measurement? An estimate? A movement? She wasn't my step-child. She was my child.

When she was nine and ten, every time she fell over or injured herself slightly, she couldn't stop crying. She would cry and cry. She thought it was her bruised knee or grazed shin. I'd sit with her and explain that she was crying because something very sad had happened to her, her mummy had died. She'd shake her head and insist it was her knee or her elbow. Then she'd cry even more. Afterwards, she'd return to her life calm; almost radiant. At peace with herself.

Her loss, which was almost tangible when she was

a small girl, turned to rage when she turned seventeen. She kicked things, physically and metaphorically. She brought home a boyfriend who was so awful it was hard to believe that she wasn't conscious of her actions. This was the jerk.

I tried to restrain myself with the thrash-band boyfriend, but she knew I disapproved. It broke my heart to see her looking worn-out and grubby. He smoked and she smelled of stale cigarettes. I bought her new clothes, as though new clothes would cover up the grubbiness. She left him once, early in the relationship, and cried in my arms at how she could have moved in with him in the first place. She went back to him the next day.

This elder daughter has been able to draw like a dream since she was a child. She has had an acute and instinctive understanding and love of art all of her life. She was having some of her own work exhibited in New York for the first time. Her father was nearly bursting with pride. Several of our friends came to the opening. So did the thrash-band boy and a clutch of his friends.

It was a small gallery. Mr Thrash held court surrounded by his friends. He was offering them connections, deals, introductions, jobs and opportunities. He'd metamorphosed into Donald Trump. I hated him. None of them gave the art a second glance.

A few days later, my daughter told me another sad story about his life. 'We all have tough childhoods,' I said. She could have told me he'd been molested by a drug-addicted, two-headed serial killer, and I wouldn't have felt sorry for him.

When she finally left him, for good, she started admitting how miserable she'd been. I asked her how she could have tolerated his smell. 'The more he smelled, the more I loved him,' she said. 'The fatter he got, the more ferociously I felt for him.'

We talked a lot in the following few weeks. We talked about why she had chosen the men that she had. We talked about how she seemed to immerse herself wholly in their worlds and neglect her own. 'Don't leap into another relationship,' I said to her. 'Pause, and try to work out what you want to do with your life.'

'I want to go to college,' she said. 'I want to get my master's degree.'

Days after she moved out of the apartment she shared with Mr Thrash, she looked years younger. Her eyes were bright, her hair moved as though it had been let loose. Even walking across a room she looked joyful. We saw each other often. We met for coffee, just the two of us. Other times we had meals with the whole family. We laughed a lot. We reminisced. We ate. The distance between us dissolved. We were a tight family unit again.

I am almost at the Cafe Dante. I am looking forward to seeing my daughter. A couple of days ago I asked a friend if she knew any eligible men I could introduce to my daughter. I know I should never attempt to introduce my children to anyone. It always backfires. If I even appear to admire a possible partner it's the kiss of death for all possibilities.

'Hmm,' my friend said. 'I think I know someone who's just right. He's thirty-two and he composes music. He used to be a money trader. He made so much money he doesn't need to work again. He spends his time reading and going to art galleries. He likes art, he's very rich and very nice.'

'How can we get to him?' I said.

'There's a slight hitch,' my friend said. 'He's involved with someone, although I think that relationship is about to end.'

I overlooked the slight hitch. I suggested she invite my daughter to dinner, with the very rich, very nice man. 'Don't mention that I know anything about this,' I said to my friend.

A book-reading, art-loving, very rich, very nice man. He sounds too good to be true. I already love him. I extend the fantasy. My daughter could have a child. She loves children. 'How tall is he?' I said to my friend, as an afterthought.

I arrive at Cafe Dante. It is summer. The cafe doors and windows are open. The fresh air smells good. Five minutes later, my daughter arrives. I'm always struck by how beautiful she is. How graceful. She bends and walks quickly towards me. Her hair is shiny. Her eyes are shiny. She's wearing a simple sleeveless navy dress. Her brown arms and legs look strong and healthy. She gives me a big kiss. We're both hungry. She chooses a fresh mozzarella cheese, prosciutto and tomato platter. She's always had a good appetite, always been able to eat anything and remain slim. I wrestle with the menu. Finally I choose half a cantaloupe and a cup of coffee.

'You look great, Lil,' she says. 'That's a really nice dress. It really suits you.' I tell her the Australian designer Graham Long sent it over for me. 'How many years has he been making clothes for you?' she asks.

'Ten years,' I say. She smiles. She loves continuity.

We begin to exchange our news. She wants to know if I've heard from G., a friend I've had problems with recently. I'm not surprised my daughter wants to know about G. My daughter has always taken my side in any rift in my friendships. She is so loyal. She remembers every slight against me and bears grudges on my behalf. I tell her G. hasn't called. 'I never liked her,' she says.

I tell her about her brother and her sister. She tells me she has spoken to them both. I tell her that I think her brother is living on jars of red pesto sauce that I've been sending to him in Chicago, where he's currently working. The red pesto is made from sun-dried tomatoes and I buy it from Joe's Dairy in Sullivan Street. 'He told me about the pesto,' she says. 'I called him the other night and he spent ten minutes telling me how fabulous the pesto is.' I tell her that her sister, who recently visited him in Chicago, reported that he was eating the pesto for breakfast, lunch and dinner.

We both laugh. We reminisce about the weird food crazes he has had over the years. Potato cakes – sliced potatoes dipped in batter and deep fried – were one of his crazes. He liked them thinly sliced. He slipped straight from a passion for potato cakes to a love of oysters, a healthier if more expensive move.

Our food arrives and we start to eat. 'This prosciutto is delicious,' she says, and offers me some on her fork. I, who have so infrequently seen the inside of a synagogue, have only recently been able to eat pork without feeling that I'll be struck down. Jewish dietary laws also forbid the eating of shellfish, yet I've been able to eat prawns, scallops, oysters and lobsters with abandon. Somehow they don't carry the same weight as a slice of ham.

This hesitancy about pork is not something that was foisted on me by my parents. My father loved ham. Every time he ate a slice of ham, he was confirming and reaffirming his belief that there was no God. Even my largely vegetarian mother enjoyed the occasional piece of ham.

Both my parents came from Orthodox Jewish homes. After the war, they each, separately, came to the conclusion that there was no God. In Auschwitz my father had watched two Gestapo officers playing football with a new baby. One of the officers ate a granny smith apple while he drop-kicked the baby. My father, who weighed about a hundred and ten pounds at the time, and who had just pinched his cheeks in order to look healthy enough to work, decided that there was definitely no God.

I eat the piece of prosciutto. Nothing happens.

I look at my daughter. She looks so good. The stoop she developed while she was with the thrash band singer – he was shorter that her – seems to have subsided. She's joined a gym. She flexes her biceps for me. 'Feel them,' she says. I feel her biceps. 'They're very impressive,' I say. After the tension of the last three and a half years, we're both keen to get on well, and both enjoying getting on well. We smile at each other.

'I feel happy,' she says. I feel happy hearing her say that. We eat our lunch. I want to know more about her life but I don't want to push her. I don't want to appear overly concerned, overly demanding, overly interested.

I finish my cantaloupe. I want to ask my daughter a question. I think of several ways of phrasing the question. I want it to sound casual. Off the cuff. Not too important. Maybe I shouldn't ask. We're having such a nice time. I should leave well enough alone. Since my daughter left the thrash singer, I've studiously avoided asking her if she's been going out with anyone. I know about her university life. I know about her working life. I know nothing about her social life.

I screw up my face in an attempt to affect a casual air. 'Have you met any men you find interesting?' I say to her. My daughter looks startled. Very startled. A piece of something she is eating goes down the wrong way. She starts coughing. I reach out to pat her on the back. She moves away.

'It's okay,' she says.

I look at her. She doesn't look okay. Her face seems to have collapsed. Her features seem to be sinking. I've made a terrible mistake, I think to myself. Maybe she thinks I'm about to ask her to meet some nice young man I've met.

'Don't worry, I'm not match-making you with anyone,' I say. 'My days of match-making are over,' I add. She doesn't look any better.

I try to rephrase my original question so it sounds less ominous to her. 'I didn't mean have you met the love of your life,' I say. She has stopped coughing. Her shoulders are hunched. She's staring at the table. I feel awful. 'I wasn't asking if you've met the man of your dreams or anything like that,' I say. 'I just wanted to know if you've met anyone at all you were remotely interested in.' The situation is getting worse. I am making it worse. I can't seem to stop. I have always over-explained everything and I do it again now. 'I was just wondering if you've met any man you find attractive,' I say.

She looks at me. She opens her mouth several times and shuts it again. She looks as though she's been hit by a truck. I feel terrible. Suddenly it dawns on me that this is not just a matter of the right phrasing or the right question. Something else is going on. I feel queasy.

There is a short time, a minute or maybe two minutes, during which I know I can change the subject. I can talk about something else. I can derail whatever it is that she's unable to tell me. I needn't know. We could talk about other things and pretend that neither of us had noticed this anxious interlude. I look at her. Her face is bright red. I feel sorry for both of us.

'Geoffrey told me a dreadful joke yesterday,' I say. Geoffrey is Geoffrey Firth, the young English hairdresser who cuts my hair. He sometimes cuts her hair, too. She really likes Geoffrey. The stiff smile she squeezes out of herself frightens me. This is obviously not the time for a joke. I push a fragment of cantaloupe around my plate. I look up again. My daughter looks as though she's going to implode. I feel sick. What is going on?

'What's up?' I say to her. There is a long silence. A very long silence. I can't bear the silence. I repeat myself again. 'I only asked if you'd met a man you found attractive. Just someone nice you feel you might like to go out with. I wasn't asking you anything more than that, sweetheart.'

Why do I think repetition brings clarity? It clearly doesn't. My daughter tries to speak, again. One word comes out at a time. There are long gaps between each of these words. 'I don't find men all that attractive,' she says.

'That's okay,' I say. 'There are not a whole lot of really attractive single men,' I say. 'Every woman in New York knows that.'

She doesn't smile. She looks terrible. And then a frightening possibility hits me. My heart pounds. I start to tremble. My legs shake. My insides, assorted stomach, intestines, kidneys and lungs feel as though they're quivering. I try to steady myself.

'Are you trying to tell me that you don't find men attractive?' I say. She shrugs. I try again. 'Are you trying to say you find women attractive?'

She bursts into tears. I feel dazed. She weeps and weeps. I reach over and hold her hand.

'I'm sorry,' she keeps saying in between floods of tears. 'I'm sorry. I'm sorry.'

We sit in the cafe in this way for several minutes. My daughter cries. I hold her hand. I look dazed. 'I'm sorry,' she says intermittently. 'It's okay,' I say. 'You don't have to say sorry. You've done nothing wrong. There's nothing to apologise about.'

I am in a state of shock. I wish this wasn't happening. I should have told her Geoffrey's joke. We could have laughed, finished our breakfast, said goodbye and parted, everything still intact and just the way it used to be. I know that this is one of those irreversible moments, and nothing will ever be the same. I want out. I want to go back to my writing, to my desk, to my study; to that safe world where the only unexpected things that happen are the things I make up.

When did this happen? This not finding men attractive? The last time I looked, she was gazing into the thrash band singer's eyes and holding his hand. And before that, she was pleading for permission to stay overnight with another boyfriend, an arrogant, stick-thin rock musician. She was nineteen. I said she could either keep her two a.m. curfew at home, or move in with him. The permission to leave home caught her by surprise. They broke-up a few months later.

So why am I surprised she doesn't find men attractive? It wouldn't have been hard to come to that conclusion, given the unattractive array of boyfriends my daughter has attached herself to. Were the boyfriends a sign? I thought they were a symptom of her tendency to drown her own ambition and her own dreams in dreadful men.

My head is reeling. It is not just a matter of not finding men attractive. She is attracted to women. My daughter wipes her eyes and blows her nose. She has almost drowned in this distress. I am having trouble not crying, myself.

I suddenly want my mother. I'm nearly fifty and I want my mother. I'm not sure that she'd be much good in this situation. I remember something that happened when I was nineteen. I'd moved back home with my parents, temporarily, after living in my own flat. A girl-friend was staying the night with me, sharing my bed. She was a tall girl – 5'10" – which in those days was considered very tall. My mother burst in on us in the morning, ostensibly to deliver breakfast. She slammed a tray of orange juices on my dressing table, waking us both up. She glared at me. 'All my friends are saying you are a lesbian!' she said, and left the room. Before she shut the door she said: 'She's got very big shoulders.' I was stunned. We'd barely heard of lesbians then.

Where did my mother pick up that word? Her English was good, but not that good. And what could her friends be saying? They'd never met this friend of mine and had hardly seen me in the last couple of years. I turned to my girlfriend. She was weeping.

I was shocked by my mother's outburst. Shocked by the rudeness. My mother, who could be charming and generous and warm, often had outbursts and they were often directed at my friends. But what caused this one?

I knew the mess and the horror and the damage of my mother's past was so vast and overwhelming that it was pointless to look for the cause of any bewildering action. My mother never mentioned the incident again, and never used the word lesbian again.

In those days, tall women were considered unfeminine. My mother felt I was too tall. I was 5'8½" when I was thirteen. 'It's because you ate so many sweets,' my mother used to say to me, in an astonishing dismissal of her quite formidable knowledge of nutrition.

I stop staring at my shred of cantaloupe. I look back at my tall daughter. 'I've always had crushes on girls,' she says. What does she mean? She has always had really nice girlfriends. And she has adored them. We all liked them. Tessa, Sarah, Caroline. We still like them.

'What's a crush?' I say almost plaintively. 'Isn't it the same as adoring someone, thinking they're wonderful?' My daughter is quiet. 'Doesn't everyone have crushes on their girlfriends?' I say.

'It's more intense than that,' she says. 'It's very intense.'

'I've felt very intensely about so many women,' I say to her. 'There's a fine line between loving a woman and being in love with a woman. I've loved so many women in my life.'

I was wildly in love with my best friend when I was thirteen. It was the only sexual relationship I've had with a woman and it was one of the most passionate sexual relationships I would have. We loved each other for years. The sex with each other stopped when we started going out with boys. And we never once brought up the subject of each other and those over-heated nights of love we shared.

We stayed best friends for decades. We fought badly, once. I can't remember why and neither can she. But the fight, and the subsequent split-up, cast a pall over my life for the couple of years it took for us to be friends again. At the time, she was married and living in a house across the road from me. This was supposed to be our childhood dream come true. I was at home with small children, she was just pregnant. The plan was to spend our days and nights together. Instead, my heart palpitated when I passed her place. I drove around the block and four blocks out of my way to get to the supermarket without driving past her house. A couple of times I glimpsed her and my heart almost stopped. Is that deep friendship? Is that love? Is that loving someone? Or is that being in love? And what is the difference? Is the difference sex?

My daughter says she has had crushes on different women. I ask her what distinguishes a crush from a lesbian leaning. 'I find them physically attractive,' she says.

'Well, on the whole,' I say, 'women are more beautiful than men.'

I understand the pleasure of looking at someone whose appearance pleases you. 'I love the way Fiona looks,' I say to my daughter. I get pleasure from looking at her pale, porcelain skin and the lush redness of her hair. I like to look at Caroline, too. Some people are just pleasurable to look at.

'Maybe you fall in love with a person, not a gender,' I say. I feel out of my depth, a bit desperate. Sure I'm being politically incorrect in this very politically correct city. I should embrace my daughter, say whatever or whoever you are, I love you. It is true. I say it to her.

For the first time since we started this conversation, I become aware of the people around me. I realise I have felt in a vacuum, isolated from the rest of the world. The cafe is very busy. It is eleven a.m. and people are still arriving for breakfast. New Yorkers eat at very variable hours. I feel exhausted.

Some instinct tells me that my daughter is involved with someone. That she is not just telling me, in abstract, her feelings. I ask her if she is seeing someone.

She seems relieved, almost eager to talk about her new lover, J. Her eyes shine and she's animated underneath her tear stains. 'She's everything you'd want in a man,' she says. This floors me, temporarily. What do I want in a man? Well, it would seem that he should be a man, for a start.

'I used to see her around the East Village,' my daughter says. 'I had a crush on her for ages.' While she was still living with the thrash singer? I ask. 'Yes,' she says.

She tells me that the thrash band man's two previous girlfriends left him for other women and that she used to say to him confidently that that would never happen with her. My headache gets worse. This is starting to sound bizarre. The thrash man's two previous girlfriends left him for women? What is happening to the world? This is not the world I grew up in. In the world I grew up in, my daughter was going to be with a man who was everything I'd want in a man, not a woman who was everything I'd want in a man.

I realise I've been holding my breath, as though if I don't breathe I won't ingest what is happening. I breathe out. I've been trying to look calm. Trying not to look as shocked as I feel. How did my daughter become girl-friend number three to leave the thrash singer for a woman?

'I feel in love with J.,' she says. I don't know what to say. Does this mean she's a lesbian? Does this mean she'll never go out with a man? My daughter doesn't know what it means either.

'I don't hate men,' she says. I didn't think she did. 'I may go out with a man again, I don't know,' she says.

'The only thing I know is that this relationship feels good. I feel really happy. J. is so nice.'

'Anyone who didn't stink would feel nice, next to Mr Thrash,' I say, and then I feel bad about saying it. But my daughter laughs. 'He did smell awful, didn't he?' she says.

'What about all our not-rushing-into-another-relationship conversations?' I say to her. 'What about all the talk of finding yourself and not immersing yourself in someone else's life? What about the plans to have some breathing space on your own?'

Why do I keep stressing this life of her own to my daughter? Is it because I've never really been on my own? I had my first boyfriend when I was fifteen and, more or less, have been with a man ever since. Mostly I've felt lucky and happy to be with the men I've been with. But occasionally I feel I haven't lived a proper adult life. I've always been buffered by a man. Haven't needed to manage a whole variety of things on my own. I've wondered what it must be like to plan your own vacations, to host your own dinners, to have to do all the work in all of your relationships.

When you're married, you can be slack. For a start, you have a built-in companion, best friend, mate. If you're tired, or flat, or unsociable in company, your partner can make up for it. As a couple you have double the number of friends, but possibly half the intimacy. It's hard to be very intimate when there are more than two of you. I have a great admiration for women who've

47

lived independent lives, on their own. I've often won-dered how they do it. It's such alien territory to me. I've been a wife and a mother for all of my adult life.

'I think it's a mistake to go straight from Mr Thrash to J.,' I say to my daughter. I have the grace to acknowl-edge, to myself, that this is hypocritical of me. Just days ago I was plotting for my daughter to live happily ever after with Mr Composer-art-lover-moneybags.

My head hurts. I feel as though we've been in this cafe forever. I don't have any headache pills on me. I never used to leave home without a full supply of pills, gadgets, dockets and documents. Enough equipment to cover any emergency. Now I don't even have a head-ache tablet when I need one and this feels like an emer-gency to me. 'Are you okay, Lil?' my daughter asks, looking at me anxiously.

'I'm okay,' I say to my daughter, and take her hand. I realise that my thoughts have been wandering. I have removed myself from some of what I haven't wanted to hear. I have done this since I was a child – escaped into a universe that was my own creation. As a teenager, I spent hundreds of hours being married to Paul McCartney. While my mother was talking to me about unbuttered Ryvita biscuits and lettuce for lunch, Paul and I were deciding what to watch on television. He always wanted to watch the same pro-grams I did. When my mother went on and on about how much weight Lola K. had lost, I was lost in Paul McCartney's arms.

Paul and I talked and talked. We were never stuck for something to say to each other. He was articulate and thoughtful. He thought I was smart and sweet. I left Paul for a boy I met at a dance. He wasn't as perfect as Paul McCartney, but at least he had his own dialogue.

My daughter smiles at me. She is looking more cheerful. The after-effects of shock, the swift heartbeat, the sinking stomach, the pallid psyche, still linger over me.

My daughter eats a mouthful of her mozzarella. 'It's funny going on a date with a woman,' she says. 'When you go to the bathroom, you're still on your best behaviour. You can't check that you still look okay, or make faces at yourself while you're fixing your hair or putting on your lipstick. You can't just hang out for a few minutes and relax. You can't have a break because she's right there in the bathroom with you. It's weird.'

I am momentarily distracted from my distress by this interesting insight. Then the feeling of not wanting to know returns. I wish this morning's revelations could vanish, and my daughter and I could be the regular mother and daughter we were, again.

I realise I've lowered my voice. I want my daughter to lower hers. I feel ashamed of having a daughter who's got a girlfriend. And then I feel ashamed of feeling ashamed.

I start feeling jittery. Something is frightening me. I'm familiar with fear. I feel it in my gut and in my heart and lungs. What am I so frightened of? Is it change? Is it my old fear of the unknown? As though everything unpredictable is a potential disaster. Am I frightened because I've been taken by surprise? Not in my wildest dreams did I expect this. I thought we may have to endure another miserable man or two, but not this, not a *woman*.

Do I feel bad because my hopes have been dashed? Years of hope that my daughter would find the right man, a man who adores her, and settle down? What does 'settle down' mean anyway? It doesn't mean this. This is decidedly unsettling.

Am I upset because, yet again, I have to face the fact that my daughter is an adult? An adult who makes her own moves. It can be very comforting to think of your children as children.

Or does my daughter's revelation dislodge other fears and taboos of my own? I was ashamed for years, for decades, of my passion for my girlfriend. She is still the only woman I feel physically comfortable with. I can sit and lean against her. I can hold her hand in the street. I feel happy being squashed together in the back seat of a car. Her body is familiar to me. I can still, thirty-five years later, remember the smell and taste of her. For years I felt uncomfortable touching other women. But then I don't go around touching a lot of men either.

My mother found it hard to touch me. She'd been touched by too much in her life. Touched by the thousands of prisoners, in Auschwitz and Stuthof, with whom she was jammed into bunks. Touched by men, in horrible ways, in those horrifying times.

I feel angry with my daughter. Just as we thought we were getting a reprieve from the thrash singer, a respite from the tension of having to watch her angry, unwashed and getting varicose veins from her waitressing jobs, she comes up with this! She was so angry during those years with Mr Thrash. Angry with him, angry with us. She waved him under our noses like a smelly rag.

She has been looking so much happier lately. She is loving and thoughtful again. Connected to us, again. And now this. 'What about children?' I say. She knows exactly what I'm talking about.

'Oh, I want to have children,' she says. 'I've always wanted to.'

She has always loved children. She has baby-sat since she was a young girl and has always been very attached to her charges. 'There's no reason I can't have children if I'm in a relationship with a woman,' she says.

I pause. I want the best for her so badly. I want to say the right thing, but the wrong words fly out. 'It's not so easy,' I say. 'It's hard enough bringing up a child, but when you start off behind the eight-ball, it can be just about impossible.'

Why did I say that? Where did that come from? I don't even know what that sporting reference means. Whose eight balls are we talking about? Although I'm bothered by what I've just said, I don't stop.

'If kids brought up in the regulation one mother,

51

one father, two and a half bedroom, one and a half siblings family have such a hard time, what chance has a donor-inseminated, two-mother household child got?' I say. Tears come into her eyes. I know I've been cruel. But I still feel angry.

What am I doing? This is the daughter who was tailor-made for me. The daughter I've laughed myself sick with. The daughter who understands every nuance of any disturbance or disagreement I have had with assorted friends. This is the daughter I've been so close to it frightens us both.

I can see her fear and confusion. I first saw it when she was an adolescent. Loving me was complicated for her. She felt disloyal to her biological mother. She found it very hard to express any anger at her dead mother, but she could rage at me. I was alive. It's tough when you can't be mad at your mother. It's hard enough when you can't be mad at a live mother, but it's very tough trying to be angry with a dead mother.

I know about not being able to feel anger at mothers. I couldn't feel angry at my mother without feeling awful, for years. Every time I'd feel any resentment or annoyance or irritation, I'd see the image of my mother, sitting at the kitchen table, when I was a small girl. Tears would be running down her face and she would put her head in her hands and say: 'You'll never know what I've been through.' And I knew I never would.

My daughter knows her mother didn't want to die,

didn't want to leave her. But she did die and she did leave her. Anyone would understand feeling mad about that.

I took all of the anger I felt at my mother, and took it out on myself. As a teenager I drove around Melbourne at night, at close to a hundred miles an hour. I used to close my eyes and not allow myself to open them until I'd counted to ten. My daughter having a female lover seems safe and sensible next to my own exploits.

I try to stop feeling angry. I should be trying to make this easier for my daughter. She is trying to tell me something that is as difficult and complicated for her as it is for me. I can see that she's not sure about what she's doing. I can see that she's confused about this new move in her life. My heart is racing. Why am I so angry?

'I do want to have children,' she says. 'I've thought about it a lot. The thought of not being able to have children would make me unsure about committing myself to a woman.' She pauses, looks at me, and says: 'Don't look as though this is a tragedy, Lil. Next to the things you did when you were my age, this is tame.'

'When I was your age I was the mother of a three-year-old living in suburban Melbourne. The highlight of my day was a trip to the supermarket,' I say. But I know what she's talking about. I had a wild youth. It didn't feel wild at the time. It felt lonely.

'I think carrying a bag of LSD pills through Australian customs when you're twenty and dressed in psychedelic robes and beads, is much more dangerous than having a relationship with a woman,' my daughter says.

'I don't think they're comparable,' I say.

My kids are shocked by some of the things I did when I was young. I'm shocked myself. And frightened, in retrospect. Why would I have brought a whole lot of LSD into the country? You could go to gaol then for smoking a joint. I was a well-known rock journalist. The world of rock-and-roll was still very suspect. I was obviously asking for trouble.

I didn't like LSD. The few times I'd taken it I'd felt awful. I was in San Francisco, in Haight-Ashbery. I'd been to the Monterey Pop Festival. Love and peace were in the air. We were all brothers and sisters, under our flowers and beads. I thought the world was changing.

This particular daughter has always been hip. She is the style maven in our family. We ask her if our dresses, jackets, jeans or hairstyle look okay. It is hip to be lesbian. At least here in Manhattan. Madonna is photographed with her gal pals and K. D. Lang is everyone's sweetheart. High school girls openly have affairs with other girls. 'Oh, she's a lug,' my younger daughter said to me about one of her school friends, several years ago. 'A lug,' I said. 'What's a lug?' 'Lesbian until graduation,' my younger daughter said. Since then, I've seen the term in magazines and newspapers. There have been many articles about the growing popularity of bisexuality and homosexuality among women. My elder daughter would be furious if I suggested this was a hip thing to do. She has always fought against being seen as hip.

What do lesbians do? Why am I thinking about this? I don't think about what my younger daughter does with her boyfriend, or what my son does with his girl-friend. I prefer, on the whole, not to think about those things. So why am I thinking about what lesbians do? I mean, what can they do? There's a limit to what any of us can do. So why does what they do bother me?

I ask my daughter if she has discussed this with her therapist. The therapist who was supposed to help her understand why she was with the thrash singer. She gives me a look that says questions about her therapy are out of bounds. I drop the questions.

All those hours of my own analysis sometimes give me the illusion that I am an analyst myself. 'You've been angry for so many years,' I say to my daughter. 'Maybe you're angry with men.'

'No, I'm not angry with men,' she says.

'Well, being with a woman is a good way of saying, "You can't fuck with me" to men,' I say.

'It's got nothing to do with men,' she says.

I persist. 'Well, I have noticed you've often screwed up your face whenever you've mentioned a penis,' I say.

'I don't like them very much,' she says.

I try to think about my own attitude to penises. Do I like them? I can't think of penises en masse. I can't even think of them separated from their owners. The only penis I can think of is my husband's.

Is my daughter reading my mind? 'What are you

going to say to Dad?' she says. 'Should I tell him? How should we tell him?' She looks frightened. I feel sorry for her. I move my chair closer to her. I can see the part of her that feels she's done something terrible. Something terrible to us.

I can also see the strength in her. She's always been strong. This slim girl has lifted heavy boxes and huge pieces of furniture. She's stretched enormous canvases in her father's studio and wrestled with large ladders and pots and cans. I can see the strength it takes to be able to talk about this. I never talked to my parents about anything. I shucked off most of their questions. As for sex, when my mother said to me one night before I went out, 'If you respect yourself, others will,' I was relieved that she'd been so brief.

'What will we do about Dad?' my daughter says again.

'Well, you could come home and tell him, except that we're going out to a big function we have to attend at one o'clock,' I say. I look at my watch. It's almost twelve. This is bad timing. 'I don't think there's enough time for you to come home and tell him,' I say.

I know I won't be able to hide this from my husband, even temporarily. I'm sure I look shell-shocked. A couple of the waiters in the cafe have looked at me a few times. They know me and I know that I look as though something is wrong. My face is flushed and I've been running my hands through my hair with more abandon than I usually allow myself. My hair is sticking out everywhere. I can feel it. I try to compose myself.

'How about I tell him?' I say to my daughter. 'I'll tell him briefly and then maybe you can see him tonight or tomorrow.' She agrees to this. I know that it's not the best solution, but reality seems to be composed of imperfections.

'You've taken this really well, Lil,' my daughter says to me.

'What did you expect?' I ask her.

'I had a scale from the most terrible reaction, to mediumly good and mediumly bad reactions, through to the best possible reaction,' she says. 'And you've had the best possible reaction.'

'Really?' I say. Her praise passes over me. Suddenly, I feel a failure. I feel that it must be my fault that my daughter prefers women to men. I feel I must have done something wrong. Intellectually, I know it's not a matter of blame. I know it's not a matter of right and wrong. But I feel terrible.

My daughter talks about all the wonderful women she's met since she's been with her lover. She talks about magazine editors, film editors, musicians, writers. Her eyes shine. 'I've met the most amazing women, Lil,' she says.

The world she's describing changes from an ordinary world of editors, musicians and writers to a world that is alien to me. A world I have no place in. A foreign universe. I feel left out. I couldn't feel more excluded if she'd been spirited away by a cult.

My daughter is still talking. She's telling me that the photo editor of this magazine and the assistant director of that film are good friends of J.'s. She's also met the woman who wrote the screenplay for a critically acclaimed low-budget movie that was recently released. All these women are so nice, she says.

I feel envious now. Envious of this new club that my daughter belongs to. I imagine everyone embracing everyone else. They're all helpful, supportive and nurturing to each other. The club feels very exclusive. I've always wanted to belong to a club. When I was younger, I formed a book club and a film club. I organised the meetings, bought the projector, provided the sweets. It was my substitute for a larger family, I think.

That's why I feel left out, I realise. My daughter's got a new family. A family I can't be part of. And they seem to be a perfect family. An attractive, successful, powerful and fun family. I was prepared for an extended family. I was prepared to be a mother-in-law. I was prepared to be a grandmother. It all seemed so straightforward. I thought all we had to do was find a better class of boyfriend.

I worry about how my husband will handle this. He's pretty unflappable, but this is an unsettling piece of news. 'Do you think Dad will be okay?' my daughter asks.

'Of course he will,' I say. 'It will come as a shock to him, but he'll be okay. Are you okay?'

'I'm okay,' she says. She looks exhausted.

'Could we have Mr Thrash back?' my husband says, a few minutes after I've told him the news. I've tried to be calm about it. I laugh. My husband has always made me laugh.

'Mr Thrash doesn't look so bad now, does he?' I say. My husband is very quiet for a while after that.

Over the next few days, he makes some out-of-character, odd remarks. When an acquaintance inquires after our elder daughter, my husband says: 'She doesn't know whether she's Arthur or Martha.' This leaves the acquaintance, an American, confused. Firstly, he's unfamiliar with the phrase, and secondly, he has trouble with my husband's accent. 'She's an author of what?' he says.

'It's been a tough week,' my husband, who is permanently optimistic and rarely complains about anything, says to a friend. 'A really tough week.' The friend doesn't ask why. 'Yeah, this has been one helluva week,' my husband says.

'I'm having trouble with one of the kids,' he says out of the blue to a neighbour in our building. This comes from a man who, despite a gregarious exterior, is very private.

Small things continue to slip out of him. It's as though his reaction to his daughter's news is seeping out of him, despite himself. Despite his effort to take it in his stride, to see it in perspective. 'If she is happy, then I'm happy,' he says to me several times.

I've been surprised at each of my husband's attempts

59

to tell people and surprised at the inappropriate moments he's chosen to do this. When my husband does discuss the subject with a couple of people, I'm surprised at myself. I'm annoyed with him. I don't want anyone to know.

This is a surprising reversal of roles. I am usually the one who indulges in intimate conversation. Intimacy is my specialty. I can talk about anything. Almost anything. I am sometimes embarrassed about the questions I ask people and even more embarrassed about the questions I restrain myself from asking. I have written about my life in detail. In fiction, in poetry and in newspaper columns. When I speak in public, I am surprised at what I reveal. I hold very little back. Except now. I want to hold everything back.

Maybe my daughter doesn't want people to know. I know that she is walking around the East Village arm in arm with J., but maybe she doesn't want the news to travel out of the East Village.

I suggest this to my husband. He looks surprised. He looks less buoyant. He looks tired. I try to cheer him up. 'Hey, at least you'll never be replaced,' I say. 'You'll always be the only man in her life.'

'I've already thought of that,' he says. He tries to be funny. 'Well, there go any dreams of golf with the son-in-law,' he says. I feel sad.

My son calls from Chicago where he's working as an Emergency Room doctor. He talks to my husband. He's known about J. for some time, he says. He tries to sound nonchalant, as if this is an everyday thing, my husband tells me later, but he can't keep a certain sadness, a slight wistfulness, out of his voice. 'Oh well, I won't have a brother-in-law to be one of the boys with,' he says to my husband. Obviously we all feel left out. 'I wonder whether there'll be a place for me in her life,' my son adds. 'Of course there will,' my husband says to him.

My younger daughter, who has also known about J., has her usual equanimity. 'I know this is a shock, Lil,' she says to me, 'but J. is very nice. I think you'll like her.'

I decide not to tell my father. I know I am missing out on an opportunity to gain his sympathy. He would definitely feel sorry for me, and that's not something to forsake lightly. After all, my parents had a monopoly on tragedy. And although I know this is not a tragedy, I know my father will feel sorry for me.

As a child, and this is true for many children of survivors, none of my painful experiences seemed very painful next to what my parents had endured. 'You think that's trouble? You don't know what trouble is,' was a familiar refrain. I think my father would agree that this is trouble, but I won't tell him.

My daughter has asked me not to tell him. 'Don't tell Grandpa,' she said. 'I don't want him to think of me as a pervert.' That small sentence almost brought me to a standstill. I had overlooked the guilt and the shame that often accompanies homosexuality. I had seen it as a thing of the past.

I don't tell anyone else, either. Our lives go on. We do the usual things. We work, we go out, we deal with all the daily things there always are to deal with.

One night, my husband and I are sitting on the sofa. It is late at night. We've had Australian friends over for dinner. It's been a really nice evening. We all complained about New York, swapped bits of Australian news, reminisced about Clinkers and Cherry Ripes, and made plans to share a house by the beach for the summer. My husband looks pensive. 'I still harbour a small hope that this thing with J. is a passing phase,' he says to me.

It is Saturday morning, and I am sitting at one of the three tables in Auggie's which serves the best coffee in SoHo. I often come here. So do most of the other people in the cafe. This is not a tourist spot. For a start, the cafe doesn't have a name. Only the locals know it as Auggie's.

A young woman walks in. I've seen her here for years. She's in her mid to late twenties, an actress. She thinks she looks like Elizabeth Taylor – I heard her telling this to a young man. She has a group of acolytes, three or four young men, who sit and hang onto her every word. What is possibly keeping them glued to her is her cleavage more than her conversation. Her necklines are always very low and she wears no bra. She always leans forward to make her points. Over the years, she has had several boyfriends in tow. Her boyfriends seem to tolerate the acolytes. She, and whichever boyfriend she happens to be with at the moment, often kiss lavishly at the back table.

I nod hello to her. She walks to the back table and greets a friend, a young woman about her own age. A few minutes later, I look up and the two women are kissing. They're kissing as passionately as she ever kissed any of her boyfriends. I can't believe it. I look again. They're wound around each other, kissing and kissing. What is happening? This woman spent her days being admired by men, flirting with men, talking about men and necking with men.

She disengages herself from her girlfriend, holds her girlfriend's face in her hands for a moment, gives her one last kiss and walks to the counter. She drums her fingers on the counter and barks out her order for coffee.

The breathy, feathery voice has gone, the plunging neckline has gone. The baby-doll dress has gone. In their place is a T-shirt with rolled up sleeves and straight, brown trousers. She is wearing cowboy boots with Cuban heels on her feet. I can't stop staring. I force myself to look away.

Over the next few weeks the former Elizabeth Taylor metamorphoses into more of a Burt Reynolds. Burt Reynolds as he was at his peak. Burt Reynolds in *Deliverance*. 'Is she gay now?' I ask the guy who works at Auggie's.

'I guess so,' he says.

'What's happening to the world?' I say to my husband, who has also witnessed the transformation.

Suddenly, everyone is a lesbian. A woman in our building shows me a photograph of her new grandchild. I congratulate her. I ask her if she likes her son-in-law who I've never met. 'I feel sorry for him,' she says. 'My daughter has just left him for a woman.'

'For a woman?' I say.

'The woman she was with before she met her husband,' she says to me.

There are half a dozen other incidents in which people mention lesbians. Lesbian sisters, mothers, aunts. Everyone seems to have a lesbian in the family. Are there more lesbians now? I ponder this question for weeks. Has feminism, with its element of anger towards men, created more women who love women?

'You better be careful,' my husband says to me. 'You're starting to sound like one of those rednecks.'

'What?' I say.

'Rednecks are always talking about blacks and gays infiltrating their schools, their churches, their communities, and being a subversive element,' he says.

'But I'm not saying anything in a bigoted way,' I say.

'You're putting it in terms of us and them,' he says.

'No I'm not,' I say. I feel furious with him.

I call a friend who is gay. She is a friend of a friend, actually. 'No,' she says, 'I don't think there are more lesbians now. They've always been there. We're just more aware of it now. Gay men have always been more obvious. Gay women are not so obvious and in part that's a reflection of women in society generally.'

I try out my theory on her anyway. 'It seems to me that possibly part of a backlash against feminism, a repercussion of the consciousness of women of years of oppression by men, and subservience to men, has produced more gay women,' I say.

'I don't think so,' she says. 'I don't think there are more gay women around now than there were twenty years ago. The difference may be that more women are openly gay.' I pause. My career as a social scientist has just come to an abrupt end.

When I first asked this friend of a friend if I could ask her a few questions, I told her that I didn't know any gay women. 'Really?' she had said, sounding surprised. I felt embarrassed. 'Well I know a few,' I stuttered, 'but not very well.' I'd badly wanted to backtrack and say, yes, I've got lots of gay women friends.

Some time passes. I find that I'm not mentioning my elder daughter in conversation. When people enquire after her I list her academic achievements. When they say I must be relieved that she's no longer with the thrash singer, I try to look pleased and then change the subject.

My husband meets J. He says she's nice, which, from a husband who always errs on the side of generosity, is less than a whole-hearted endorsement. 'I don't think the relationship with J. is going to be a very long-term relationship,' he says, later in the day.

I tell a few people about my daughter. About my

daughter and J. I feel annoyed with the friends who look as though the news is a disaster. Some friends look positively pleased. They rush to reassure me that everything will be all right. But their cheerfulness is palpable. They've found the chip, the crack, and it is in someone else's family.

I feel very annoyed with a friend who says she suspected my daughter was this way. We didn't suspect anything. I decide the friend is lying.

My daughter writes me a letter. It is a response to my essay on ageing in this book, which she took home and read. 'I've heard you tell some of these stories again and again,' she writes, 'and yet locating them in the entire context of your life and your life's struggle, I find them shocking all over again. The thought of you calculating and recalculating your diets, a story which you have told me so many times and which I have thought about often, made me want to cry.'

She ends the letter: 'You are so clear-sighted and strong and you think about your life with such a lot of clarity, finding sense in what might have been such a hopeless confusion.'

I am very moved by her response. If only I did have the sort of clarity that cut through confusion. She goes on to tell me that she has been given an assistant teaching position at Rutgers University for next year. This will not only give her a salary, but will reduce her tuition fees by fifty per cent.

I swell with pride. This is the same girl who refused

to even think about going back to university a couple of years ago. I write back to her. I write out all the love I feel for her. If only I could be as nice in my real life as I can in my writing. I wish I didn't feel as though the news of my daughter's homosexuality was a tragedy. Intellectually I know it's not.

A few weeks ago, my husband and I were on Shelter Island, which is a small island enfolded by Long Island. It is a five-minute ferry ride from the Hamptons, where Steven Spielberg and Barbra Streisand and half the upwardly mobile population of Manhattan, spend their summers. Shelter Island is everything the frantic Hamptons are not. It is quiet and tranquil. There are no movie theatres and no cash machines. The locals call it the UnHamptons.

We arrived just before sunset and went for a walk along Wades Beach on the south end of the island. The beach was deserted. We walked, coated in the deep pink light of the setting sun. We walked with our arms around each other. From somewhere in mid-air, we thought we heard a Schubert sonata. The poignant and vulnerable tones seemed almost surreal. Then we came across the source. Two men in their forties were on the beach. The Schubert was coming from a CD player on a table which was set with linen and silver. The two men were eating clams on the half-shell and toasting each other with martinis.

We all said hello. 'I've seen you here before,' one

of the men said. 'You two always seem so in love with each other.' My husband beamed. 'We are,' he said.

'So are we,' the man said. We all beamed.

If I can feel uplifted by the two men on the beach, why do I feel so distressed about my daughter? Gay people have good lives, on the whole. Their created families, their friends, their tribe, often seem to me to be more functional than society's regular families.

I watch a Canadian documentary about gay and lesbian youths on television. All the mothers of the gay and lesbian youths cry when they talk about how they found out that their child was homosexual. One mother after another cries. I cheer up. I feel better about my own reaction.

Part of me has looked down on myself, chastised myself for my reaction to my daughter. Part of me thinks I should have been able to incorporate the news as no big deal. In exactly the same way that I think it is no big deal when someone other than my daughter is gay.

'He took all my dreams of having grandchildren away from me,' one mother in the documentary said. I can identify with that. I feel as though my daughter has taken something away from me, but I am not as clear about what that thing is.

A young Chinese girl in the documentary says that her father said that if they hadn't left Hong Kong, his daughter would never have become a lesbian. This makes me laugh. I'd suggested something similar to my daughter. 'Maybe if we'd never left Melbourne it

68

wouldn't have been so easy for you to slip into this lesbian lifestyle,' I'd said to her. She had laughed. 'Melbourne is one of the epicentres of lesbian life,' she'd said.

Can you have one of the epicentres, or is an epicentre, by its very nature, the only one, I'd thought. I'd decided not to take up that semantic issue with my daughter. I made a note to myself to mention it another time. Growing up with parents who spoke broken English seems to have translated itself, in me, into a need for my children to speak perfect English.

The mothers in the documentary stopped crying when they joined a parent support group. In the group, they were told, over and over again, that homosexuals are born that way, not made. This removal of parental guilt seemed to be very powerful. By the end of the documentary, all of the parents, except the Chinese father, had adjusted and were blossoming in roles that began as disasters.

It is six months later, now. I think I am adjusting to the situation. I no longer feel a sense of shock when I think about my daughter. I've seen her quite a lot. We've talked and, on quite a few occasions, seem to have got back to the best we can be with each other. A best that is composed of ease, familiarity and joy. She has mentioned J. now and then. But we don't dwell on J. or the subject of homosexuality. I haven't met J. yet. I'm not in a rush.

One morning my husband tells me, quite casually,

in the course of a conversation about something else, that my daughter and J. are going to share a house by the sea for a week or two next summer. I feel shocked, as though the fact that I hadn't met J., and the fact that we didn't talk about her much, meant she and the lesbianism might have gone away.

I am ashamed of the sick feeling this piece of news has given me. How long will this sense of shock keep lingering? What do I want for my daughter anyway? Wasn't it happiness that I wanted for her? And isn't happiness so elusive that we should all be grateful for every way in which we feel it? My daughter certainly looks happy.

I am sitting in my study writing a poem to my younger daughter. It is a poem about my death. I tell her:

> *Throw out and discard*
> *the storage*
> *that comes with death*
>
> *separate the dresses*
> *and shoes*
> *and perfume*
>
> *they were not*
> *parts of me.*
> *I was made with many parts*
>
> *and all these parts*
> *are*
> *in your heart.*

I am not ill, just melancholy. My elder daughter arrives unexpectedly. In New York, no one arrives without calling first. Even your children. So I know something is up. It is. She has broken up with J. I am so pleased. All my melancholy evaporates. I try not to look cheerful. I force myself to look sombre. I worry that the forced sobriety comes across as sinister. 'I never really loved her,' my daughter says. I try not to nod in agreement. 'I liked her very much and I was happy with her, but I wasn't in love with her,' she says.

The effort of appearing neutral is taking a toll. My facial muscles are paralysed. 'Are you okay?' my daughter says. 'I'm fine,' I say. I'm more than fine. I'm elated. I feel positively light-hearted.

'When I told her I wanted to break up, she had a really bad reaction,' my daughter says. 'She went to pieces. She almost begged me to stay with her. It was awful. It really put me off her.' I can barely contain myself.

'That must have been hard for you,' I say. My daughter looks at me strangely. 'No, it wasn't hard. When she reacted like that I just wanted to get away from her.'

I can't think of anything to say. The act of repressing myself has rendered me speechless. I look down at the dress I am wearing. 'Do you think I should wash this dress or take it to the dry cleaners?' I say. My daughter looks at me in astonishment. 'Is that all you've got to say, Lil?' she says.

Summer arrives. We all have a wonderful summer. We rent a house on Shelter Island, a place I've become very attached to. Before this, the only attachments I've formed in my life were to people. I've never even been fond of dogs.

The house we rent is a modest three-bedroom cottage on an acre of land, five minutes from the beach. If I stand on my tip-toes, from the highest point in the garden, I can see the sea.

The house is just big enough for the girls' bedrooms to be out of earshot of ours. I, who get up very early, don't have to ask them to be quiet at night, or ask them what time they are going to bed.

My husband paints a lot. A young Australian architect, Jeremy Edmiston, has designed and erected a white canvas tent for my husband to paint in, in the front garden. The tent looks very middle-eastern, as though it belongs on the banks of the Nile or in the Sinai desert.

Both of my daughters love to swim. While my husband paints, we swim and swim. We swim in a freshwater pond. Islands of yellow waterlilies float around us. The water is like liquid silk. Better for your skin than Estée Lauder, Origins or Lancôme.

At its centre, the pond is over six hundred feet deep. I try not to think about that. I knew we were not the only inhabitants of the freshwater pond. But I banished all thoughts of the snapping turtles who have lived there for years. The locals said the turtles never bothered anyone. They said they were scared of people and wouldn't come near us.

The lake is a quarter of a mile wide. One day we were three-quarters of the way across, when my younger daughter, who was in the lead, suddenly shouted: 'Something slimy!' The three of us panicked. We turned and swam frantically back.

Occasionally, one of the girls checked that I was still afloat and still on my way back to the shore. We had caused a commotion. A few people were waiting at the edge of the pond for us.

'What was it?' several people said.

'Something slimy,' my younger daughter kept saying.

'Could have been a snake,' one man said. A snake. I made a note never to go into the pond again.

'Could have been a snapping turtle,' someone else said. My elder daughter shrieked: 'I'm not swimming in there ever again!'

An elderly woman walked up, holding a lily pad. She pressed the underside of the pad against my daughter's arm.

'Is that what you felt?' she said.

'That's it,' my younger daughter declared.

'Every summer there's someone who gets terrified by a lily pad,' the elderly woman said. All three of us looked embarrassed.

'Do you think there really are snakes in there?' my elder daughter said to me.

'I'm sure there aren't,' I said. We lined our towels up side by side and lay on the bank of the pond and dried off.

We played netball and table tennis. We worked out how to use the barbecue, and barbecued everything we could find. Swordfish, scallops, fresh tuna, red and yellow peppers, eggplant. We barbecued bananas stuffed with chocolate and became addicted to them. At night we played scrabble and went for walks. It was idyllic. It was as though we had gone back to the family we were when the kids were small. No one mentioned relationships. No one talked about the future. What to eat for dinner, and which beach to go to, were the most contentious issues we tackled. Our only tense moments came when a word was called into question around the scrabble board. It was bliss. We rode our bikes all over the island. We removed small turtles from the middle of the road, and oohed and aahed at the ospreys and the swans and the piping plovers and their new families. We watched a family of six dumpy, clumsy cygnets grow into elegant swans. We were so happy.

The happiness lasted back in Manhattan. My younger daughter went back to college ready to take on a new year. The aches and complaints left over from last year were almost invisible. I met my elder daughter for coffee and a movie. 'That was the best summer holiday I've had for years,' she said. 'Can we do it again next summer?'

The next time I speak to her, my daughter tells me

that she and J. are back together. I try to be pleased about it. It's a bit of an effort.

I notice that my husband and I no longer talk about this daughter in terms of her having children, having a family of her own. We have switched our focus to her career. But her lesbianism, her having an affair with a woman is no longer a shocking thing.

Although, there are small shocks. The first time I meet J., I am shocked at how obviously gay she looks. She is so clearly a gay woman. I'm not at all sure why this surprises me. Perhaps it's related to my fantasy that this isn't a mature lesbian love affair, but just two girls having fun.

Then comes the other shock. My daughter, in J.'s company, looks decidedly gay. Her hair, which has been growing steadily shorter, is very short. She is wearing low-slung men's trousers and thick brown leather sandals. I am shocked at how gay she looks. It was never visible before. Maybe it wasn't there before? Who knows. It is there now. I look at her several times. Her mannerisms are more manly. Her demeanour is more masculine. Her gestures more assertive. When she gets up to go to the bathroom, she walks with a slight swagger.

It takes me a while to recover from this small shock. When I calm down, I see that she hasn't changed into somebody else. She is still there. She is still my daughter.

It is a year later, now. A year after that fateful breakfast

in Cafe Dante. My daughter is still with J. The relationship is not perfect. Sometimes she complains about J.'s
domineering ways. Other times she has other complaints. They have fought and made up. They have
broken up and reconciled. Much like any other couple,
I guess.

I stay out of it. I have learned, belatedly, to stay out
of my children's relationships. All three children have
benefited from this.

My transvestite is standing on the corner of West
Broadway and Spring Street again. I am totally bowled
over by her outfit. She is in red. Several different shades
of red. She is wearing a scarlet, satin dress. The skirt is
tulip-shaped, with a scalloped hemline. The bodice is
also scalloped, and low-cut. On her head is a crimson
silk hat. The hat has a dark crimson net which dips down
over her eyes. This small veil is very fetching. It creates
a demure look, despite the false eyelashes and vermillion
lipstick. I love the outfit. I wish I could wear it.

'You're very regular,' the transvestite says to me.
'I've seen you three weekends in a row at exactly this
time.' I am astonished. You think you are anonymous
in Manhattan. Just one of so many people. But you are
not. In Manhattan, everyone notices everything.

The young Englishmen who run a flea-market stall
near my building used to tell me, if I'd been out in the
afternoon, what time my daughter got home from
school. They used to tell her how many times I'd been
out that day. Occasionally, they'd volunteer some extra

information like: 'Your mum didn't look in a very good mood today.'

The man who cleans the windows of the corner store asked me this week why I'd missed my early-morning walk on Thursday. And the postal worker, who delivers mail on West Broadway, stopped me to congratulate me on my weight loss. Two days later, she stopped me again and asked if I had a special diet. I made one up on the spot.

'I've been here, at the same time, three Saturdays in a row?' I say to the transvestite.

'Yes,' she says. I'm surprised. Surprised that I didn't notice this myself.

The transvestite looks at me. 'You've been here at exactly the same time,' she says. 'And you're wearing the same outfit you had on last week.' I look startled. 'You don't want to get stuck in a rut,' she says.

She looks me up and down. 'You want to expand your horizons, darling. Trust me,' she says. I laugh. 'That's very good advice,' I say to her. I walk away. A few minutes later, I am still laughing.

SEX

MY MOTHER LOOKED LIKE A cross between Sophia Loren and Gina Lollobrigida. She was all low-cut necklines, backless and strapless dresses. In summer, she wore bikinis at the beach, in the garden and around the house.

When she went out at night, her eyes smouldered, even when she lowered her lashes. All that allure and heat was contained in a strangely restrained person. My mother could display her body, but except for being able to comment about whether people were slim or fat, she couldn't talk about bodies or bodily functions.

When she said to me, when I was seventeen, 'If you respect yourself, others will,' I knew what she meant by that quick, cryptic dispatch. But I'd already not respected myself. I'd been having sex with my boyfriend. In his bed, in my bed, in his parents' bed, in the car. My mother's admonition was too late. I was already all out of respect.

I tried to be more prescient with my daughters. More direct, or at least less oblique. We began talking about bodies and reproduction and love at an early age.

My younger daughter startled me when she announced that she'd like to use Justin Derry's sperm to make a baby. She was four at the time and so was Justin Derry. She said it was because he had such nice blue eyes. I made a note to keep an eye on her.

Talking about bodies and bodily functions became even more imperative with the advent of AIDS and the emergence of a slew of sexually transmitted diseases. Over the years we had many talks.

My younger daughter left home at seventeen. She left home to go to Bryn Mawr College in Philadelphia. That's the American way. Americans don't think of it as leaving home. They think of it as going to college. I found it hard to think of it as anything other than leaving home.

An irritated neighbour snapped at me, when I was looking particularly morose one day, 'Your daughter has got into one of the top colleges in the country. Stop looking as though it's a tragedy.'

The day I took my daughter to this top college, I tried not to look as though it was a tragedy. I helped her to unpack the 156 boxes of essentials she had packed to bring to Philadelphia. I thought I should run through a checklist of essentials, myself.

'You know I love you,' I said.

'Of course I do,' she said.

'You know you can ring me whenever you want to,' I said.

'Yeah, I know that,' she said.

'You can write to me too,' I said. 'And I'll write to you.' She nodded.

'When you get a letter from me, highlight any questions in the letter,' I said. 'That way when you write back you can answer all the questions.' I paused. I was feeling uneasy. Letters suddenly seemed an archaic and inadequate method of communication.

'Maybe I should buy you a fax machine,' I said.

'So you can fax me and write to me?' my daughter said. 'I'd be highlighting day and night.'

I took a deep breath and thought of my neighbour. I tried to snap out of the tragic mode I could see I was slipping into. I picked up a medicine bag I had packed for my daughter. 'There's some cortisone cream in here if you get another eye infection,' I said. My daughter looked at me in disbelief.

'I had that eye infection when I was nine,' she said.

'It could come back,' I said. 'And I've packed some Advil, that seems to work best when you get a headache, and calamine lotion, some antiseptic cream, throat lozenges and cough medicine.'

81

My daughter stopped unpacking. 'Lil,' she said, 'this is a college, not a sanitarium.'

'Don't forget you're allergic to penicillin,' I said. My daughter took the medicine bag and put it under her bed.

'There's nothing you want to ask me about sex, is there?' I said, trying to sound relaxed.

'No,' she said.

'About contraception?' I said.

'No,' she said. 'I'm an expert. Not that I'll ever get a chance to put that expertise into practice. I can put a condom on a cucumber in ten seconds flat, and that includes squeezing the air out of the tip. Last year, the whole class had to practise putting condoms on a cucumber. We had to roll the condom over the cucumber as soon as the cucumber was erect, before continuing with any foreplay. The teacher said we should never wait until the last minute to put a condom on a cucumber.

'We practised removing the condom after ejaculation, before the cucumber could become flaccid. We had to hold it, carefully, by the rim and discard it in a tissue.' I started laughing. I knew that all the thought we had put into choosing the right high school for her, in Manhattan, had been worth it.

We were both laughing. I should have dropped the subject then and there, while the going was good. But I've never been good at knowing when to stop. 'You know it's worth waiting for someone you really care about before you leap in and have sex,' I said to my daughter.

'I'm not leaping,' she said. 'There's no one in sight to leap to.'

'I'm serious,' I said. 'When you have sex, you're so close to the other person that it's easy to believe you really are close. The reality could be that you know nothing about them other than what they feel like.'

'Isn't that quite a lot?' my daughter said brightly. I glared at her. 'Just joking,' she said. I felt irritated. I was getting a headache. I wasn't looking forward to saying goodbye to my daughter. I have always found goodbyes difficult. I see them as permanent. I see the smallest separation as a split. Especially with this daughter, my youngest, my baby, despite her adult appearance.

'I wasn't joking,' I said. 'I meant it. Instead of fleeting and awkward sex with someone you don't know, it's worth waiting to experience the full majesty of making love.'

I stunned myself with that sentence. Where did those words come from? My anxiety about leaving was turning me into Barbara Cartland.

My daughter looked at me as though I'd just turned into E.T. 'Lil,' she said, 'you sound like someone straight out of *The Young and the Restless*.'

'I thought you never watched soap operas,' I said. We spent the rest of the afternoon sorting socks, and assorted underwear and outerwear, into drawers and cupboards.

The day before, my closest friend in America, Mimi Bochco, had called me from L.A., where she lives. She knew I'd been dreading this day. 'Darling,' Mimi said, 'I know you're feeling bad. I remember when my children left for college. It feels terrible for a few days. And then it feels wonderful.'

I tried to keep Mimi's words in mind. She's lived a lot longer than I have and she knows what she's talking about.

After my daughter and I unpacked, we walked to one of the college's large auditoriums and listened to the President of the college give her Freshmen Address. It was a very moving speech and I was not the only parent who was tearful.

Afterwards, we walked across the beautiful grounds of the college to one of the halls of residence, and had afternoon tea. By then my head was splitting. 'I've got to go,' I said to my daughter. 'I've got to get this goodbye over with.' She looked a bit trembly.

'Maybe you could stay another half an hour?' she said.

I looked at my husband. He was happy to go or to stay. 'Okay,' I said. 'I'll go through the stuff in your drawers and tell you what's where.'

'Maybe we should just say goodbye,' my daughter said.

When I got home, I called Mimi. I said hello and started weeping. Mimi made me laugh. 'Helen Bloomberg rang me yesterday,' she said. 'She asked after you.

Then she said that I am a mother substitute for you. I said to her, "So what. She couldn't have a better one".'

'You're right,' I said.

Mimi is probably older than my mother would have been if she were still alive. I don't know exactly how old Mimi is. I've known her for ten years. We talk several times a week. She says she loves me. She tells me everything. But she won't tell me her age.

I think Mimi is more or less eighty. Some years she is less — last year she was seventy-two. Some years she is more — four years ago she was seventy-five. Mimi's son Steven, the writer and producer of such television shows as *Hill Street Blues*, *L.A. Law* and *NYPD Blue*, wants to give Mimi an eightieth birthday party. 'When I decide to be eighty, I'll let you know,' she said to him.

'I didn't do all that well,' I said to Mimi. 'I cried and I talked about sex.'

'That doesn't sound bad,' Mimi said.

'It was bad,' I said. 'I sounded like Danielle Steele. I talked about the full majesty of making love as opposed to just fucking with someone.'

'I agree there's a full majesty,' Mimi said. 'But it depends on whom you're fucking. Some people have a small, thin majesty.'

Mimi is incorrigible. She says exactly what she wants to say. To everybody. She decides to distract me from my distress by telling me about a mutual friend, a woman in her fifties who has been single all her life. 'She finally met a wonderful man,' Mimi says. 'He's intelligent, kind, very good-looking – I saw him myself – and very successful. And they share a lot of interests. But, when push came to shove, he couldn't push and he couldn't shove.'

'Oh no,' I say, laughing.

'Oh yes,' Mimi says.

'So what's happening with them?' I ask.

'She's not seeing him anymore,' Mimi said.

It seems like a severe solution to the problem, to me. 'Surely they could have worked something out?' I say. 'If he's intelligent and kind and they share a lot of interests. A lot of people share very little with each other and don't do much pushing and shoving either. This guy seems to have a lot going for him.'

'Except that one thing which isn't going anywhere,' Mimi says.

'Does it matter?' I say.

'Of course it matters,' Mimi says.

Mimi speaks with a thick Lithuanian accent. This makes me feel very at home. It reminds me of my child-hood in Carlton, a community of migrants and refugees. Everyone had accents, and mangled and inventive English.

Some of the happiest moments of my childhood were at Mr Kurop's grocer store. On the corner of Amess and Pigdon streets, Mr Kurop stocked food that you couldn't buy anywhere else in Melbourne. Big barrels of dill pickles and olives were on the floor. Huge stacks of rye bread, dark bitter chocolate and halva were on the counter. There were shelves filled with sausages and a fridge packed with fresh herring, sauerkraut and rollmops.

On Saturday mornings the shop was always crowded. All the women I saw walking their children to school or rushing in and out of their houses during the week, seemed to be in Mr Kurop's on Saturday morning.

Everyone knew each other, if not well, at least by sight. And everyone talked. They talked about everything. And they complained. It's a Jewish thing to complain. When I wake up in the morning, I give my husband a run down of what's wrong with me. I might have had an unpleasant dream, or slept badly. I might have woken up with a sore neck or a sore psyche. But, after I've listed my various complaints, I feel much better.

The women in Mr Kurop's complained about everything. They complained about their husbands. Everyone knew who was a good worker, who wasn't and who was being paid what. They complained about their sex lives. The women knew who was having too much sex and who wasn't having enough. They talked about sex easily, as though it was as much of an everyday subject as their shopping. They talked about what their husbands wanted in bed last night and what they didn't want. What was good and what wasn't so good.

They spoke Yiddish. They used strong, robust words. They dispensed with polite phrases and words, like making love and intercourse. Their talk was street talk.

I was mesmerised. My women friends, my contemporaries, never talk to each other about what happened last night. And maybe that's not such a good thing. Not only do we not talk much about sex, I think we are not supposed to write about it, either. There is a lot of sex in my last novel, *Just Like That*. Or is there? I'm not sure what constitutes a lot of sex. Sex on what percentage of the pages? What I do know is that men clear their throats, constantly, when referring to that aspect of the book. 'There's a lot of hum, um, uh, ah, um,' male journalist after male journalist said to me. 'It's very, um, very, um, gritty,' said a butch-looking reporter for a suburban newspaper.

'You've got a very modest demeanour for a girl who writes like that,' a radio announcer called out to me across the lobby of the radio station. I decided to dwell on the pleasure of being called a girl rather than be unnerved by what 'like that' could mean. All this awkwardness came from men. Women talked about the love in the novel and the fact that the love and the lust were between a married couple.

I do understand the awkwardness. Sitting on my own, in my study, writing an intense and long description of two people making love, I realised I was feeling aroused. I felt embarrassed and awkward. My response surprised me. The embarrassment, not the arousal. Why did I feel embarrassed? Who was I embarrassed in front of? Part of me felt there was something forbidden, something illicit about feeling sexual, on my own, in the middle of the day. As though my sexuality was somehow separate from the rest of me, and could be tucked away and brought out at the appropriate times.

This constraint is something that I don't feel when I write. When I write, I feel a great palpable freedom. I can fly, I can leap, I can take risks.

When I stop writing, I return to my fearful, cautious, self-conscious self. When I am asked to read from my work, I have a problem. I can't read a lot of what I write. Not out loud, anyway. I can't read anything that is too sad or I start weeping. I can't read anything that is about my mother, or the same thing happens. I can't read anything to do with sex or bodily fluids. That leaves me with just the funny bits, and it's hard to read them without laughing.

Last year, I was invited to read at The Harbourfront Festival in Toronto. My New York agent suggested I read the first chapter of *Just Like That*, as it is self-contained.

I stood in front of the bathroom mirror for hours, and practised saying 'He sucks all the cum out of me' in a nonchalant manner. I practised and practised. I tried to stop flinching as I said 'sucked'. And I tried not to rush over the word 'cum'. I tried smiling as I read, but the smile looked slippery. I tried to be expressionless but my discomfort slipped through.

Finally, I gave up. I found a section about New Yorkers and their dogs. And I read that. But, even then, I skipped the bits about how the various dogs shit.

My children don't have this trouble. They discuss orifices, their own and others', with ease. I listened to a discussion about dental dams between my two daughters, for ten minutes, before I asked what dental dams were.

'They're a covering to protect your mouth during oral sex,' my younger daughter said. She looked at me as though I must have been living on Mars, not to know what dental dams were.

'Where have you been, Lil?' she said.

'Obviously not hanging out with the same crowd as you' I said, loudly.

'Some people use a plastic wrap,' she said. 'Regular or microwaveable.'

'Have you ever heard anyone talk about dental dams?' I asked my husband, when he came out of his studio.

'Never,' he said. I felt better.

'You can use Gladwrap,' I said. 'Regular or microwaveable.' I then told him about latex gloves and finger cots, and their various uses, information which the girls had felt obliged to pass onto me. 'I thought I'd brought them up to be more reserved,' I said to my husband.

My son has the same lack of restraint. I was talking to a friend, with great pride, about my asymptomatic menopause. My son, who was working at a computer at the other end of the room, called out, 'You've got no symptoms at all, Lil?'

'No, none,' I said.

'What about vaginal dryness?' he said. I was taken aback. Firstly, I thought he was too far away to be able to hear the conversation, and, secondly, he had seemed engrossed in his computer. 'What about vaginal dryness?' he said again. 'You've got no vaginal dryness?'

I took a deep breath. It's not easy to shout across a room about vaginal dryness. Especially to your son. He *is* a doctor. But, still, who wants to talk about vaginal dryness with their kid? 'No I don't,' I said to him.

'Really?' he said.

'Really,' I said.

This was the kid who asked me, when he was four, if he could look and see where the tampon I was inserting was going to. The question took me by surprise. I didn't want to appear prudish, or make the tampon's absence any more mysterious or interesting than it already was. I didn't want to appear uncomfortable with any part of my body either, particularly that part. And I didn't want to show him where the Tampax went. I didn't know what to do. I pretended I was in a hurry. 'We have to go out,' I said. 'But you can have a quick look.' He looked, and looked unimpressed.

It's a touchy subject, sex. My husband has had to cope with me writing about sex. He has had to tolerate seeing very intimate parts of his life appear on my pages. Luckily, he continues to love me.

Writers are always observing themselves as well as observing others. It's terrible, in a way. You can be doing something very intimate, like making love, and you can find yourself making a mental note of a certain sound or gesture.

Being able to expose myself on paper, doesn't mean I am uninhibited in real life. I can't even watch R-rated movies with anyone other than my husband. These are movies with wholesome, academy-award-winning actors. Movies that gangs of teenagers and groups of adults go to together.

On screen, when people make love with varying degrees of heat, lust, love and athleticism, I feel edgy. I look at the audience. They watch as pelvises thrust, thighs thunder, mouths water, legs grip and skins snap and clap together. Few of them look uncomfortable about what they are watching. They're there with friends, with family. I have to censor what I see with friends and with family. I would choose *The Sound of Music* as our family outing if it was up to me.

When I was in Australia last year, I decided to go to the movies with my father. My father really wanted to see *Heat*. He loves Robert DeNiro. *Heat* is R-rated. I persuaded my father to see *Babe*. He didn't like it.

'What a sweet movie,' I said to him when the film ended.

'Ugh,' he said.

I decided that I was a prude when I felt embarrassed at feeling aroused after watching the only porno movie I've ever watched.

'They're supposed to arouse you,' my husband said.

'But it was so bad. Such a tacky movie,' I said.

'I don't think it's the intellectual content of the plot that's supposed to work on your libido,' he said. I felt deflated. I thought my libido was more discerning.

The prudish part of me wasn't evident to my father when I was a teenager. He used to call me a prostitute if I came home late at night. He would greet me at the door, in his pyjamas. He'd look at his watch – it was probably 11:15 p.m. – and say, 'What are you? A prostitute?'

I often wondered if the words wouldn't have seemed so harsh in Polish, in Poland. Maybe there was a level of affection in the phrasing that I was missing. In English, the question and the accusation felt awful. Especially as I was so innocent. I spent my days dreaming about falling in love. And I was so virginal.

This very virginity lost me the first serious boyfriend I had. I was fifteen when I met him at a dance, at a seaside resort in the summer. I was overwhelmed and overjoyed when he asked me to dance. He had shoulder-length hair, in the days of short back and sides, just before the Beatles. And he wore jeans and no shoes. He told me on our first date that he owned three pairs of jeans and five white shirts and that was it. I decided against listing my own more elaborate wardrobe.

I let my parents know that both his parents were doctors and that he was Jewish. They overlooked his hair, his bare feet and his unvarying wardrobe. They embraced him.

But I wasn't embracing enough. One night he told

me he could no longer go out with someone who wouldn't have sex with him. He was too old, he said, to have a relationship that excluded sex. He was eighteen. For a moment I contemplated keeping him by losing my virginity, but it didn't seem right. It seemed too cold-blooded for what I still hoped would be a romantic occasion. I looked a bit sad, but he wasn't moved. He went back to his former girlfriend.

I felt a bit of a failure. For months after he left me, my parents kept hoping he'd ring. 'Maybe you could lose some weight,' my mother said every time the phone didn't ring.

'Don't you experience lust?' said a school friend when I told her about the break-up. This friend was one of the most sophisticated girls at University High School. While other girls talked about letting boys go all the way, she talked about making love, outside, in the open air. At one with, and connected to, the earth. She wore black shifts and Bandit perfume. Did I experience lust? I'd never thought about it. I felt inadequate all over again.

I experienced an overload of lust when I met the man I am now married to. There was a slight problem. I was married to someone else at the time.

I left my first husband, not only because I was besotted about the man I am now married to, but because I realised that I no longer lusted after my husband. I realised this when my knees went weak, the first time my current husband touched me. Weak knees are a reliable indicator of lust. They may also make a good marker for love.

I was thirty-two when my knees made their move. I loved my husband. We'd been together since I was nineteen. We seemed to have a good marriage. We had shared interests, beautiful children, reasonable sex. And that was what shocked me. The reasonable sex. I was shocked to have lost my lust at such a young age. To have settled into some sort of workaday easiness about making love. Sex was certainly no longer the powerful, explosive force it had been briefly.

I didn't know this until I felt the pull of that power. The pull that made me, someone who was happily married, overlook my married state and leap into someone else's arms. Luckily, I landed in the right place. I'm still wild about him.

Sometimes you land in the wrong place. Until I was about forty, I used to weep when I read about children who were sexually abused. I sometimes still do. I thought I wasn't one of them. I knew I had been sex-ually abused. But I never thought of myself as the victim. I thought it was my fault. I thought I was a bad child. I thought it must have been the bad part of me my mother was talking about when she sometimes said: 'You'll drive me to my grave.'

I was very young when it began. Six or seven. It happened regularly. Two or three times a week. He was an adult and I was a child. I knew there was something wrong with what happened, but I thought I was the criminal.

He was the man who lived next door to us in Nicholson Street, Carlton. He had things I had never seen before. A glass paperweight with snowflakes that floated over the Leaning Tower of Pisa after you turned it upside down.

He had another gadget. It almost makes me ill to recall it. It was a toy slide viewer. You pressed a button on top of the blue plastic box and a series of photographs of various parts of Italy came into view.

He also had a kaleidoscope. You turned the end and an endless parade of colours and shapes fell into extraordinary configurations and patterns.

I sat on his lap and looked at the colourful display while he masturbated me. I shook snow all over the Leaning Tower of Pisa with his hands in my pants.

I got to know Italy. I looked at slides of the Trevi Fountain, the Vatican, the Sistine Chapel, the ruins of Pompeii, the canals of Venice, the bay of Naples, while he rhythmically moved his fingers around my vagina.

No one else was ever there. He lived in a small, bare cottage that was almost a mirror image of the cottage we lived in. As my mother cooked or cleaned or sat behind her sewing machine, I was sitting ten feet away, separated by two walls and an entire universe.

How old was he? Thirty, forty, fifty? I don't know. He wasn't a kid and he wasn't an old man. I don't remember talking to him, ever. He never offered me a drink or a biscuit or a sweet. He offered me his lap and his hands.

I never saw him outside his house. I never saw him in the street. I never saw him playing pinball in the milk bar a couple of doors away. Italian men often gathered there after work to play the pinball machine.

I never saw him at Mr Keech the butcher's or Mr Canals the fishmonger. I never even saw him in his backyard, which was separated from ours by a thin paling fence.

This was happening in Carlton, Australia. A friendly, safe inner-city suburb of Melbourne. A suburb made up, mostly, of migrants and refugees. Germans, Maltese, Italians, Jews, Chinese. A friendly, safe suburb in a friendly, safe city. But it was clearly not safe to be too friendly. Even if you were only six.

Why did I keep going back day after day? I must have wanted the attention so badly. I must have wanted the affection so badly. I must have been trusting, like a lot of little girls. I must have wanted it, and it must have felt good.

I still feel more disgusted with myself than I am with him. I obviously colluded. I didn't tell anyone, even when I sensed it was wrong. I never mentioned it to my best friend and I told her everything.

I didn't tell anyone for years. I didn't tell my first analyst, I didn't tell my first husband. I didn't tell my best friend. I didn't tell my children. I didn't think about the ramifications. I think I thought it was part and parcel of growing up. Part of the uncomfortable part of growing up.

Like the juggling, when I was a bit older, to not be left alone with the distant relative who always grabbed my developing breasts, whenever I passed him. Sometimes he offered me a chocolate bar. I was smarter by then, I always said no.

I was pretty smart too, to avoid being raped when I was an adolescent. My parents left us, some nights, with a brother and sister who lived down the street. They were newly-arrived migrants and must have seemed like reliable baby-sitters. While my sister slept, they had sex with each other, on a couch in my parents' bedroom.

He made me watch. He kissed her and touched her. He shoved himself into her. He grunted and sweated and slammed himself against her.

After he had fucked his sister, he would tell me to give it a try. His English was limited, but he let me know I'd like it. I don't remember what I said. I only remember my terror.

I kept all of this to myself. I think the subject was too unsavoury to bring up. I think I was frightened of being tainted, by virtue of the fact that I had been present. I didn't want my parents to know what I had witnessed. I thought it was better to appear innocent. And I think I kept quiet, too, because I didn't want to add to my mother's troubles. As an overweight daughter, who ignored all her implorings to lose weight, I already felt enough of a burden.

I remember all of this so clearly. The cousin twice-removed, the baby-sitters, the man next door. I don't want to remember. I have tried to forget. Yet, I remember each detail vividly.

Why is the memory of these events so clear when my memories of so many wonderful moments are almost erased? And why do these memories return to me, so unexpectedly and so relentlessly and so unpleasantly? I can be reading a book, at home at night, and suddenly an image of a detail of the Sistine Chapel comes into my head. I see God, with his long grey beard stretched out across space, his finger touching Adam's finger. The flesh tones are distorted in the cheap reproduction. Instead of siennas and ochres, God and Adam are an electric orange and shrill yellow. It looks like a scene from *South Pacific*. 'Some Enchanted Evening' with a gay cast. I know that the next slide is going to be the Trevi fountain. And I see the neighbour, the man next door, and his incessantly moving fingers. Sometimes I think the feeling of grubbiness will never leave me.

Why are these memories so potent? It is as though the experience itself is always active and viable when other parts of my past have long since disappeared. It is as though the grubbiness, the mess of my own needs and collaboration, is intertwined with the grubbiness of his hands.

I may think I am no longer the six- and seven-year-old who watched those snowflakes as they descended over that Leaning Tower of Pisa. I may think it is part of my past. But it is the one part of my past that has stuck with me, intact and new. Untarnished and unblemished.

What was my father doing while I was visiting the man next door? He was working. In factories. Stitching fabrics and carrying parcels. On weekends he delivered parcels of work to piece-workers who worked at home. He was always working.

What was my mother doing? She was working, too. At home, behind a sewing machine. But she was also preoccupied. Preoccupied with hundreds of dead. Her dead mother and father, her dead brothers and sisters, her dead nieces and nephews, and aunts and uncles. Once, in Stuthof, she had been taken for one of the dead herself. She had typhoid and was lying outside, on the ground, in mid-winter. They threw her onto a pile of dead bodies. A school friend pulled her off and took her back to her bunk.

My mother had a lot to shut out. In her preoccupation, she lost sight of me. She shut out my long absences. Maybe her negligence was aided by her ambivalence. She loved me fiercely. She told me things she never talked to anyone else about. My mother, who never confided in anybody, who held herself aloof, confided in me. She talked to me, in this confidential way, from the time I was a small child. The most horrific things I know about her years in the ghetto and in Auschwitz and Stuthof, are things I've known since I was a young girl.

Then, they were all part of an incomprehensible and

terrifying part of something awful that I wished would go away. Now I know that that something awful was her life, and all the terror and horror was part of her. It couldn't go away.

On the one hand, my mother guarded me ferociously. My diet, my hair and my piano lessons were the subject of her undivided attention. On the other hand, she neglected me. Unconsciously, of course, she wanted me to know some of what she had felt. Maybe exposing me to danger linked us even more closely.

It was a huge relief for my mother to bring up a child in a peaceful, safe, free country, so far away from Europe. And it tormented her to have a child so removed from her own past. Her constant refrain: 'You will never know what I went through', still rings in my ears.

I knew that what my mother had been through wasn't ordinary. I knew that our goal, in Australia, was to lead an ordinary life. The man next door looked ordinary. A new migrant living in an ordinary house, in an ordinary street.

My mother often told me that she knew what ordinary people were capable of. My mother knew it was ordinary Germans who murdered and brutalised millions of Jews. Her experience had been so extraordinary, that she was separated, permanently, from ordinary life. She scrutinised, carefully, some ordinary details of my life. The length of my skirt, every crease in a shirt, every spot on a dress, whether I was fatter or thinner.

But when I wasn't there, no one asked where I was. I wandered around Carlton. I knew every lane and alleyway. I sat on somebody's front fence and watched as the drunks poured out of the pub on the corner of Nicholson and McPherson Streets, at six o'clock every night. Some of them were so drunk. I was fascinated by their wobbly legs and the way they weaved across the footpath. Sometimes they spoke to themselves. Sometimes they groaned and looked like they were about to weep.

One of them vomited right in front of me once. He vomited up baked beans. I'd never seen baked beans. We never had Australian food in our house. I was fascinated. I bent down to examine the baked beans. Mrs Dent, who lived on the other side of us, was just coming home from her volunteer work at the Methodist church around the corner.

Mrs Dent was a real salt-of-the-earth Australian. She baked apple pies and brought them in to us. She made jams and marmalades. And she was always helping somebody. She tried to help my mother adjust to life in Australia. She taught her how to make a meat pie. But my mother substituted sauteed veal and beef slices for the minced meat filling, and they never tasted right.

My mother was grateful to Mrs Dent. I think she was relieved to know such an inherently good human being. My mother taught Mrs Dent to make gefilte fish, ground fish formed into balls and boiled in fish broth. Mrs Dent had acquired a taste for it. Gefilte fish is traditionally eaten at Passover. It is a difficult dish to master.

But Mrs Dent's gefilte fish, which she served in its own jelly, was very good. She once made a batch of it for some friends of hers from the church. They hated it.

I felt very comfortable with Mrs Dent. I ate her apple pies and I watched television, sometimes, in her house. The Mickey Mouse Club, and Tom Terrific.

Mrs Dent stopped in the street. She looked at me, bent over the regurgitated beans. 'That's a filthy thing to do,' she said, and dragged me home. 'I caught her doing a filthy thing,' Mrs Dent said to my mother. My mother didn't seem too disturbed. She told me to wash my hands for dinner. My mother had experienced real filth.

Once I ventured outside Carlton. I rode my bicycle to Northcote, three or four miles away. I was gone for half a day. No one asked where I had been. In a poem, 'Growing Up', I wrote about my parents that:

> they knew
> extraordinary danger
> ordinary danger
> eluded them

The ordinary Germans, who erased everyone my mother loved and who eroded my mother's capacity to be connected to her present, were just that. Ordinary Germans. The men in the German police battalions were not chosen for their ideological allegiance to the Nazi party. There was a shortage of German police man-power. The Germans took all the men they could get.

These ordinary men had children, wives, lovers. They had love affairs while they were murdering Jews. They had good appetites and relished their meals, at the same time as they burned Jewish bodies. They listened to musical concerts and they went to church.

No one had to incite these ordinary men to work hard in the slaughtering of Jewish men, women and children. No one had to encourage them to be more enthusiastic in their round-ups of Jews. They carried out their jobs with vigour. They did more than was asked of them. They used their ingenuity. They set Jewish men's beards alight. They unzipped themselves and urinated on Jewish women. They shot Jews, often before they were given orders to shoot, and when shooting Jews proved to be too slow, they burnt them alive.

Some of these ordinary men were sensitive. They shielded the wives who were with the battalions from some of the more gruesome sights. These ordinary men weren't reflecting a Nazi sensibility. They hated Jews.

My mother, who was seventeen when she was herded into the Lodz ghetto and twenty-three when she was liberated from Stuthof, the concentration camp she was sent to from Auschwitz, found it difficult to distinguish between ordinary and extraordinary. She gasped when the phone rang. She braced herself every time there was a knock at the front door. If one of my children caught a cold, my mother acted as though it was pneumonia.

My mother spent her life chronically distressed. She

covered the distress up with elegant clothes and a beautiful tan. But her distress was always there. Sometimes it was temporarily relieved by the sun or by grandchildren, but it never left her for very long.

I didn't feel entitled to feel distressed. Nothing that terrible had happened to me. Certainly nothing that could compare with a fraction of what had happened to my mother and to my father. As a child, I was terminally cheerful. Even as a teenager, I laughed a lot. I hid my distress, from myself as well as from others.

I pretended I had had a childhood of Sao biscuits and sunshine, which was a bit of a stretch given my parents' history. And a bit of a stretch given that everyone around me was damaged, bereaved and grief-stricken.

After all they had been through, my parents were still living in barracks when I was conceived after the war. They were in a D.P. camp, Feldafing, in Germany.

For years, I remembered such a happy childhood. Visits to the zoo or trips to Luna Park with my father. Ice-creams. Lots of friends at school. Being invited to their homes after school. I dislodged and dispersed any unpleasantness. I eliminated all my bad memories. I forgot about feeling like a foreigner despite my Australian accent. I forgot about my amazement and my humiliation when Caroline B.'s whole family sat down to a meal of toast and chops and left me in the living room on my own.

'I don't know whether you people eat toast,'

Caroline B.'s mother called out to me through a partition. 'And I'm sure you don't eat chops.' I loved toast and I loved chops. I sat in the living room and pretended it didn't matter.

I was good at pretending. For decades I pretended that nothing bad had happened to me. Nothing really traumatic, anyway. I read articles on child abuse and felt so grateful that I hadn't experienced any.

When I first told my analyst, and this was my second analyst, I shook and I wept. I felt so grubby and so humiliated. Years later, with my third analyst, I lay on the couch in dread. As much in dread of what I remembered about the man next door, as what I may not be remembering about him. Did I see his penis? I wondered to myself on the couch, and then trembled so much it was hard to stand up when the session was over. Did he have an orgasm? I don't know whether he came or not. Thinking about it makes me feel ill.

Part of the agoraphobia which I had, on and off, for many years, was a fear of being alone with a man. I couldn't get in a cab, in New York, on my own. I thought that it was my fear of the driver. It was my fear of myself. What would I do if I was left alone with a man? I thought what I did with the man next door might be what I did if I was left alone with any strange man.

Writing about this bothers me. Suddenly my study feels airless. I feel a need to get out and walk. I walk and I walk. I walk eight miles. It takes me just under two hours.

I feel better. I've walked along the Hudson river. I've inhaled some fresh air. And I've exhaled some parts of the past that seemed to coat even the lining of my lungs.

I'm happy to be out on my own. Happy to be able to go out on my own. My agoraphobia seems at last to have gone. I can shop on my own, I can catch cabs on my own, I can sit in cafes on my own.

Sometimes, being on your own has its drawbacks. In cafes, people feel more free to chat to you. I stop at Auggie's for a coffee after my walk. A man in his mid to late thirties sits at my table. I've seen him around before. I know he lives locally. I'm not very friendly. I don't talk easily to people I don't know. I nod to him and pretend to be engrossed in a copy of the *New York Post*. That's quite a feat, as I usually want to throw this right-wing tabloid into the nearest rubbish bin.

He puts his caffe latte and a small laptop computer on the table.

'Hi,' he says. 'I'm Joe. You are really looking great. Are you working out?' I am annoyed that he is speaking to me. I try to be brief.

'Yes, I work out,' I say.

'I thought so,' he says. 'I can tell by the shape of your shoulders.'

Vanity gets the better of me and I smile.

'I see you in the area all the time. You're always with your husband. The two of you look so in love,' he says.

'I'm not always with him,' I say, before I can stop myself.

'I wish I was in love,' he says. 'I'm looking for a relationship.'

I can't believe this. I just want a quiet cup of coffee.

'Well I'm married,' I say as a joke. He doesn't get it.

'Of course you are. I see you with your husband all the time. I just told you. Do you know any women who'd be interested in meeting me?'

I put down the *New York Post*. In New York, you become very adept at brushing people off. 'No, I don't,' I say loudly, and I pick up the newspaper again.

'I'm a professor,' he says. 'I've got a nice apartment in Sullivan Street and a 1969 Mercedes convertible. And I'm serious. I want a relationship and you look like the kind of person who would know people that I like.'

I put the paper down. I have been an incorrigible and unsuccessful matchmaker all of my life. The news of my miserable matchmaking record obviously hasn't spread to Sullivan Street.

'I'm very serious about looking for a relationship,' he says again. I look him over. He is quite presentable. Regular symmetrical features, a hip haircut, Banana Republic clothes. He is about 5'11", with dark brown hair. And he is a professor. A professor of what? I am just about to ask him, when he starts speaking, again.

'It's not a cheap process looking for a relationship,' he says. 'By the time you have several dinners out, buy extra clothes, have to pay extra dry-cleaning bills, the cost can run to $200 per date. And that's for the relationships that don't last too long. If they last longer, you can be in for a lot more expense. It's a very costly procedure. I always go Dutch.'

I am speechless. Joe interprets my silence as sympathy. 'I'm a professor,' he says. 'I have students falling in love with me all the time. It's a problem that professors have. But I'm not interested in young girls. Some of them are very attractive, but I'm looking for a more mature woman. And she has to be geographically desirable. New York's a town where you can go for months without getting to see a friend. People in your life have got to be geographically desirable. You're not going to travel to Queens for an impulse late-night chat.'

I shook my head. Geographical desirability isn't a quality I have thought about a lot. 'Everyone in New York is in a rush,' Joe says, 'so you have to make decisions early on in the relationship. It can be tough to evaluate a possible future in one or two dates.'

Joe clearly has no need for me to speak. He hasn't paused for breath. Luckily I haven't said anything. Luckier still, I haven't volunteered one of my single friends as a possible date. He looked normal to me, when I used to see him in the street. Maybe he is normal. Maybe what is normal in New York is not normal anywhere else. I suddenly feel very normal.

My friend Mimi calls when I get back home. I can hear her husband, Win, in the background. Win is ninety. He is prompting her about bits of news he wants her to relay. Win and Mimi were married when Win was eighty-one and Mimi was sixty- or seventy-something.

When Mimi's son, Steven, asked Win why it was necessary for them to get married, as opposed to just living together, Win looked at Steven and said: 'Your mother is pregnant and I want to do the right thing by her.' I used this line of Win's at the end of *Just Like That*. It still makes me laugh.

I tell Mimi about Joe and the cafe. I tell her the account of his escalating expenses as he searches for a relationship. And I tell her about the matter of geographical desirability.

'Relationship?' Mimi says. 'Sounds like relationshit to me. The sort of relationshit that starts to stink pretty quickly.' This sounds twice as impressive in Mimi's Lithuanian accent.

Mimi has just come back from a work-out with a personal trainer. 'He's killing me,' she says. 'He makes me stretch and stretch. I can stretch my legs like this.'

I can hear all sorts of bumps and knocks on the line. I know Mimi is stretching her legs. I can almost hear how far she is stretching them, over the phone.

I hear Mimi exhale. 'I said to my trainer,' she says, 'what good will it do me to stretch my legs like this now? Twenty years ago, it would have been helpful. But now?'

Mimi stops stretching, and tells me about a program she watched on television about things that can go wrong with plastic surgery. Some of the details are grue-some. 'Still,' Mimi says, after she has described a cata-strophic mistake that occurred during a face lift, 'I wouldn't mind a little tuck.'

I tell her to forget the tuck. Not after the story she's just told me. She turns away from the phone, to Win, and asks him what he thinks. 'Honey, sure have a tuck,' he says, 'if that's what you want. Personally, I'd prefer a fuck.'

NEW YORK

WHEN WE MOVED TO NEW YORK eight years ago, my younger daughter was thirteen. I timed how long it would take her to walk from our apartment to her school. I timed it twice, once strolling, once walking briskly. At a leisurely pace, the walk took two minutes and thirty-five seconds. At a brisk clip, it took just over one minute.

I thought of New York as a city where you dodged bullets and stepped over used syringes. In the street, I gripped my handbag so tightly my knuckles were white. I avoided eye-contact and ignored anyone who spoke to me. I was alert and on guard at all times. I glared at the doorman of the building we lived in. I thought he was a stranger, loitering in the lobby. He snubbed me for months after that, and went out of his way never to be helpful to me.

I practised being street-smart. When someone shouted hello to me on First Avenue, I looked away and walked faster. By the time he caught up to me, he was breathless. He was a former editor of mine, someone I've known since I was eighteen.

We chose the apartment we lived in because of its proximity to Friends Seminary, the Quaker high school my younger daughter was enrolled at. The apartment was so close to the school, but still I looked at my watch, anxiously, if she was a few minutes late coming home.

Before we left for New York, several well-meaning friends had said, 'You're not taking the children to New York?' in tones that suggested gross, if not criminal, negligence. 'They're not really children,' I replied, meekly, to each accusation. And they weren't. They were thirteen, eighteen and nineteen.

The children were fine. My younger daughter met her three best friends on her first day of school. Tina, a delicate Cambodian girl whose mother and father had been murdered by the Khmer Rouge; Makeeba, a tall, buoyant African-American girl whose mother, a single mother, worked hard to give Makeeba everything; and Daryl, a gorgeous Chinese boy whose father was a dentist in Chinatown. They were to become an inseparable quartet.

My elder daughter was enrolled at the Studio

School, an art school with an impressive history, and my son was at New York University. I was the one who was not fine.

Our apartment in New York was unfurnished. I had left a home with years of accumulated kitchenware and other accoutrements and equipment. I burst into tears in Macy's department store when I couldn't find a grater.

'I feel like a refugee,' I said.

'Refugees don't have American Express cards,' my husband said.

When I objected to the older kids going out at night, my husband intervened. 'This is not downtown Beirut,' he said.

I slowly became less scared. I spoke back to the drug dealers who lined Eleventh Street and hissed, 'Coke, coke, crack, crack,' at me. 'No thanks, no thanks, no thanks,' I said to each dealer. They all looked startled. 'You have very good manners,' one of them said to me one day. 'Thank you,' I said.

That was eight years ago. I don't look so well-mannered now. New York has changed and so have I. I first noticed I had changed when I accosted a man in the street. He was a slight man in his sixties. His scruffy-looking mongrel had just relieved himself in the middle of Prince Street. 'Hey, clean up after your dog!' I shouted at him. I stunned myself by doing this. A second later I thought, 'Wow, I'm a real New Yorker now.'

'Lady,' the man said in a very loud voice, 'I already

cleaned up after him. The dog's got diarrhoea. I came out with four pieces of paper.' I looked sheepish and started to walk away but he kept talking.

'I'm worried about him,' he said. 'Last week he was constipated. I got a neighbour who's got the same thing. Doctor said it could be Irritable Bowel Syndrome. That happens when the contractions that propel the waste through the intestines to the rectum are disrupted by irregular contractions. Then you get constipation or diarrhoea or alternating bouts of both. So lady, think before you shout at people.'

'I'm sorry,' I said.

I knew then that I wasn't a real New Yorker. Real New Yorkers never back down. I've become tougher since then. The change in me is nearly as dramatic as the change in the city.

New York is not the place it was when I moved here. You hardly see any drug dealers any more. There has been a dramatic decrease in crime. There are more police in the streets, and they are prosecuting small crimes in the belief that this prevents larger crimes. We had a burglary in our loft six years ago, just after we had moved in. It was my fault, really. I was trying to diminish the fear I felt about living in New York. I adopted a casual attitude: I went away for a weekend and didn't set the burglar alarm, and I told a cleaner I had never used before, that we were going away.

When we got back, everything was in a mess. All my jewellery was gone. Bracelets the kids had when they were small, some of my mother's things, rings my husband had bought me.

We called the police. 'Could you call back? We're busy,' they said. It was eight p.m. We called back at eight-thirty p.m., at nine p.m., at ten p.m. Finally, at eleven p.m., two cops from the First Precinct arrived. 'We're just here for insurance purposes,' one of the cops said. 'We no longer investigate burglaries.' He handed us some forms.

'Could you tell me how they got in?' I asked the cops.

'Hard to tell,' he said.

'There's a window open in my study,' I said. 'Could you have a look at it and tell me if it was forced open?' We walked into my study.

'Are you a writer?' the taller policeman asked me. I nodded. 'My wife wants to be a writer,' he said. I smiled. 'I think she's quite good,' he said. 'She's taking a course at the moment.' I smiled again.

'How could anyone have got in through this window?' I said. 'There's a thirty-foot drop outside.' No one moved towards the window.

'How many books have you written?' the cop said.

I finally agreed to read his wife's manuscript when it was finished. This stood me in good stead. For months the policeman waved from the patrol car every time he saw me. I felt very safe. His wife never finished the manuscript. And we never saw any of our stolen things again.

When we arrived in New York, it was the twelfth most dangerous city in the United States. Now, according to the *New York Times*, New York is the twentieth most dangerous city.

'People aren't trying any more,' my husband said after he read the article. 'The mafia are behind bars, muggers have moved into the middle class.' I couldn't laugh. I'm still not that relaxed about how safe it is.

Part of my general fear came from a language problem. We all spoke English, but not the same English. There are certain vowels that we Australians pronounce in a way that is incomprehensible to New Yorkers. 'A' and 'I' are the two worst offenders.

'Can you tell me where the rice is?' I asked a man loading shelves in the supermarket.

'Where what is?' he said.

'Rice,' I said.

'What?' he said.

'Rice,' I said.

He looked totally bewildered. I tried some alternative pronunciations. 'Raice, reece, roice.' Nothing worked. He called over another man.

'What do you want?' the other man shouted at me.

'Rice,' I said.

'Oil?' he said. 'Olive oil?'

I tried to describe rice. It's not an easy thing to do. Especially if you want to avoid Is and As. 'It's a grain,' got me nowhere. I finally left the two men, shaking their heads.

There is also the way we phrase things. 'Could you please turn left at the next set of lights?' I said to a cab driver. Too late. There's no time for 'could you please' in New York. As for 'turn left at the next set of lights', by the time I got to 'turn', he was on the other side of the street, heading in the wrong direction. 'Make a left,' is what I shout now.

In New York, Koreans, Indians, Jamaicans, Americans, Israelis, Europeans and Africans all understand each other. They just don't understand us.

My father, who moved to New York a year after we did and stayed for four years, was understood by everyone. His thick, Polish accent, which had burdened him for years in Australia, was perfect in New York.

'Where's the Blinker Street?' he asked a man on the street. I went to correct him, but the man was already pointing him in the direction of Bleeker Street.

When my father encountered an argument on the subway, he said, 'Don't take your shirt off', and everyone quietened down. I asked him whose shirt was off, when he told me the story, and he looked at me with disdain. 'It's a saying what we have in Australia,' he said.

Three days later, I got it. '"Keep your shirt on" is what my dad said to those guys in the subway,' I said to my husband. 'We must remember that,' my husband said.

My father felt at home in New York for many reasons. The pace of life, the constant action in the streets, the cops with revolvers in their holsters, were all familiar to him. He has been reading about cops and crimes for almost all of the time that he wasn't working, all of his life. He has read *thousands* of detective fiction books.

The books my father read had gory titles and worse covers. He borrowed them, half a dozen at a time, from various libraries. The crime writer Sue Grafton knew what those books did for my father. 'In detective fiction,' she told me, 'all the danger is contained.'

And then I understood. He could feel all of his fear and all of his terror, quite safely, in the confines of the pages of books named *The Last Bullet*, *Blood Strike*, *Night Killers* or *A Stranger in the Mirror*.

'They saved my life,' he has said to me many times. And I've known what he meant. The books took him away from his own world, in which he was always trying to forget about something. The things he needed to get away from were horrendous. Like my mother, my father lost his mother and father and brothers and sister, and just about everyone he was related to. They were murdered by the Nazis. And, like my mother, my father was in Auschwitz before they shipped him off to a labour camp. When he was liberated, he weighed just over one hundred and ten pounds and had fluid on his brain. He had a lot to forget.

'When I read them, I feel every moment. I am living inside the book,' he used to say to me. Inside the books was the best place for him to be reliving his nightmares. Much better than inside his head.

Seeing my father so at ease in New York helped me to calm down. In small doses, often imperceptible to me, and often in spite of myself, New York began getting under my skin. I began to form an attachment to the city as intense and volatile as any love affair.

New York is teeming with people. It is drenched in mankind. Every store counter, subway strap, door handle and elevator button is touched hundreds, if not thousands of times a day. Every inch of street surface is walked and driven on. And there is a living arrangement in every square centimetre of space. There is something happening every second of every day. There are births and deaths and marriages. There are huge failures and enormous achievements. There is massive wealth and terrible poverty, and the repercussions and ramifications of both of these states. There are passions and hatreds and tragedies and triumphs. And everything is happening at top volume, and often in full view.

Every New Yorker is inextricably entangled, in the most intimate manner, with the city. They bark at the city, they shout, they hurtle huge accusations, they complain, they berate. And then they melt. They embrace the city, they stroke the city, they love the city. They speak of it with great pride as if it belongs to them. The city's presence is potent and encompassing, and it belongs to all of us who live here.

The noise adds to the feeling of chaos. There are omnipresent car horns and police and ambulance sirens. And then there are the road works. The roads are always being worked on. They should be as smooth as marble. Early in the morning and late at night, pneumatic drills break up bitumen on roads and sidewalks. After weeks of work, trucks arrive and smooth new tar over the old surfaces. In a second, new potholes appear.

There are also teams of workers, fixing and installing cable lines, and gas, oil and water pipes. It is a city that is perpetually trying to repair itself, and to keep growing. There is building construction and renovation all over Manhattan.

And there are deliveries: bricks and timber and plaster and machinery; air-conditioning units and water towers and grand pianos. In peak-hour and pre-dawn, there are deliveries to sixth floor walk-ups and pent-houses on top of skyscrapers. The city never gets any beauty sleep, and you can see the fatigue in its inhabitants.

Mother nature adds to the unruliness of New York. The weather is erratic and extreme. Spring and autumn slip by in a second. Now you see them, now you don't. Winter is interminable and summer unbearable.

Last winter was the longest winter on record. The psychiatric departments of hospitals had long lines of depressed people. I longed for summer. I prayed for summer. When it came, it was awful. I had forgotten about that winning combination of high temperatures and high humidity with car exhausts, air-conditioning outlets and high-rise buildings. I had forgotten how thick the air becomes, how you can't breathe, even early in the morning. I had forgotten how enervating it is. Everyone looks damp and flat. When you kiss someone, you stick to them. That's okay if you're in love, but it's awkward if it's an acquaintance in the street.

With all of this disorder and disaccord, you'd think the city couldn't function. But it does. Everything works with an efficiency that is astonishing and exhilarating.

You can do anything in New York. The best of everything is available: theatre, opera, art, museums, dancers, singers, actors. You can sit six feet from writers Philip Roth or Seamus Heaney, or musicians Wynton Marsalis or Luciano Pavarotti, or just about anybody you've ever admired.

I heard the comedienne Roseanne speak at the 92nd Street Y, one night last year. The Y is a cultural and educational institution for the people. It has lectures, concerts, films, forums, classes and a health club. Rosanne attracted a huge and diverse audience. She walked out onto the stage, slowly, and on her own. I was stunned to see how human she looked. Her complexion was flushed and she had bare, blotchy legs.

She spoke for over two hours. She talked about women and feminism in a more potent way than any feminist I have ever heard. She talked about her past with such brutal honesty that I started feeling anxious. So much of her damage and struggle seemed to mirror my own. Perhaps that was true of a lot of people in the audience.

There was not a sound while she was speaking. Later

she took questions from the audience, and her extraordinary sense of humour, which obviously doesn't rely on script writers, shone. It was such an intimate night.

This sort of intimacy is part of what is unique about New York. In a fast and frenetic city, you don't expect to be able to share small, quiet moments or personal revelations and reflections. But New York audiences are intense, informed and appreciative, and the people on stage know this.

You can get to everything that is on here, on time. Somehow the traffic jam clears, the subway arrives, and the bus appears. There are few delays. Even in the worst weather. Against all the odds, the city works.

Part of the efficiency is an extraordinary system of communication. Everything is communicated in abundance: minute-by-minute road, rail and bus reports; bridge and tunnel reports; cultural reports on concerts, readings, street fairs, and gallery openings. From the weather reports you can anticipate changes in the weather from hour to hour, and for the rest of the week. There are parking reports and public holiday reports. On each public holiday you are informed about the sanitation, banking, post-office and parking arrangements.

In winter there are reports on precisely how many inches of snow will fall, and have fallen, and what time what streets will be cleared by. When the weather is very hot, the city prepares its occupants for heat emergencies.

There is an efficient information network among

New Yorkers themselves. Anyone in the street can tell you the weather forecast. Today's, and the long-range, five-day forecast. People also exchange information about apartments available, jobs, where to buy the best of anything, where to jog, where to swim, where to park your car. It's one of the most efficient ways of finding things out. New Yorkers pride themselves in knowing all they can about how to function in the city.

If you can't get to the sales, if you can't get to anything, you can have it delivered. You can have anything delivered. Your next meal, your underwear, your vitamins, your dry-cleaning, your medication, your make-up, your office supplies, your furniture. You can order salmon from Alaska, steak from Ohio and oranges from Florida.

It all arrives immediately. In twenty minutes, in an hour, or in a day. Most things can be delivered overnight. Nothing takes more than a week.

You can have your pets, children or elderly parents picked up and delivered. One of my younger daughter's school friends was brought up by a single father, a cellular phone and a limousine company. Her father booked the limousines that dropped her off and picked her up and ferried her around. And he rang her, on her cellular phone, almost hourly.

There is an ease and fluidity of movement that is surprising, too, in this crowded metropolis. It is so easy to socialise. Everyone meets out of their homes. It means no cleaning up for visitors. You don't have to hide your old toothbrush or tidy the toothpaste tube.

People are very appreciative when you do invite them to your home, however. New Yorkers love to see how other New Yorkers live. This curiosity cuts across all socio-economic lines. Someone else's apartment is an endless source of fascination for all New Yorkers. Someone else's foyer, someone else's elevator, someone else's view and someone else's space is something that New Yorkers want to see. This interest is not merely in order to check out how your own place rates, by comparison. It is an endless quest to know the city, to know what is available, to be informed.

There's a lot to keep up with. The city is difficult and swift and you have to be nimble. It forces you to acknowledge things about yourself you may prefer to ignore. Faced with competitive New Yorkers, I have had to face how competitive I am. It's hard to be complacent here. There's so much activity, you are forced to examine your own actions and ambitions.

I am much tougher than I used to be. I'm not cowed by some of the awful things people in the publishing industry can say. I've spoken to literary agents and book editors who've made me feel like a used carpet salesman. And this is the book business. A business that supposedly involves the more sensitive aspects of life.

But I also take with a grain of salt the extraneous praise that New Yorkers dish out. New Yorkers are extreme about everything. I am becoming that way myself. I'm still slow and polite by New York standards, but I speak more speedily and I walk faster. I grimace at tourists who stop in the middle of the footpath, and, last week, I grabbed someone else's cab. I paused long enough to feel embarrassed before I jumped in.

In New York, people are as unguarded about their ambition as they are about their philanthropy. New Yorkers are open about who they are and who they want to be. By definition, New York is the place where you arrive from the old and redefine yourself as the new. There is an extraordinary social acceptance, cultural tolerance and political freedom. It is the combination of the culture, the money and the social fluidity that allows people to reach their potential. Everyone is emboldened.

I am not emboldened enough to drive. The free-form weaving and dodging that comes naturally to New York drivers frightens me. I like order in traffic. Lines and lanes.

I used to love to drive. I started driving when I was fifteen. My father sometimes used to leave the keys of his pink Pontiac in the glovebox of the car for me. After school, I'd go to the top of Flinders Street, where he parked the car, and drive home in my green and tan checked Uni High School uniform.

One morning I was driving to school. It was 7:35 a.m. We had just turned into Storey Street, Parkville. 'Oy a broch,' my father said. Loosely translated, that is Yiddish for 'oh shit.' Literally, it means 'oh, a curse.' A cop was telling us to pull over.

I stopped the car. My father hopped out. 'Stay there,' he said to me. He ran towards the policeman. 'I'm sorry officer,' he said. 'I know she's not eighteen. She's nearly eighteen.'

I tried to add some years to my age by adding some inches. Despite the fact that I was already tall, I sat up very straight.

'I'm sorry officer,' my father said again. 'I was driving the car until the Swanston Street when I did get a terrible pain here.' He grimaced and pointed to his stomach.

'Oy cholera,' he said to the officer (a stronger version of 'oh shit', and, literally, 'oh cholera'), 'it was something shocking. I did eat a chulent last night. Maybe you don't know what is a chulent? It is beans and meat and potatoes and fat and stuff, and kishke. You know what kishke is?' he said, pointing in the general direction of his intestines.

I looked up. The policeman was open-mouthed. He was staring at my father, who was still jabbing himself in the stomach.

'It's very good,' my father said. 'And that's the trouble. I always eat too much. My wife said "Moniek don't eat so much chulent," but I am a pig, officer. My wife said, "Moniek you won't feel so good in the morning," and she, like usual, was right. I don't feel so good. So what should you do, officer, if you are driving a car and you feel shocking? In Swanston Street in the morning you can't park. In Elizabeth Street you can't park. I stopped the car and said to my daughter, "I'm sorry, darling, you will have to drive to the school and I'll leave the car in Storey Street where I can park the whole day."'

The officer, a young, red-haired, fair-complexioned Australian, looked bewildered. It was clear he'd had trouble keeping up with the culinary details. I could see the ingredients of the chulent had gone right over his head. Especially when my father, in his enthusiasm to explain kishke, had been pointing at his groin. I knew he'd meant to isolate his intestines.

My father saw the cop's confusion. He seized the opportunity to cement his case. 'Officer,' he said, 'if you were following me from the Swanston Street, you have to admit there is no doubt my daughter is a good driver. No doubt.' My father always pronounced 'doubt' with a loud emphasis on the 'b'.

The officer looked over at me, dazed. 'No doubt,' he said, echoing my father's full-throttle 'b.' I decided the cop was in a state of shock. My father knew he was on the home run.

'Officer, if you ever get the chance to try a chulent,' he said, 'they have a good one at the Scheherezade, in Acland Street. But don't eat too much.'

'Don't let your daughter drive again until she's eighteen,' the officer said.

'Oy a broch,' my father said when he got back into the car. 'Next time you drive, take off that stupid school hat. And why didn't you see him? If he was behind me from the Swanston Street you should have seen him.'

My father has always loved cars. He often talked to me about the Skoda sportscar he had in Poland, before the war. When I was young, he couldn't talk about any other aspect of his life in Poland. His parents, the deaths of all of his family, the ghetto, the camps; but he could talk about his Skoda.

He managed to find a Skoda sportscar in Melbourne, and bought it for me when I was eighteen. It was a terrible car. Impossible to drive, and always breaking down, but my father loved it.

His real love was American cars. Big American cars. When he moved to New York, he bought himself a big Buick. It was a 1982 Buick. It felt a bit loose and wayward to me, but my father loved it. He got his American driver's licence and drove everywhere in his Buick. He negotiated the Brooklyn-Queens Expressway, the Holland Tunnel, the F.D.R. Drive, Fifth, Sixth, Seventh Avenues. He was so happy in his Buick.

The year before he returned to Melbourne, he went to Florida for the winter. I should have known something was up. We always spoke regularly, but he started calling me every day, from Florida. And then I noticed he was talking about cars and how cheap they were.

At first it was general conversation, and then he began bringing in individual cars. I didn't twig until it was too late.

'I saw a beautiful Cadillac,' my father said to me. 'It

is in perfect condition. Do you know what such a car would cost in Melbourne? Thousands of dollars. Maybe twenty thousand. Guess how much it costs?'

'I don't know,' I said. 'How old is it?'

'A 1986 model,' my father said.

Car prices are not my forte. I took a guess. 'Six thousand dollars,' I said. My father was thrilled.

'Guess once more,' he said.

'Seven thousand,' I said.

He was overjoyed. 'One thousand eight hundred!' he shouted. 'One thousand eight hundred for such a beautiful car. In perfect condition.' I suddenly comprehended.

'Dad, we don't need a car,' I said. 'Nobody needs a car in Manhattan. And we can't afford to have one here. Garaging a car costs nearly as much as renting an apartment.'

'You can leave it in the street,' he said.

'It'll get stolen,' I said.

'I left my car in Queens for two weeks and nothing happened to it,' my father said.

'In Manhattan everything gets stolen,' I said.

'You always see the black side,' he said. I didn't want to explore this theme, so I said I had to go.

He rang me at seven the next morning.

'I will buy the car for you,' he said. I thanked him profusely and explained, again, that we didn't need a car and couldn't afford to keep a car in Manhattan.

'It is in perfect condition,' he said. 'Like new.'

'You don't know what it's like, mechanically,' I said.

'I drove it,' he said. 'It was beautiful.'

'I'm sorry Dad,' I said. 'It's just not what we need.'

That night he called back. 'I spoke to the mechanic,' he said. 'He told me he knows the owner. An old Jew who can't drive any more.' I wondered how old this old Jew was. My father was seventy-nine at the time.

'As a matter of fact,' my father said, 'I have got the car at home with me. The mechanic said I could take it for a day. He said he trusts me.'

I knew I was in trouble. I pulled out all the stops. 'Dad, I couldn't possibly drive in Manhattan,' I said.

'What are you talking about?' he said. 'You are a very good driver.'

'I used to be,' I said.

'Rubbish,' he said. I didn't know what to do.

'I want you to have this car because I know how happy it will make you,' my father said. His voice faltered, uncharacteristically.

'I can't, Dad,' I said. 'I'm sorry.' He was worryingly silent.

'All right,' he said. He sounded heartbroken.

I tried to get back to my work. I couldn't concentrate. I talked to my husband. I called my father back. 'We'll take the car,' I said.

'Oy, is that good news,' he said. All of his spirits returned. 'I am very happy,' he said. 'And you will be very, very happy.'

The next day he called. His voice was ringing with excitement. 'Guess what I have got in my pocket?' he said. He didn't wait for me to answer. 'I got car keys,' he said.

He shipped the bright red 1986 Cadillac with its maroon roof and maroon interior to us from Florida. We frantically searched around for a cheap place to park the car. The cheapest parking we could find was outside, on a ramp, beside the Hudson River. The car would be cold, but it would have a spectacular view. It enjoyed that view for two years.

I took it out, once, early on. I took it out because my father had asked me ten times if I had driven the car yet. I think he may have asked me twenty or thirty times.

I drove the car down the ramp of the parking station, and was almost at the Westside Highway entrance, when a red light came on. In bold capital letters it said **CHECK**.

Oh, shit, I thought. Check what? I looked around the car. There were no other lights or signs on. I read the sign again. It still said **CHECK**. Check what? Check mate? Check the tyres? My hair? My make-up? I felt frazzled before I'd even hit the street.

There was an attendant at the exit, a young man. I asked him what the **CHECK** light meant.

'I'll check into it when you bring the car back,' he said.

I drove down the Westside Highway. I turned left

into Canal Street, and then turned left on Lafayette Street. I was trying to use only one-way streets. I didn't want to be disoriented by driving on what felt like the wrong side of the road.

I wasn't going anywhere in particular. I was just driving the car. I got to Union Square. Little drawings of grids with arrows showed you which way you could turn. I couldn't understand any of them. I made a guess and turned left, slowly. Two seconds into my turn, I heard a whistle and a traffic cop was beckoning me to pull over. I spent ten minutes explaining that I couldn't understand the sign, and ten minutes explaining that I thought it was legal to drive on an Australian driver's licence even though I was an American resident.

I started to sweat. I wanted to cry. The cop was half my age. In the end, he felt sorry for me. He told me to study the road signs and get an American licence. I crawled up First Avenue and parked outside Essa Bagels on 21st Street.

I called my husband. I said I was coming home without the car if he couldn't come and pick up me and the car. He said he would meet me at Essa Bagels.

Essa Bagels, on 21st Street, has the best bagels in New York. They make the bagels in front of you, thousands of them a day, in the store. Poppyseed bagels, sesameseed bagels, plain bagels, onion bagels, garlic bagels, raisin and cinnamon bagels, wholewheat bagels.

I love watching the bagels being dropped into the boiling water, then rolled in their various seasonings before they are baked in the ovens. It's quite mesmerising.

I had been at Essa Bagels for ten minutes before my heartbeat slowed down. I wouldn't be able to tell my father how I cowered in front of the cop. My father loved New York cops. He spoke their language. It was the language of his crime books. Lines filled with broads and dames and blood. Once when he called out, 'Did you catch a few perps today?' to a cop on Fifth Avenue, I cringed. I wanted to pretend I wasn't with him. 'You betcha buddy,' the cop answered with a big smile.

'Good on you,' my father said.

'Thank you. Have a good day,' the cop said to my dad.

A man in front of me in the queue at Essa Bagels ordered one cup of Coke and one cup of ice. I ordered a poppyseed bagel and a cup of coffee.

I sat down. The man who ordered the cup of Coke and the cup of ice was sitting, with another man, at the next table. The men were in their early sixties. They were both wearing suits – not the smartly-tailored, dark suits of Wall Street; more the middle-grey suits of insurance agents and accountants. The man who had ordered the Coke and the ice was saying to his friend: 'Two objects can't occupy the same space at the same time. I learned that a long time ago. Why should I pay double?'

'That's not true,' his friend said. 'You can pour a

half a cup of alcohol into a full cup of water without the water running over. The molecules of the alcohol fit in beside the molecules of the water. We did it at school, in physics.'

How can you pour a half a glass of alcohol into a full cup of water? It doesn't sound possible, to me. But then physics is not my forte. And this man looks as though he knows what he's talking about. But so do all New Yorkers. I decide to do a small experiment when I get home.

Essa Bagels is full. It is always busy. I get out my notebook. I often write when I'm by myself in public places. I write notes for poems, notes for novels, shopping lists, lists of things to do. I am just about to write out a list of ingredients for a frittata I am thinking of making, when I notice a man sitting against the wall. He is very thin. He has hollow cheekbones, black, lank hair and blue-white skin. He is wearing dark glasses and has headphones in his ears. He is looking around nervously. There are five or six large, bloody sores on his face, each about half an inch in diameter.

They look awful. I look away. I try to sit so that I am facing away from him. I try to concentrate on my list of ingredients, but the thought of a frittata is not as appetising as it was before.

I look up at the man. He is picking at the sores with his thumb and forefinger. One by one. He digs and digs. His fingers never seem to come up for air. They remain implanted, burying into the bloody openings in his flesh.

136

His eyes look down at the table. Occasionally, he glances up.

Everyone ignores him. A table of black and Hispanic schoolgirls are talking flat out. One of them is laughing and flirting with the man behind the counter. They don't look at the gaunt, black-haired man, who is just on their left. Two Jewish women in their sixties are having lunch. They tell each other how good their respective whitefish and tuna fish sandwiches are, several times. They're not distracted or put-off by the man in the corner. They take no notice of him.

But I can't stop looking at him. I twist my body and turn my head; I hunch over my chair. All of this is in the effort to get him out of my line of vision. But every time I look up, I see him digging and digging into his skin. My Essa bagel, which I had so looked forward to, is tasteless to me.

I want to leave. But I am trying to be more mature, to require less than a perfect environment before I can feel happy. So I stay and feel miserable. I have to wait for my husband, anyway. I'm not going to get behind the wheel of a car, in Manhattan, again.

'This city is driving me nuts,' I say to my husband when he comes to pick me up.

Seventh Avenue and 12th Street is one of the windiest corners in New York. I was standing there, trying to hail a cab. A cold day on this corner feels even colder. I was smiling to myself. 'How are you, young lady?' the doorman in a friend's building had just asked me. In New York, you can be called a young lady at any age. And everyone calls you miss. Excuse me miss, they say. It always makes me feel youthful. 'Miss, I miss you,' a homeless man who I pass on my daily walk along the Hudson River, said to me recently.

I saw a cab on the far side of Seventh Avenue. The driver saw me and slowed down. I crossed Seventh Avenue. I opened the door of the cab and was about to get in, when a young woman, her nostrils flared and steaming with anger, came around from the other side of the cab.

'I was here first!' she screamed. 'You know I was here first!' I was too stunned to say anything.

'You know it!' she screamed. 'She knows I was here first!' she shouted at the cab driver.

'I didn't see you at all,' I said to the young woman.

'You saw me!' she shouted. 'And you know it. You saw me.'

She blocked my way so that I couldn't get into the cab. I was still stunned. This woman looked like a normal young woman in her early thirties. She was wearing a business suit and carried a briefcase.

She grabbed the door handle of the cab. 'This is my cab and you know it!' she screamed.

'I didn't see you,' I said.

'You're a liar!' she shouted.

'She's a liar,' she said to the driver. I stepped back and she jumped into the cab.

I stood on the corner in a daze. What was wrong with her? Why did she have to shout like that? My heart was pounding. I felt a bit shaky. It's stupid how a perfect stranger shouting at you can make you feel shaky. I wondered why I felt so trembly. It probably had something to do with being afraid of my own rage.

It's usually easy to get a cab. For some reason, this morning, all the cabs were full. I saw the bus coming down Seventh Avenue, so I walked to the bus stop. The bus was very crowded. I had to stand up. I wished I'd waited for a cab. I don't like crowded buses. I feel claustrophobic. I remind myself that it's only a short ride to Spring Street, and after spending so many thousands of dollars on analysis, I should be able to tolerate a crowded bus.

People are talking very loudly on the bus. I can't understand why New Yorkers are so loud. Two people are talking about a play rehearsal. 'You did very well,' the first woman says.

'Did I?' her friend says.

'You could have been an actress,' says woman number one.

'I tried to give it my best,' says her friend.

'You did give it your best,' said the first woman.

From somewhere in the middle of the bus, a man starts to sing. His voice is strong and clear. It rings through the bus. 'Jack and Jill went up the hill to fetch a pail of water, Jack fell down and broke his crown and Jill came tumbling after.'

My mouth drops open. I can't believe this. Why is everyone in this city crazy? I'm in a sweat. I haven't unbuttoned my coat or taken my scarf off. And the heating system on this bus is overly efficient.

'Sing that again,' a woman says, 'that was beautiful.'

The man starts singing, again. 'Jack and Jill went up the hill . . .'

I've had it. I'm sick of the noise, I'm sick of the crowds, I'm sick of the crazies, I'm sick of New York. I'm going to London for two weeks, in a few days, for the launch of one of my books. I'm so glad to be leaving. I decide to get off the bus and walk the rest of the way home. Just then, the bus driver announces that we have reached Houston Street. He enunciates each word carefully and then repeats the announcement. This must be a particularly enthusiastic bus driver, I think. Street announcements are not the norm on a bus.

Three-quarters of the bus stands up. People pick up bags and backpacks, button up their coats and put on gloves. Most of them are moving slowly and deliberately. I look around the bus. This is a group of retarded adults.

I feel ashamed of myself. I feel terrible about my impatience and intolerance. 'I thought it was just another busload of New Yorkers,' I said to my husband when I got home. 'I couldn't tell the difference.'

When I lived in Melbourne, I used to think life in London was swift and sophisticated. Coming from New

York on this visit to London, I see what a relaxed, civilised city it is.

London is so civilised. Such a polite city, from its population to its public signs. On the number ninety-four bus there is a notice which is headed: 'Beware Pickpockets'. It reads: *There have been a number of incidents of pickpocketing on board our buses recently. With your help, we can make it as difficult as possible for them to prosper, and stop these unfortunate incidences from happening again.*

Another sign says: *We would prefer you not to eat or drink on this bus. However, if you do, please take your litter home with you.*

You can gauge the pace and soul of a city by its public signs. In London, they apologise to you in their signs. In parks there are signs saying: *Sorry. No skating allowed.* Contrast this with the New York directive: *No Parking. No Stopping. No Kidding.*

I don't understand why drivers don't toot their horns in London. I noticed the absence of that omnipresent sound immediately. There seem to be as many cars around in London as there are in New York. And the traffic is as congested. But it is so quiet. I'm not used to this quiet. Silence leaves me wondering if something is wrong.

And I don't understand why everyone is so orderly. I'm amazed by it. Over a hundred people are on the escalator, coming out of the Camden Town tube station. I am one of them. Everyone stands on the right. This allows those who want to walk up the two-storey escalator to move ahead. Not one person blocks the left passageway.

I tell my husband about the different signs, the queues and the order. I am bubbling over. I listen to myself. When did I become someone who is excited by orderliness and cleanliness?

'I'm looking for more than well-scrubbed manners and polished elocution,' my husband says tersely. I know he's bothered by my unexpected love affair with London. I try to tone down my enthusiasm.

The pigeons in London look more lustrous to me. Less scruffy and with more gloss on their feathers than their New York counterparts. I keep this observation to myself.

People in London have ordinary dogs. Cocker spaniels, terriers, poodles. Black dogs, brown dogs. Dogs that look like dogs. In New York, dogs are an accoutrement. There are dogs that look like wolves, dogs that look like horses. There are dogs that resemble spiders, and dogs that match their owners' coats and purses. I watch two cocker spaniels running around Hyde Park. London dogs look less stressed than New York dogs, I'm sure of it.

On my last day in London, trying to savour every moment, I have lunch in a Portuguese cafe near Camden Lock. Afterwards, I go to the bathroom. There is a window open in the bathroom and the cold air hits me. This is the cold air of London. It is not New York cold or Melbourne cold. It is London cold. It reminds me of other cold London days.

Cold days long ago when I was twenty-two and pregnant with my son. He was born in London. I was overwhelmed when he arrived. I knew nothing about babies. I kept him by my side day and night. In my free time I read Dr Spock.

The first time I took him out of our apartment he was six weeks old. We had an appointment at the local Baby Health Centre. I got him ready for the trip. I dressed him, and wrapped him in a new blanket his grandmother had sent. I carried him down the three flights of stairs to the ground floor, where his pram was kept. When I got down there, I opened the front door. It felt cold. I worried that I hadn't dressed him warmly enough. I went back upstairs and added an extra hat and an extra blanket. I went up twice more, for booties and mittens, before it felt safe enough to take him out in the street. We walked six blocks to the Health Centre.

When the nurse unravelled all the layers I had around my son, she held him up in the air. 'Come and have a look at this,' she called out to another nurse on duty. 'This is the first case of heat rash we've had in winter.' Sometimes I think that my son feels that this incident is a metaphor for many things that followed.

I breathe in the cold air in the cafe bathroom. How can cold air smell so different in different places? Is it the different components of the landscape? The composition of the earth, the position of the planets? There's so much I don't know.

I miss London when I leave. For a few days after my return to New York, I talk about London to anyone who will listen. This doesn't please my husband.

There is a panhandler who's been standing on a street near us for six years. Every day he holds out his cup and repeats the same thing. 'The key word is please,' he says, over and over again. He pounces on people as they walk by or come out of a store. 'The key word is fuck off,' I said to him when he startled me badly one day after I'd returned from London. I knew I'd acclimatised myself to New York again.

Australians either love New York or hate it. My husband is an Australian who is crazy about the city. He grew up in Gymea Bay, a then poor, working class area south of Sydney. His mother was sixteen when she gave birth to him, and his father was nineteen and illiterate. The family lived in a small garage. Until he was twelve, my husband walked the four miles to school and back in bare feet. His father wanted him to be a boxer and his grandmother thought that as he was good with his hands he might be able to be a hairdresser.

In this humpy town, this community of poor, English migrants, my husband slept in a corner of the garage and dreamt of salons in New York. He dreamt of nights of poetry readings and discussions of art and literature. I don't know how he even knew where New York was let alone what happened at a salon. He was reading books of Chinese and Japanese poetry in Gymea Bay. He was reading Christmas Humphrey's *The History of Buddhism.* He'd read a biography of Leonardo da Vinci when he was ten. And he was particularly interested in Bertrand Russell. I was in Carlton, Melbourne, seeing how high I could tease my hair.

My husband often used to say to me that he'd love to live in New York. I never used to hear him. I think I nodded or said, oh yes, but the information went in one ear and out the other.

He first said it to me days after we met, and then for years afterwards, but I didn't hear. One day I heard what he was saying. He was saying, 'I'd love to live in New York.' I heard it very clearly. And then years of him saying, very quietly, 'I'd love to live in New York,' came into my head. I couldn't believe how long I'd managed to block it out. I took a deep breath. 'Could you give me nine months to leave my analysis and organise the kids?' I said. 'And then we'll go.' And we did.

Australians who live here are often divided and anguished about what they are doing. Was it the right decision to leave Australia? How long are they here for? Will they ever go back? What are they missing?

Possibly Australians in England don't feel the wrench and the division so acutely. England is more familiar to Australians. They're understood there, too. They don't have to change their vocabulary. They don't have to remember to say sidewalk not footpath, bathroom not toilet, sweater not jumper, vacation not holiday. And they don't have to wince at phrases such as 'tornadic activity', 'focalise on the work', or 'deplane the aircraft'.

We Australians smile while we exchange American-isms. The Olympic Games in Atlanta stretched the Americans' creativity with language to its limit. We heard broadcasters bounce with announcements of 'medalise,' 'winless' and winningest'.

When one of us returns from a visit to Australia, the first thing we're asked, by other Australians, is: What was it like? Was it really wonderful? Are we mad to live here?

On my most recent return from Australia, I reported that I'd seen a couple that most of us know. Australians who'd lived in New York for years, and who moved back to Australia last year. They both looked wonderful. The man, a journalist in his forties, looked ill at ease in New York. You never knew if he was going to spike you or smile at you. In Australia, he looked happy. He was wearing a beautiful suit, his skin glowed and so did his demeanour.

I reported this to several people in New York. They took the news in silence. They were pleased for him and his partner, but what did it mean for them? 'He said his sperm count has gone up since he's been in Australia' I added, to a couple of the people who knew him well. There was no laughter. Just more food for thought.

You can't tell Australians here enough about Australia. 'Who else did you see?' my friend Rachel asked. 'What was the weather like?' There is a thirst for news about our homeland that seems strangely out of place in this electronically hooked up and connected age.

At the same time, there is a very quick and efficient distribution system for all sorts of news from Australia. Two hours after I'd stepped off the plane from Melbourne, I was shopping for food in SoHo. I bumped into an Australian friend. 'Did you see Caroline?' she asked.

'Yes,' I said. 'She looks great.'

'Did you meet her new boyfriend?' she said.

'Yes,' I said, 'he's really nice.'

Then I stopped. I couldn't believe I was discussing Caroline's boyfriend, in the middle of the vegetables in Gourmet Garage less than a day after I'd had dinner with Caroline. Two days later, another friend said she'd already heard my report on Caroline's boyfriend.

At the moment, my elder daughter is in Australia for a month. She calls and says how wonderful it is. She says her friends live so well. They have organic fruit and vegetables delivered to their house, every week. A huge box, she says, for twenty dollars. She says she was driving with a friend along Brunswick Street, Fitzroy, when their car broke down. It was peak-hour. The traffic was held up for blocks. No one tooted their horn. Several people asked if they could help with the car. It's such an easy life here, she said.

'How did that make you feel?' my younger daughter asked me when I gave her this news from her sister.

'Like going home,' I said.

And where is home? For my first couple of years in New York, I cried when people asked me if I lived here. I cried in front of perfect strangers, at dinner parties, and standing on the street. I couldn't bear the sense of departure, the separation. When I heard Tom Waits singing 'Waltzing Matilda', I wept.

A patriotism I wasn't aware of emerged and wouldn't go away. I missed everything Australian. I missed the weather I complained about, I missed the pies I never ate, I missed people I never spoke to. I was hopeless.

'I want to go home,' I said, every time I was miserable. I'm not sure how my husband survived those first two years. I didn't expect it to be such a wrench. I loved Australia, but I didn't think it would be that hard to live away from it. But it was. It was home. And it is always hard to leave home.

Even my father was forced to say something to me. This is a man who won't hear a word of criticism against Australia. A man who will never stop being grateful for being given a home, and a life of freedom, when he thought he would never have either.

This is a man who would come home, after working two shifts in a factory, and say, 'This country is Paradise.' Until I was six years old I thought we lived in Paradise.

But, listening to me whine about wanting to go home forced my father to be reckless. 'Stop talking like

Australia is perfect,' he said to me several times. 'You can't get such good hot dogs in Australia,' he said. He was right.

I tried hard to pull myself together. I started by trying not to call Australia home. 'I'm going to Australia,' I'd say, instead of I'm going home. But I kept slipping. I tried to call New York home. The first time I did, I was triumphant. I'm going home, I said, and I meant, home to New York.

It's not easy to switch the notion of home. Australia feels like home, to me. And, no matter how much I like New York, I'm not sure I'll ever feel completely *at home* here.

Most Australians here can't get that sense of belonging to Australia out of our hearts, no matter how long we've been here. 'Are you going home?' we say to one another. And we all know which home we're referring to.

I stopped trying not to call Australia home. It was a lost cause, anyway. Instead, I learnt all the words to all the verses of 'Waltzing Matilda'. I sing it to myself, sometimes, when I'm walking along the Hudson River.

MY BODY

'YOUR BODY MUST FEEL STRANGE to you,' my husband said, lying next to me in bed. We were in a motel in Wainscott, in the Hamptons, where New Yorkers spend their summer. I love motels. Even the ones where you always find someone else's pubic hair on your blanket.

This was a real motel. Your parking space was in front of your door, ten feet away from your bed. There was even a breakfast hatch in the wall. Orange juice and a muffin could be delivered to you any time between seven a.m. and eleven a.m.

I could see outside from the bed. The sky was blue. There was a slight breeze. It looked like one of those days when everything feels all right with the world.

I knew what my husband meant. He was touching my quads – my quadriceps. Two years ago, I didn't even know I had quadriceps. Now I know about deltoids and gluteals and lactic acid burn.

'I'm getting used to it,' I said to him. But I am still sometimes startled when I feel my hips or arms or legs in bed, in the middle of the night. I think I am someone else.

I have biceps, triceps, pecs, glutes and hamstrings. I had them before, but I never noticed. Now they're more noticeable. More powerful.

This has happened because I took up weight-lifting. My taking up weight-lifting was as unexpected and unpredictable and unlikely an occurrence, as anything could be. I would have been less surprised if I'd enrolled myself in a rocket science program.

I am getting used to the change in the shape of my body. It was a body that needed to be changed. I spent years in analysis making changes of another sort. Clearing my head, rearranging my thoughts. The analysis freed me to look after my body. I started eating properly. I started walking. And I started to lift weights.

This wasn't something that happened overnight. It took me years, decades, half of my life. Walking, eating properly, looking after my body. It sounds simple. If only it was.

I was never athletic. Even as a child I didn't run around,

I didn't play rounders or softball. No one in our family did. We regarded sport as something strange that Australians did. I didn't run or skip or play hopscotch. I talked a lot. I made up stories. Stories about being too poor to afford more than one blanket for the whole family. The other kids at school, who were as poor as we were, used to be wide-eyed. Most of them had their own bedding.

I made up friends and relatives. I needed to: I had a shortage of both. I invented conversations and histories and daily lives. I invented illnesses and afflictions. More sophisticated kids might have picked holes in my stories, but at Lee Street Primary School in Carlton, my stories were a big drawcard.

I was so busy making up stories that I started forgetting the truth. I volunteered to swim in the under elevens' freestyle race at the annual inter-school swimming carnival.

I stepped up to the edge of the pool at the Carlton Baths on the day of the big race. The starter's gun went off. All the competitors dived into the water except me. I held my nose and jumped. Underwater, I panicked. Water went up my nose, in my ears, down my throat. Heather Rice, the school swimming champion, had to dive in and fish me out. I had forgotten that I couldn't swim.

I still can't dive into water, but I can swim. And I feel better about swimming now that I'm a better shape. I used to keep my towel wrapped around me until the last minute, then submerge myself as soon as I got into the water. I would try to look nonchalant. I'd hold the towel loosely and let it drape a little, as though the towel wasn't essential, as though it wasn't hiding me. I'd grab it as soon as I got out of the water. It's terrible to be so self-conscious about your body.

I'm half the size I used to be and twice as strong. I can't get used to my size. I keep thinking there's something wrong with the mirror. 'This is one of those slimming mirrors,' I said to my husband, when we were staying at a friend's place. I made my husband look at my reflection and look back at me. 'Is that what I look like?' I said. 'That's what you look like,' he said. I didn't believe him.

I knew I had lost weight, but the weight that was gone seemed quite abstract. Numbers on a weighing scale. Pounds and half-pounds. I looked at myself so infrequently that I made no connection between the diminishing pounds and my diminishing size. As I lost weight, my clothes stopped fitting me. I kept wearing them. I wore dresses that were so big, they fell off my shoulders. I still didn't make the connection. 'The dry-cleaner has done something very strange with this dress,' I said to my husband.

It was a big day when the truth hit me. So much of me was gone. I packed up my wardrobe as though I was packing away a dead relative. I folded things up lovingly. I said goodbye to each item. Then I rang up the Salvation Army.

I felt terrible when the Salvation Army van came to collect the clothes. I felt as though they had taken me, not my wardrobe. I cheered up at the thought of lots of large women having a selection of idiosyncratic clothes, somewhere in New York. I bought a range of exercise clothes – unitards, leotards, leggings, exercise bras.

Sometimes I want to cry when I look at myself in the mirror. I can't believe this is me. It's not that I look that wonderful. Many women would cry if they weighed what I weigh, and I have to add inches to my height to get to my ideal weight in all those weight-for-height charts. But, I look so much happier, much better, much freer.

I love being strong. I can lift my husband, who is not small, up in the air. This isn't the sort of thing you would often have a pressing need to do, but it impresses me. It impresses others too. I did it at a party, once, when a young movie producer friend said he didn't believe I could do it. My husband said he'd rather not be an accessory for a party trick, so I haven't done it since.

Being strong makes you a better shopper. I can carry loads of groceries. I can buy a week's worth of fruit and vegetables and walk home with them. I'm sure I could carry lots more Bloomingdales and Bergdorf Goodman bags, too.

Having muscles is exhilarating. I can feel the strength of my body. I can feel it when I walk; I can feel it when I climb stairs; I can feel it when I make love. I can feel it when I am just sitting.

We start losing muscle early in life. The muscle mass of a thirty-year-old is less than that of a twenty-year-old. The more muscle you have, the more energy you burn. This amount of energy is your metabolic rate. Mine must have been at a standstill.

A lower metabolic rate contributes to an increase in body fat. A higher metabolic rate means you can eat more and not increase your body fat. The only way you can avoid losing muscle is by strength training. That is, weight-lifting. Strength training also increases your bone density, which is particularly important for post-menopausal women. And there are studies that suggest it helps with arthritis, and the stiffening of joints and tendons that occur as we age.

When you diet, while strength-training, you lose fat, not muscle. You can start weight-lifting at any age. Thirty, forty, fifty, sixty, seventy, eighty or even ninety. The results are almost instantaneous. This building of muscle doesn't take much time. Forty-five minutes, twice a week, is enough. And there are studies that suggest once a week is effective.

I do it three times a week, not because I want to look like Arnold Schwarzenegger (which I'm coming around to thinking could be quite a good thing), but because I love it. I love the concentration and the focus. I love the challenge. I love grunting. The sounds that come out of me sound so primitive. I've always been so polite and well-mannered. I'm the sort of person who would never burp or fart in front of anyone. When you're lifting two hundred pounds, you can't think about any bodily functions except getting that weight off the ground. You can't worry about perspiration running down your face, or the sweat patches around your armpits or your crotch. I like being able to sweat freely, and being red-faced.

I feel so good after my weight-lifting work-outs. I think weight-lifting must have an anti-depressant effect, in the same way that aerobic exercise has. I leave my sessions feeling buoyant.

When the work-out is over, it's over. There's nothing you have to do until the next session. I used to feel uncomfortable about this. As though I wasn't doing something I should be. Maybe this was after years of analysis in which it's a good idea to stay vigilant, and keep working, in between sessions.

I started, in an almost flippant way, to compare my analysis sessions with my weight-lifting sessions. Especially on those days when I left my analysis feeling wretched. The weight-lifting was so uncomplicated. So straightforward. And so much easier. I thought I detected a slight note of annoyance in my analyst's voice when I made these comparisons.

I know I never would have taken up weight-lifting or power walking if it weren't for my analysis, but for a while I was ready to shuck all interpretation and introspection. I wanted to take up boxing, rock-climbing and tai kwon do.

I need to walk and I need to lift weights. I feel this need as strongly as I used to feel the urge to eat. I started feeling hungry when I was so young. And I remember it so clearly: I lusted after another girl's chocolate custard when I was in kindergarten. This was the chocolate custard they gave us every afternoon. I ate my custard quickly. She ate hers slowly. Very slowly. When there was not even a smear of custard left in my bowl, she still had heaps to go.

I have a photograph of myself, then, with the rest of the kindergarten class. I am staring at the slow eater. Maybe the photograph was taken just after, or just before, our bowl of custard.

Food has played such a complicated role in my life. What to eat. What not to eat. What to eat more of. What to eat less of. How to get more. How to have less. What I'm about to eat. What I've just eaten.

What I ate occupied a lot of my mother's life, too. She was always feeding me. Grilled chops and salad, grilled chicken and salad, grilled fish and salad. She made sure I was never offered latkes, cartoffle kloiskes, chulent or any other of the more calorific Jewish dishes she cooked. She kept the chocolates locked in a safe, and the chocolate biscuits in a locked cupboard.

The one thing my mother wanted me to be was slim. Other mothers had different aspirations for their daughters. My mother didn't dream of me becoming a lawyer or a doctor. Her dream was for me to be slim. 'She's so slim,' was the highest praise my mother could bestow on another woman. Perhaps tall and slim was marginally better. The matter of slimness was omnipresent for my mother. Her own slimness, and my lack of slimness.

Like all complex issues, it was double-edged. On the one hand, my beautiful mother wanted a slim daughter, and on the other hand she didn't want any competition.

I was torn. Torn between the part of me that wanted to please her, and understood that her beauty was one of the few things she had been left with after the war, and the part of me that was furious, and wanted to wield the power I had over her, in this battle of to bulge or not to bulge. I never thought about the cost.

'You'll never get a boyfriend,' my mother said to me when I was thirteen or fourteen. 'Boys don't like fat girls.' She was right about that. I wasn't fat, then, just chubby. But chubby was fat enough to disqualify you as girlfriend material.

'This is your last chance to lose weight before it's too late to get a boyfriend,' my mother said. I wasn't moved. I wasn't in a rush to have a boyfriend. I had invented a whole lot of friends, boys and girls. I used to sit in my room and daydream for hours of dialogues with the various invented friends. Every one of them adored me. I felt really popular. I couldn't understand why my mother was so panicked.

I did get a real boyfriend, and then another. Neither of them seemed bothered by my chubbiness. 'Okay, so you got a boyfriend,' my mother said when I was seventeen, 'but he won't marry you. Boys don't marry fat girls.' Thank God he didn't. He was bisexual and unfaithful. A bad combination.

I married my first husband when I was twenty-one. By then, I was considerably bigger, and he was probably bothered by that. But in the general confusion of why you decide to get married at such a young age, and what you're going to do with your life, the issue of weight got lost. Not with my mother, though.

'Well, you're married,' she said, 'but you won't be able to get pregnant. Fat women find it very hard to get pregnant. Liebala, lose weight now.'

Eight months after I got married, I was pregnant. 'Liebala,' my mother said – she called me Liebala when she wanted to make an important, but intimate, point – 'you are pregnant, but you could have a terrible child-birth. Liebala, it's not easy for a fat woman to give birth. Please, now is the time to lose weight.'

Any woman who has been pregnant, knows that this is not an easy time to lose weight. You feel more hungry, not less hungry. You have more cravings, more irrational desires to eat.

After I'd given birth to my son, I inadvertently looked at myself in the mirror when I was undressed. My stomach had hardly gone down and my thighs were huge. I was stunned. I didn't know how that had happened. I knew I'd had a few licorice all-sorts too many, but I thought I'd been moderate. Obviously I had a long way to go to moderation.

When my mother saw me, eighteen months later

(I'd been living in London since early in the pregnancy),
she took me aside. 'Liebala, you have a beautiful son,'
she said. 'He needs a mother. You need to live for him.
Fat people die young.'

The Nazis caricatured Jews as short and fat. The old
saying, that if you fling enough shit, some of it sticks,
was true in this case. My mother didn't want to be a
short, fat Jew. She didn't even want to look Jewish. She
thought she didn't. She thought her dark eyes were too
light to be Jewish. And she lightened her hair for so
long, she was convinced it was blonde.

In the ghetto and in the camps, any Jew who was
fat was eating the food of someone who was dying of
starvation. My mother couldn't bear greed. When my
father ate his dinner quickly, she called him a greedy
pig. If I ate with relish, I was a little piggy. If the dog
gulped his dogfood *he* was a greedy pig.

She had seen piggish behaviour. The Jews in the
ghettos and camps were starving, diseased and dying.
The situation brought out the worst in some people.
People stole their children's food rations, their parents'
food rations. Some people kept the bodies of relatives
who'd died, in order to use their ration cards to have a
little extra food.

My father would often say, out of the blue: 'Friends
are good for good times. When things go bad it's
goodbye Charlie.' Goodbye Charlie was a phrase he
loved. I'm not sure where he got it from. My father
stayed shocked for decades about the large problems and

petty squabbles, and deceit and greed and grievances, that began on the first day in the ghetto.

Of course, it makes sense. The Jews in the ghetto were in a state of terror. They had had to leave their homes and their possessions. Many had already experienced gross brutality and loss. Why would that bring out the best in anyone?

Both of my parents had experienced the extremes of human behaviour, and most of it was bewildering and unpredictable. In Stuthof, the concentration camp, on the Baltic Sea, near Gdansk, a female Nazi Kommandant took a liking to my mother. She said that my mother reminded her of a friend.

This Kommandant was feared by everyone. She had a German Shepherd which she used to unleash, as she walked in between the lines of prisoners. 'Show us what you can do,' she used to say, in German, to the dog. The dog would jump and sink his teeth into the thin, shrivelled neck of a Jewish woman. The Kommandant would laugh and pat the dog.

This Kommandant saved my mother's life. She gave my mother a thick woollen coat. The coat saved my mother when she lay dying of typhoid on the iced earth, in Stuthof. A girlfriend who survived Auschwitz and Stuthof with my mother chipped some of the ice and fed it to my burning mother. My mother had herself carried pieces of ice to this girlfriend, weeks earlier, when she, too, had typhoid. Two years later, the horror of what my mother's girlfriend had lived through proved too much for her. She jumped off the top of a building and died instantly.

Occasionally, the Kommandant gave my mother a couple of potatoes. My mother shared her potatoes with a mother and daughter, in her barracks. She told me many times how happy it made her to see a mother and daughter. 'You can't imagine how excited I was to see a mother and daughter,' she used to say. 'It was such a special thing. No mothers had daughters then and no daughters had mothers.'

After the war, the mother and daughter told the story of my mother sharing her potatoes to a friend of my father's. It meant a lot to my mother that people knew she had remained human in the most inhuman circumstances. Being human meant having control of yourself. My mother saw fat people as having lost all control.

Whenever my mother gave me one of her talks about losing weight, she would take me aside. Sometimes into her bedroom, sometimes in my room, but always somewhere where she could shut a door behind us. I used to feel trapped in a clash of threats ricocheting around me. Sometimes they'd hit and stick, and I'd feel the aches and pains for hours. My head used to hurt. Sometimes my stomach seized up. Other times, I deflected the blows and arrows and emerged just exhausted and unnerved.

I always needed to eat after these episodes, and would walk to the milk bar for a Cherry Ripe or a

163

Pollywaffle or a White Knight, which always calmed me down. Gradually my fear would subside and I could go back home less scared.

What was I scared of? I was never sure. But I had a nightly routine to ward off all evil. I had to touch the four corners of each of the built-in cupboards in my bedroom, twice over, before I could go to sleep.

There were three large double doors and three small double doors. Forty-eight corners to touch, twice. Ninety-six corners every night. Sometimes I'd be just falling asleep, and I would wake up in fright, not sure if I had touched every corner. I'd have to get out of bed and start all over again.

When I was thirteen, my mother took me to see a gynaecologist. After examining me, the gynaecologist asked my mother to leave the room. She stood up. She was a tall woman and I was sitting in a particularly low chair. She looked down at me, sternly, and told me that I would lose my periods if I didn't lose weight.

The significance of what she was saying went right over my head. I wasn't that keen on having periods, anyway. I thought it wouldn't be that bad to never have to carry another sanitary pad, wrapped in a paper bag, to the toilet with me again.

I must have looked as unresponsive as I felt, because she became angry. 'Young girl,' she said, 'do you realise that that would mean you may not be able to have children?'

I started to cry, more at the tone of her voice than

at the thought of not being able to have children. She called my mother back in. 'The doctor is only doing this for your own good,' my mother said to me.

I have often wondered what other misinformed advice this gynaecologist passed on to other young girls. I have had a fear of being alone in rooms, with doctors I don't know, ever since.

I upped my eating after that visit. I started by having an extra breakfast. I would meet my best friend at the Elizabeth Street and Flinders Street tram stop in the city. This was the tram that took you straight to University High School. We would meet at seven-thirty a.m. That gave us three-quarters of an hour to eat. Some mornings we'd have a cheese and salami and lettuce roll, other mornings mixed sandwiches and a milk shake. It balanced my earlier breakfast of a boiled egg with unbuttered toast perfectly.

My best friend and I loved eating in the city. By the time we were fifteen, we had graduated to breakfast and dinner. We ate an early dinner in small cafes and restaurants, all around the city. Spaghetti bolognese was one of our favourite meals. I was perfectly ready for my mother's grilled chop and salad by the time I got home.

This extra eating was okay for my best friend. She was slim. Once when we were having a midday barbecue on Elwood Beach, a group of boys, who must also have sneaked out of school, started a loud chorus of 'Fat and skinny went to war. Fat got shot and skinny swore.' We were so happy with our barbecue and so happy with each other, that we both laughed.

I was the better liar of the two of us. So I invented the textbooks I needed to buy, and the fees I had to pay for certain school events, in order to subsidise our daily dining.

Before I was able to buy my own food, I stole it. I stole another girl's snack at the dress rehearsal for our ballet class's gala performance. She was a ballerina in a pink tutu, and I was playing a young man in blue cotton trousers and a checked shirt. I had to dance and sing 'I'm just a fella, a fella with an umbrella'. I couldn't dance and I couldn't sing. I was given the role of the man because of my height – I was already, at twelve, 5'8" tall – and because of my short hair.

My mother had taken me to Mr Brown, the barber across the road from us in Nicholson Street, and cut off most of my hair. Inches of dark curls were snipped in an instant. At my mother's insistence, he cut shorter and shorter. It wasn't short enough. My mother asked him to use the clippers on the back of my neck. I emerged a shorn pin-head.

I don't even remember feeling miserable. I knew my mother had once looked worse than this. When they'd shaved her head in Auschwitz, they'd left no hair at all.

I knew my mother hadn't done this to me out of ill-will. I knew it was an unconscious gesture. An unconscious need for me to experience something of what she had experienced. I don't know how I knew this, but I did.

The ballerina whose food I'd stolen started weeping when she found out her jam tarts were missing. The ballet teacher lined up the whole class and asked who the thief was. I stayed silent. I was sure I was turning bright red. I hoped there were no crumbs on my face.

I used to wipe the cream and custard from the layered cake my mother bought when she had visitors. I'd start with a layer of cream, then a layer of custard. By the time I was finished, the once high mille-feuille cake was as flat as a pancake. My mother never said anything. If there was no cream or custard left at all, she unlocked the chocolate biscuit cupboard and served chocolate biscuits with the coffee.

This stealing of food was just one part of a life of crime. I had displayed a criminal tendency at an early age. I forged my bank book when I was seven. I took the money I was supposed to bank every week, and spent it on broken biscuits and pens. I forged the initials of the bank official who initialled the weekly deposits.

I slipped up and was caught one day, when I decided to bank my two shillings. The man from the bank took one look at the columns and columns of his initials, and became suspicious. He looked at my bank book for a long time, then asked me to stay behind after class.

They called my parents to the school. I remember sitting outside the headmistress's office, eating a sugar-coated Nice biscuit someone had given me. My parents looked sombre and distressed. The school decided to give me another chance. I wouldn't be expelled. My parents were so grateful.

I wasn't deterred by this narrow escape. I went on stealing. I stole pens, nibs and fountain pens from the local newsagent. I had the most beautiful collection of pens at Lee Street Primary School and no one ever asked how I got them.

My life of crime came to an abrupt end when I was arrested for shoplifting. I was ten years old and it was the first time I had been allowed to go into the city on my own. I took the ninety-six tram on Nicholson Street and went straight to Coles. I stole some stuff from Coles, and then I went across the road to Myers where I helped myself to more. I went home on the tram and put all my bounty into a drawer. Then, as this had been such a successful trip, I headed back. When the store detective gripped my arm and told me to follow him, I knew the return trip had been a mistake.

What was I stealing? Things I didn't want, things I didn't need, things I didn't like. Fake pearl earrings; garish gold necklaces; pink lipsticks, hair bands and hair rollers. I think I wasn't stealing. I think I was screaming. Screaming for attention. And I got it. My parents were hysterical and furious.

The chief store detective, a large, tough woman, told me she had put her own daughter in reform school for shoplifting. I started to be afraid. They took my watch away from me – they thought I'd stolen that, too – and I started to cry. 'Crying will get you nowhere,' the head detective said. 'They'll take no notice of your tears in reform school.'

I don't know how I got out of being sent to reform school. There was a court case. A friend of my father's, a Jewish man who'd migrated to Australia before the war and spoke good English, spoke up for me, and I was allowed to go back to Lee Street.

At home no one spoke to me for weeks. They spoke to each other in hushed tones. I felt as though someone had died. Me. For years I read the word shopfitter as shoplifter, and felt sick. I wasn't able to walk past Coles until I was well into my thirties.

My parents never mentioned the incident again. When I tried to bring it up in a light-hearted way a few years ago, my father said, brusquely, that it was not a laughing matter. I knew then, that neither shoplifting or weight-loss would ever be a laughing matter.

My mother was always up with the latest developments in the world of weight-loss. One day, when I came home from Uni High, she told me she had enrolled me in a course at Slendertone, or Slenderama, or Slenderella.

Slender whatever-it-was-called, a slimming salon, was located at the top end of Collins Street. They had vibrating couches in small cubicles. All you had to do was take off your shoes, lie down and vibrate. Twenty sessions, they said, would take care of most people's problems. I think it was only weight problems they were referring to.

I lay on their couches and vibrated every Monday and Thursday for several months. My best friend sat next to me, in a chair in the cubicle. We shared a family-sized block of Cadbury's Fruit and Nut chocolate while I waited for the vibrations to whittle away my hips.

My mother found a more severe solution when I was sixteen. I was in my final year of high school, the year that determined which university you would get into, when my mother told me I would be going into hospital for two weeks.

Just writing this down gives me the creeps. All the shame and confusion and isolation comes right back to me. I can smell the hospital, and my loneliness.

My mother's solution was to starve my excess weight off. I was to be on a five-hundred-calorie-a-day diet. I don't actually remember eating any hospital food. The menus that came with my breakfast, lunch and dinner all had 'no' ticked in front of every food in every category. No cornflakes, no milk, no toast, no butter. No bread, no cheese, no chicken, no jelly, no sugar. No meat, no potatoes.

It must have been the Royal Melbourne Hospital as it was so close to my school. I don't remember. I do remember the shame I felt, and the lies I had to tell to explain my absence and my hospitalisation. For the only time in my life, I found it difficult to come up with a lie. I couldn't work out how to explain why I was in hospital. And, for the only time in my life, I lied to my best friend. I told everyone that I was having an

170

operation on my throat and wouldn't be able to speak.

This was smart as it stopped me having to come up with the details of the throat operation. And it also meant that I wouldn't have to explain the lack of surgery scars.

I let people peer down my throat, afterwards. Several girls said they could see the scars clearly. The results showed on my hips. I lost quite a few pounds. It took me several weeks to replace them.

I took over the management of my weight-loss when I was twenty. I started by having injections of something, when I was in London. I never asked the Harley Street specialist what he was injecting into me.

In between interviewing Stevie Winwood and Mick Jagger and Manfred Mann, I was rushing to the doctor's for injections. The doctor gave me a printed diet. He told me to stick to the diet if I wanted the injections to work. Breakfast was one soft-boiled egg and a cup of black tea. Lunch was two slices of unbuttered bread, one slice of ham and an apple, and dinner was poached chicken breast. Poached chicken breast? I was sharing a house with Normie Rowe and the Playboys at the time. Dinner was often fish and chips. How could I poach a chicken breast, in the kitchen in front of them, every night?

I did my best. I peeled the batter off the fish, and left the buns of my Wimpie burgers. But it was tough going. The doctor didn't think I was losing enough weight. He started jabbing the needles in a bit roughly, so I left.

I tried hypnosis next. I was back in Melbourne. I went to a hypnotist who kept telling me how relaxed I was feeling. It was news to me. I felt so tense my jaw was aching. In the end, he said I wasn't an easy subject for hypnosis and recommended that I try Lee Saxon. Lee Saxon was quite famous and had rooms in St Kilda Road. I tried my best to relax. 'You're not relaxing,' he kept saying to me. 'I'm trying,' I kept answering.

If marijuana had had the relaxing effect on me that it seemed to have on other people, I would have smoked a joint before my hypnosis sessions. Pot made me feel sick and disoriented.

Lee Saxon finally gave up. He sent me to a friend of his who had a blue light. I stared at this blue light twice a week for months. The blue light hypnotist sat down one afternoon and told me I was beyond his help. I felt desolate and a failure.

I cheered up when I saw an ad for a muscle-exercising machine. I was back in London, working in the rock world again. I was interviewing Cliff Richards when I spotted the ad in a magazine on a side table. I asked Cliff if I could borrow the magazine for a day. He told me to take it and keep it.

I ordered the muscle-exercising machine that after-noon. It would take three weeks for delivery, the man said, but once I got it, the weight would begin to fly off.

There were so many suction caps to attach to my skin, and so many leads to link them back to the machine, that it took me another three weeks to work out how to use it.

Finally, I figured it out. First I did my thighs. Prickly small stings flicked at the front and back of my thighs. I ignored the discomfort. I knew that losing weight was never painless.

It took me an hour to do both thighs. It was the fastening and unfastening of all those caps and leads. At this rate, it was going to take me a month to get through my whole body, once.

I kept trying. I persevered. I missed an interview with Lulu because I couldn't bear to untangle myself when I'd only just got myself hooked up. I lay on my bed, in my flat, in London, for hours, while different parts of my body throbbed. It wasn't as thrilling as it sounds. It took up most of my evenings and all of my spare time.

After two months, I was the same size I was when I started. But my career was going downhill and I'd lost most of my friends. I wrapped all the cords around each other, and threw the machine away.

I decided diet was the answer. But as soon as I decided to go on a diet, I ate more. I started feeling hungry as soon as I thought about dieting. So for days before my diet started, I ate the last of all the things I knew I would be deprived of. I had to have lots of bread with inches of butter, as I knew it would be dry toast with every meal, any minute. I had to have chocolate and I had to have ice-cream. There were so many things I had to have, that I often had to delay the start of the diet. I know I was pounds heavier at the start of each diet than in the weeks before the decision to lose weight.

I have been on every diet known to mankind. I've been on the Grapefruit Diet. I ate grapefruit with every meal. I ate grapefruit and fried bacon, grapefruit and fried eggs, grapefruit and fried sausages. I don't like fried bacon, fried eggs or fried sausages but they were the foods that were prescribed with the Grapefruit Diet. I craved a carrot or an apple. My breath began to smell. I ditched that diet when people turned away from me.

I tried the boiled egg diet and became so constipated I had to swallow two packets of prunes to rectify things. I tried the Israeli Army Diet, the banana diet, the Scarsdale diet. I tried the low carbohydrate diet and the no carbohydrate diet. I tried the high carbohydrate diet. I tried the eat-all-you want-of-one-kind-of-food-diet, the fruit juice diet and the celery diet.

On the whole, I remained pretty much as I was: very overweight. People assumed that I had a thyroid condition of some sort, as no one saw me eat much. I did most of my eating at home alone, or in the car.

I felt miserable now and then especially when my clothes didn't fit. But on the whole, my size didn't bother me. Many things that *should* have been bothering me were not bothering me. I started to find this out when I went to my first analyst and began five years of psychotherapy.

My mother had given up on me. She no longer took me aside for those this-is-your-last-chance-to-lose-weight talks. Even her ambition was not broad enough to encompass the sort of weight loss that would leave me slim.

She tried to look past the large, full-length tent-like dresses I lived in. Occasionally she couldn't help herself and would suggest that we go shopping for clothes. But she never insisted. I think it would have been hard to find my size in Myer's or Buckley's.

Anyway, my mother had my children by this time and luckily, they were slim. She was so happy with her grandchildren, that I think she decided she could live with the imperfections in her children.

A couple of years into my psychotherapy, when I was wrestling with the issues of food and weight, I thought I would skip some understanding and deal with the symptoms. I joined Weight Watchers.

I listened carefully to the Weight Watchers lecturer. I read the literature. I bought weighing scales. I cooked five-ounce portions of chicken and fish and liver, and put them in the freezer. I bought loads of radishes and zucchinis and celery and tomatoes.

They weighed me in front of all the other members. Everyone knew each other's weight. They set a goal. I don't remember how many pounds I had to lose. I just remember it was a lot.

I stuck to the diet. I ate my Weight Watchers breakfast, my two slices of bread and cottage cheese for lunch and my five-ounce portions of fish for dinner.

It seemed a long time between meals. I made up the free soup. It was called free because you could eat it at any time. It was largely composed of zucchini and radishes. I ate a gallon of the soup every day. This meant that I was pissing all day.

At my second Weight Watchers meeting I weighed in at two pounds lighter. The lecturer was thrilled. She told the rest of the meeting. Everybody clapped. I wasn't that thrilled myself. At two pounds a week I thought it was going to be a long haul.

I decided to take things into my own hands and fast. I had nothing but water for the whole week. The first two days were the hardest, after that the challenge of losing weight properly took over.

When they weighed me, I'd lost seven pounds. Everybody was elated. I got an extra round of applause for the biggest weight loss of the week. I fasted for another two days. By the tenth day, I was starving, and I didn't feel great. I broke my fast with a dozen cream buns from the Hot and Crusty Bread Shop on the corner of Glenferrie Road and Barkly Street, in Armadale.

I ate the cream buns as I walked down Barkly Street. Each mouthful tasted delicious. I had icing sugar all over my face by the time I'd walked home. I finished the last cream bun as I walked into my front gate. I felt happy.

I'd come a long way from the chocolate custard. My former kindergarten teacher, the one who dished out the chocolate custard, was at one of my readings at the

Adelaide Festival two years ago. She wanted to reassure me that I was not as fat as I've described myself. 'You were not that fat,' she whispered in my ear. Maybe I wasn't at four, but I made up for it later on.

Remembering all of this has made me edgy. I feel swamped by the past. I need to see that things have changed, that I'm not that poor Lily who rarely moved, never looked in a mirror and pretended that her body wasn't part of her. I feel a bit adrift in images of myself wearing enormous dresses and unattractive underwear.

I put on my running shoes and walk. I am on Shelter Island. I walk along Peconic Avenue. I pass box turtles and small rabbits and deer. There are deer everywhere on this island.

I can see the sea now. I feel better. I walk along West Neck and out onto the peninsula. There are large and small boats in the water. I walk past Silver Beach and Crescent Beach. I inhale the clear air of the island. My husband, who is on his way home from the studio he is renting above a former petrol station on the marina, passes me in the car and stops. I ask him to measure my speed with the speedometer. I'm doing five miles an hour. I'm really pleased. That's fast. I start to feel less unsettled.

Two hours later, I come back. I'm covered with sweat. My hips and legs and lungs and arms feel alive. I feel happy. While I was walking, I thought about all the strange foods I ate in order to lose weight. What they had in common was their volume. Large portions. I was eating more and more, all in the hope of becoming less and less.

For about six months, when I was somewhere around thirty, I lived on tuna salad. I made up the salad every morning. I tried to stretch one large can of tuna, packed in water, as far as it could be stretched.

I packed the salad with radishes, lettuce, cucumber, celery and parsley until it was so dense it was hard to find the tuna. This way, eating one can of tuna took me all day. The vegetables I'd added, added a negligible number of calories, and I hoped all the chewing involved used up a few extra calories as a bonus.

There was another drawback to this can-of-tuna diet. I was hungry most of the time. So I doubled the quantities. Two cans of tuna, four bunches of radishes, two heads of celery, two lettuces, four cucumbers and a bunch of parsley.

The diet had now become very time-consuming. I barely had enough hours in each day to chop all the ingredients, and then eat them. I was dying for real food by the time I ditched the tuna diet. I spent the six months after that eating all the food I'd missed.

'I think my body's deprived of iron and thiamine and niacin, and I need some complex carbohydrates,' I said to friends as I grilled slices of calf's liver and toasted rye bread.

I had an encyclopedic knowledge of calorie values and could tell you the nutritional composition of most foods, so people assumed I knew what I was talking about. If only I knew what I was doing. I can produce a demented list of dishes that I thought would make me slim. It's not the list that was demented, it was me.

I once carted an electric food heater from Melbourne to Sydney, so that I could stick to my current fad, a cabbage stew. The stew was made from half a cabbage, two pounds of zucchinis, one onion and one cup of rice, cooked in a large can of tomato juice. It was quite tasty.

We were staying at the Sebel Town House, in Sydney. The Sebel Town House, in Elizabeth Bay, is a discreet yet hip hotel. When I heated up my cabbage stew, the entire fourth floor of the Sebel Town House smelt of cabbage. No one said anything.

The following night I heated the cabbage in the bathroom. The electric food heater set off the fire alarm. The resultant chaos turned me off cabbage for quite a while.

My eating was so disordered. I rarely ate the same meals as my children. I would serve them normal food and then bring my portion of whatever it was that I thought was going to solve my problems, to the table. My kids can amuse each other for hours by going through a list of my crazes and phases in food. I don't find it quite so funny.

Today my children are still sometimes surprised to see me sitting down to three ordinary meals, every day. They will be helping to dish out the food at a family dinner and go to ask me where my food is.

I am sometimes still surprised at myself, too. Surprised that I can eat what other people eat. That I can eat anything I want to eat. And I do. What I want to eat has changed. But sometimes I want what I used to want. Chocolate, cheesecake, chopped liver. And I have some.

Separating my own food from what my family ate was another way in which I was mimicking my mother. And again, it was unconscious. My mother never ate with us. She didn't eat what we ate. She ate remnants. The leftover celery, onion and carrots from the chicken soup, the stale rye bread with caraway seeds.

She ate her food when she was alone. I think my mother never stopped feeling guilty for being alive. Guilty for living when her mother and father and four brothers and three sisters had all died. Eating requires life. I think my mother was trying to tone down the life involved in the act. If she ate her leftovers while she washed the dishes, she could almost not notice she was eating. Sometimes I'd see her sitting at the table eating her stale bread or over-cooked carrots. She always looked sad.

My kids didn't escape my neurosis about food. My son, a very smart kid, saw my anxiety and capitalised on it, when he was just months old. He became a very fussy eater. I would spend hours trying to feed him. When he went onto solids, I would spoon the food in and he would spit it out. This routine could take up most of the day. I thought he would die if he didn't eat all of his food, and I must have looked as though I would die if he didn't.

I used to make faces and make up stories to distract him, in order to get him to eat. He thought it was a great game. He'd laugh at my faces, and look involved in the stories, and spit the food right out again. He became such a fussy eater that he ate only yogurt and strawberries for most of his third year.

I took him to a pediatrician. An awful man with a large bow tie. He called me mother. 'Mother, what's the problem?' he said to me. I told him about the yogurt and strawberries. 'Mother, you're the problem,' he said. I decided his communication skills were limited, and went home and wept.

My son survived. He grew into an adult who has a penchant for oysters, escargots, lobsters and eye-fillet steak. I'm sure this is a reaction to some part of his childhood. And there were extreme moments.

I sterilised everything my poor son touched until he was about two. I had raw welts on my hands from constantly dipping them into Milton solution. Milton solution was what we all sterilised our nappies in. I also sterilised everything else.

I thought I was frightened of germs and bacteria. But I was frightened of motherhood, and what it meant, although I would not recognise either fear for years. I was on guard for germs.

I was more flexible by the time I had my daughter.

I had been reluctant to have a second child. I thought I couldn't possibly love another child as much as I loved my son. And then I had my daughter. I adored her. I wanted to give her all the freedom that I had denied myself. I gave her a name that to me was a symbol of freedom. When she was two, I found her eating her lunch on the floor. She had tipped her food onto the floor, and was picking it up, piece by piece, and eating it.

From then on, she wanted to eat all of her food on the floor. She liked to get bread or potato or a slice of cheese and smudge it right into our cork tiles. She would press the food firmly into the tiles, then dig it up and eat it. She did this for months, with every meal. I tried to keep the kitchen floor as clean as I could.

I'm not sure why I tolerated her need to eat off the floor. I used to think it was because I wanted to please her. But, I think I was overrun by motherhood without knowing it.

Other people complained about the boredom and loneliness of motherhood. Not me. Other people complained about their children. I never did. Not once. Having children wasn't a problem, my children weren't a problem, being a mother wasn't a problem. What was? I had a variety of answers. Being fat was one of them.

My father had a problem with fat, too. My mother thought he was too fat. This was not as serious a problem to her as me being fat, but it was a problem.

My father wasn't really fat. He still isn't. He's always eaten more or less what he wanted to. And that included a lot of chocolate and a lot of spaghetti bolognese and a lot of gelati. He's rarely been sick. He's eighty years old now, and looks seventy.

But he feels fat. Nobody other than my mother thought he was fat. Years after her death he continues to feel fat. My father also can't admit to hunger. I have never heard him say he was hungry. In fact, he always says he is not hungry, even when he's hovering around the kitchen.

My father often told me how one day, in Auschwitz, he was first in line for the soup. This soup was not clam chowder or vichyssoise. This was a watery broth thickened with sawdust. If you were lucky, there were a few turnip or potato peels floating in the soup. If you were unlucky, there were pieces of tin and the odd dead rodent. He was so hungry and so excited about being first in line, that he put his bowl to his mouth and gulped the whole lot down all at once. The soup was still boiling and my father's blistered mouth and throat took a long time to heal.

I inherited my father's inability to voice hunger. If you overlooked my size, I appeared to be a person with no appetite. Today, my father laughs when I say I'm starving. He's still not hungry. For two people who were rarely hungry, we did pretty well.

We were travelling with the kids and my father, nine years ago. It was not long after my mother had died. My father had been very depressed. For nearly a year he'd refused to go out anywhere. In the evenings, he sat in his chair, at home alone.

He'd wanted to die with my mother. 'I should have died,' he said, over and over again. 'Your mother looked after herself,' he said. 'She ate such healthy food, and look what happened, she got cancer. And I did eat like a pig, and I'm still here.' And then he would weep.

Not only did he not want to leave the house, he didn't want to be a burden on us. Each time I asked if he would make the trip overseas with us, he would say he didn't want to be a fifth wheel. This must be a Polish saying.

My younger daughter finally persuaded him by saying that if he didn't go, she wouldn't go. She'd stay in Melbourne and they could go to Luna Park and McDonalds together.

My father started to look like his old self in New York. He loved it. He felt very at home. We ate mounds of chopped liver and brisket and pickles. Before each meal, he said he wasn't very hungry.

In London, we stayed at the Hilton. A buffet breakfast was included in the price of the room. My father took one look at the buffet breakfast and said: 'What, are they crazy? Who eats this for breakfast?'

There were chefs cooking omelettes and grilling steaks and sausages. Others were cooking waffles and pancakes. 'I'm not hungry,' he said. 'I'll just have an orange juice.'

'We paid for this meal,' I said. 'At least have some cereal.'

'Don't noodge me,' he said.

Noodge is a Yiddish word. To noodge is to pester, to bother, to irritate. 'I'm not noodging you,' I said. He got up, reluctantly, and went off in the direction of the cereals.

He came back with a bowl of cornflakes. 'Not bad,' he said when he finished the bowl. 'This Kelloggs is just like the Kelloggs in Australia.' I was eating some fruit. My father looked at my bowl. 'They got prunes here,' he said. 'I think I'll have some.'

After the prunes, he had some fried potatoes. My husband persuaded him that the sausages were worth trying and he tried several. Then he spotted the chocolate sauce. He came back with a plate of waffles drowning in chocolate sauce. After each dish, he announced loudly, 'That's it, that's enough for me. I'm not hungry. I'm finished.'

My son was going through a croissant craze at the time. He had five or six croissants on his plate. My father took one. 'These are very good,' he said, and wandered off to the buffet again.

My father couldn't finish his croissants. He pushed his plate, with a half-eaten croissant still on it, away. 'That's it,' he said, and rubbed his hands together as though he was brushing away the whole breakfast. It was a gesture that distanced him from what he had eaten. He did it after every meal.

Later that day, when we were discussing lunch, he asked my son how he could think about lunch after he'd eaten so many croissants. 'I myself didn't eat so much,' he said. And I knew he believed it. Food was so complicated for us. For my mother, for my father and for me.

When I was a kid, and as a teenager, we ate such different food. School friends would be agog at the sight of my father sitting at the dinner table with a fish head hanging out of the side of his mouth. My father loved sucking the juices and jellies out of the gills and the eye sockets.

My mother cooked liver and tripe. She cooked chicken. Chicken feet and chicken stomachs and chicken hearts. The chicken feet terrified quite a few of my friends. I loved the feet. I loved separating all the small bones and chewing the gristle between the joints.

When he turned seventy-five, my father decided to tackle what he saw as his weight problem. He wasn't really overweight. I think he was keeping my mother's priorities alive. He announced he was going on a fast.

'That's stupid,' I said to him.

'Thank you, my daughter, for that compliment,' he said.

'No,' I said. 'It's a mad idea to go on a fast.'

'What do you know about mad?' he said. 'You are the one who has to see a psychiatrist.'

'An analyst,' I said.

'It's the same thing,' he said.

I tried to talk him out of the fast. But he was adamant. He was not going to eat anything. That way he could lose weight, once and for all.

I felt worried about him. I decided to watch him carefully. He'd been eating dinner with us, several times a week, up until then. He said he'd come around at dinner time anyway, and sit with us so that he could see the children.

The first night, he watched everything I ate. 'Good klops?' he said. A klops is a meatloaf. 'It's a good klops,' I said. 'Good carrots?' he said. I offered him klops. I offered him carrots. I offered him everything. He said no.

The next day, he came early. I was still writing. I put away my work and came out of the bedroom, where I worked, to talk to him. On the way, I picked up an apple.

'You're eating an apple and I am eating nothing,' he said. I offered him an apple. He shook his head. 'Please have an apple,' I said. He shook his head, again. 'Not for me,' he said.

Dinner the following night was the same. He watched what everyone ate. He patted his stomach. 'I'm getting thinner,' he said.

A couple of days later, I felt more worried about him. He wasn't his old self. He was starting to look flat. I tried to persuade him to give up the fast. He left the house in a huff. I started calling him, first thing in the morning, to make sure he was all right.

On the fifth day of the fast, my father rang me at seven a.m. 'I'm finished with the fast,' he said.

'That's great,' I said.

'It's not so great,' he said. 'I did eat nothing for four

days and I lost not one pound. What's the use of fasting if you don't lose any weight?'

'You didn't lose any weight?' I said.

'Nothing at all,' he said.

'That's impossible,' I said.

'That's the truth,' he said.

'Maybe it's the scales?' I said.

'No,' he said. 'I have got two scales. The both scales say the same weight like they always did.'

'I can't understand it,' I said.

'Who could understand such a thing?' he said. 'To fast for four days and not to lose one pound?'

My father was working in a print studio, making etchings with my husband, at the time. I was worried that he might feel deflated at the failure of his fast. I called one of the young printmakers who worked at the studio and asked him to keep an eye on my father. I told him the story of the fast. 'Fasting?' he said. 'I don't think he was fasting. He asked me to buy him two blocks of chocolate yesterday.'

Two blocks of chocolate! I couldn't believe it. I called my father. 'Bill said that you asked him to buy two blocks of chocolate,' I said. 'I thought you were on a fast.'

'What are you talking about?' my father said. 'Of course I was on a fast.'

'But you were eating chocolate,' I said.

'I didn't have breakfast. I didn't have lunch. I didn't have tea. That's a fast,' he said.

'But you had chocolate,' I said.

'I only had chocolate,' my father said. 'Dark chocolate and nothing else. Now I'm going to have some more chocolate. What's the use of fasting if you don't lose any weight?'

'He's mad,' I said to my husband.

'You're mad,' my younger daughter said to me when I asked her to ring Essa Bagels, on 21st Street, and ask them what the calorie value of one of their bagels was.

I didn't want to drive them mad by ringing myself. I had asked them twice in the store, and rung them several times. Each time I got the same answer. A hundred and nine calories.

This didn't seem possible. They were huge bagels. One slim slice of white bread can be a hundred and nine calories. I'd questioned two of the people serving at Essa Bagels, separately, about how this low calorie count was possible. 'We use a special low-starch flour,' they said.

'How low-starch can flour be?' I said to my husband. I weighed one of the bagels. It was nearly five ounces.

I called Essa Bagels again. 'Could you tell me how many calories there are in one of your bagels?' I said to the woman who answered the phone. 'It's still the same,' she said wearily. 'A hundred and nine.'

'I've rung them for you, before,' my younger daughter said to me. 'Just ring again,' I said. They were still a hundred and nine calories.

I had been travelling to Essa Bagels for two years

when the *New York Times* came out with an article on bagels. They analysed the nutritional content and calorie value of New York's most popular bagels. One Essa Bagel was five hundred and eight calories.

I was in a state of shock after I read this. I couldn't work for the rest of the day. I ran into my husband's studio to tell him. He tried not to laugh. He'd watched me weighing the bagels, then adjusting the scales and weighing them again, in the hope of lowering their weight. I called the kids and told them. They couldn't stop laughing.

'What did you expect, Lil?' my younger daughter said. 'They are ginormous.'

'Some days I had two,' I said to her. 'And occasionally three. Three bagels. Fifteen hundred calories. I was eating a day's worth of calories as a snack.'

'Could we sue Essa Bagels?' she said.

'I wonder if business has dropped off since the *Times* article came out,' I said to my husband the next time we passed Essa Bagels. He laughed. 'No,' he said. 'New Yorkers are pretty unflappable.'

The first time I came to New York, I was nineteen. It was 1966. The only person I knew in New York was the late Lillian Roxon, an Australian journalist who'd been living in New York for years. She'd introduced herself to me, several months earlier, in London.

Lillian took me over in New York and took me everywhere with her. She took me to a small club to see Jim Morrison and the Doors. Lillian, her friend Linda Eastman and I, sat ten feet away from the band. In between sets Linda (who two years later would become Linda McCartney) and Jim Morrison had short, volatile, private conversations. The Doors were not yet very famous. Jim Morrison was a mesmerising and hypnotically seductive performer.

Lillian introduced me to everyone as Australia's best journalist. I hardly felt I was a journalist, let alone Australia's best. I used to say, with embarrassment, that I wasn't really Australia's best, until Lillian told me to grow up.

At the time, I thought Lillian was quite old. She must have been about thirty. There was a peculiar separation in my generation. No one I knew, knew anyone other than people their own age. I was puzzled by why Lillian had sought out my friendship. Puzzled but grateful.

When I called her a couple of years later to say I was getting married, she was the only person to ask me why. I thought it was a crazy question.

Lillian was short and tubby. She bought her clothes in the Chubby Teens department of Macy's. I went there once with her. I felt very uncomfortable. Lillian tried on endless dresses. I said everything looked wonderful. I couldn't wait to get out.

Lillian also introduced me to a low-calorie world. She knew where to buy low-calorie ice-cream and low-calorie sweets. We had low-calorie milkshakes in a cafe with booths. We sat in our own booth and had two chocolate milkshakes each. I'd never seen a cafe with booths. I thought the booths were for privacy, so fat people could enjoy their low-calorie milkshakes in peace.

When I look at the array of low-calorie products in my fridge now, I often think of Lillian, who died of an asthma attack before she was forty.

I was forty-five before I could differentiate hunger from needing to fill myself up. I couldn't tell when I was hungry and I couldn't tell when I was full.

The gaps I was trying to plug with food became fewer. I felt more solid within myself and had less need for a solid exterior. I was no longer pretending to be someone nicer, smarter, kinder. With the loss of many of the illusions I had about myself, came the loss of my need to overeat.

Slowly I began to learn when I was hungry and when I was full. I stopped thinking about food constantly. Sometimes, I'm still surprised that I don't think about food in between meals. I think about what I eat. I try to eat as healthily as I can. It's not hard. I love fruit and vegetables.

Weight-lifting makes you very aware of the connection between what you eat and who you are. If I haven't had enough protein for a few days, for example, I'm just not as strong.

It's very easy to separate yourself from what you eat, especially for women. Women believe that eating haphazardly and skipping meals has no effect. The brightest women I know muck around with their food. They skip breakfast, they often overlook protein altogether and exist on green salad. This doesn't happen with men. Even the most stupid men seem to eat regular meals.

Dog breeders know the importance of nutrition. In the *New York Times* today the Vice President of Communications for the American Kennel Club is quoted as saying: *Breeders are obsessed with food because what a dog eats is almost immediately reflected in how he looks and performs.*

All those young women who smoke and miss meals will probably look like cigarette ash in a few years' time. Why do we women have to damage ourselves so? I don't know. I've been working hard to undo what damage I can. With exercise, with good nutrition, with vitamins.

I'm not an expert on vitamins. I take a multi-vitamin and mineral supplement every day in the belief that it could help and it can't hurt. I also swallow a daily capsule of Evening Primrose oil. I do this because a former editor of mine swore Evening Primrose oil was a cure for everything.

I get into habits easily, so I just kept taking the Evening Primrose oil. I was about to give it up, recently, when I read that Cher takes it. On a less than scientific basis, I decided that Cher probably knows what she's doing. Now, I have to stay abreast of Cher's moves. At least in the Evening Primrose oil department.

Cher has probably never had any trouble measuring her hips. Last week I had to measure my hips. Graham Long, the Australian designer, has made clothes for me for over twelve years. Ever since I first saw his sign in the window of his shop in Brunswick Street, Fitzroy. The sign was in very artistic lettering. I thought it said Graham Zong.

Graham has made my clothes in so many sizes. This size after that diet, that size after another diet and the sizes in between diets. Over the last few years the clothes have been getting steadily smaller.

Graham was making me a dress to wear to a friend's wedding anniversary dinner. He called me and asked me to measure my hips.

I don't like measuring any part of me. My bust, my blood pressure, my pulse, my weight. When I weigh myself, I take off all my clothes, have a piss, exhale, and step as lightly as I can onto the scales. I don't inhale until I get off.

I got the tape measure out. I checked to see that it wasn't stretched. Tape measures can stretch. It looked okay. I went to put it around my hips. But I encountered a problem immediately. Exactly where were my hips?

It wasn't that they were so small that they were hard to find. They were quite broad. And that was the problem. I was trying to minimise the breadth without giving Graham an incorrect figure.

Do you measure your hips around your bum? I wondered. Around the top of your thighs? Probably at their widest part, I decided. I looked at the measurement, wow, my hips were still pretty wide.

Maybe I was holding the tape measure too loosely. How loose should it be? I rang Graham. Loose enough to be able to move the tape measure, he said, and not so loose that it slipped.

I tried again. Maybe this time it was too tight? After fifteen minutes, I decided on a measurement. I called Graham. 'That's good,' he said. 'You must have lost more weight.' 'Maybe I'm not measuring the right place,' I said. 'I'll ring you back.'

I rang him back four times. I gave him eight different hip measurements. Finally, he said he'd average them out. I was so flustered after all the measuring and positioning that I had to go for a walk. 'Obviously decades of analysis doesn't teach you to deal with a tape measure,' I said to my husband, on my way out.

I have changed in so many ways, yet I am still the same person. Curiously superstitious. Not wanting to push my luck. 'Are you well?' a friend said to me recently. This is a friend who is also a collector of my husband's paintings. I like him very much. He's a reserved man, my age.

Understated people often bring out the excess in me. I become louder than I am, more emotional than I am, and less certain than I am. Not a pretty picture.

I hadn't answered him, so he repeated the question. 'Are you well?' he said. What a question. No Jew could answer that question without a few questions of their own. 'I hope so,' I said uncertainly. Why did he have to ask me that? I wasn't even thinking about my health, or about all of the perils and risks there are to all of our well-being. Am I well?

I pictured my insides. All that blood surging and circulating. Was my haemoglobin concentration on track? Was my liver eliminating whatever it had to from my bloodstream? Were my intestines transporting and absorbing nutrients? Were my kidneys flushing? How did I know?

'I think I am,' I said. I amended this to, 'As far as I know, I am.' I must have looked worried because he was looking at me quizzically. 'I can't answer that question,' I said to him. He started laughing.

'I could have coped if you'd said, "You look well",' I said. 'Then I would have said, "Thank you." But "Are you well?" is a serious question. "How do I know?" is the answer.'

'You could just say "yes",' he said.

'I can't,' I said. 'I might be pushing my luck. Invoking the evil eye.'

He rolled his eyes at me and looked at my husband. I could see he was really glad that it was not he who was married to me. I offered him another explanation. 'It's like not buying baby clothes before you've delivered the baby,' I said to him. I could see by the expression on his face that I'd lost him completely.

'You're not pregnant?' he said.

'God, no!' I said. He looked at me carefully. I tried to look as normal and composed as I could.

'You look well,' he said.

'Thank you,' I said.

FOOD

THE DAY MY HUSBAND CALLED me to say he wanted
to marry me, I had sixteen frozen pheasants floating in
the bath. I was trying to defrost them. They were supposed to have been delivered fresh, not frozen.

I had thirty-two people coming to dinner that night.
It's not easy to defrost poultry, hygienically. I was trying
to thaw the pheasants while keeping them cold. The
pheasants were a sad sight. Sixteen naked, puny little
bodies bobbing up and down in the bath water.

'I love you,' he said to me on the phone. 'I was
born to be with you.' I took off my rubber gloves. You
can't participate in a conversation like that with rubber
gloves on.

'I've got sixteen pheasants defrosting in the bath,' I said to him. He didn't seem to hold this against me. 'I've never cooked pheasant before,' I said. I didn't want him to think I was the sort of person who was always cooking pheasant.

I felt a bit nervous and wasn't sure of what else to say. 'Only a maniac would cook sixteen pheasants on their first attempt to cook pheasant,' I said.

'I love you,' he said. 'I want to marry you.' I stopped talking about the pheasants. The pheasants were not my biggest problem. I had a more pressing problem. I was married to someone else.

Food seems to have been at the centre of quite a lot of my life. My mother was a very good cook. When she cooked, she was in a world of her own. It was a volatile world. She was always in a hurry. She placed saucepans on the stove with a bang; she slammed cupboards. She opened and shut a revolving cupboard in the corner of the kitchen with such speed, that I lived in dread of it, one day, revolving right through several of her fingers.

There was a lot of noise in my mother's kitchen. Her Mixmaster whirred and the meat grinder roared. My mother chopped and mixed and stirred and kneaded. While things were cooking, she washed up with the same volume and vigour.

Out of all of this turmoil, my mother produced beautiful food. Not only did it taste good, it looked wonderful. My mother arranged her food artfully. And this was well before the days of Martha Stewart and *Vogue Living*.

She cooked far too much food. Too much for us, on a daily basis, and too much for the dinner parties she had regularly. The amount of food needed, on any given occasion, was a loaded question for my mother. I have inherited this dilemma. When I cook a meal for four, I make enough for at least twelve, and feel worried that I haven't made enough. I've tried to force myself to make less, but I haven't yet succeeded. I write two pounds of ground veal on a shopping list, and then in the butcher's, I hear myself ask for four pounds. Of course, I then have to double all the other ingredients. I am genetically incapable of cooking a meal for two and I wouldn't even attempt a dish for one.

When we caught the train to Philadelphia recently to see the major Cezanne exhibition, I packed a three-course lunch for the two-hour train trip. 'We're not going to Mozambique,' my husband said when he saw the food I'd packed. I looked so offended he ate two mozzarella and sun-dried tomato sandwiches, before we'd even left Penn Station. 'These are really good,' he kept saying.

We all knew to keep out of the kitchen when my mother was cooking. Sometimes my father made the mistake of creeping in for a drink, or a book he'd forgotten. Inevitably, it would be when my mother had a sponge cake in the oven. My mother's sponge was a cake that could detect a footstep at a hundred paces. Any shift in the air, and this cake would sink. My mother prided herself on her perfect sponge cakes. 'The cake, the cake, Moniek!' she would shout, when he intruded.

Cooking was a solitary activity for my mother. She didn't want company in the kitchen. She didn't like to talk while she cooked. She didn't want any help, either. 'Go and study,' she would say to me, if I offered to do anything. She liked to be on her own with her pots and pans and spoons and spatulas. And she kept her recipes to herself. If friends badgered her, she gave them diffuse measurements. A handful of this, a piece of that. None of them could ever replicate whatever it was they were enquiring about.

Although I wasn't included in the cooking, and my mother never once told me a recipe for anything, I grew up able to make all of the meals that she made. I often marvel at this. How did I know how to make a kapush-niak? A sauerkraut and potato soup made with veal bones. I just knew. I closed my eyes and I saw my mother frying onions until they were golden. Then she added flour and pepper before pouring in the water. Next came the bones which were boiled until they were cooked and their juices were flowing. Then the sauer-kraut was added, and last of all, the peeled potatoes. The first time I made it, my father pronounced it to be just like my mother's. This was a compliment he didn't give out lightly.

How does that knowledge seep into you? By osmosis? I can make latkes, tsimmes, klops, matzoh brei, farfel and kasha. I can make a veal brisket and my mother's roast chicken. We obviously take in much more than we know. Many of my memories of my mother are of her in the kitchen, cooking. I bring my mother to life by cooking her dishes. I find myself handling utensils in the same way that she did. I peel apples and potatoes with the same movements and gestures.

I have similar hands to my mother's. Sometimes when I watch my hands chopping an onion or quartering an apple, I forget who I am. I think I am my mother. This is sometimes disconcerting, sometimes distressing and sometimes comforting. And it is sometimes so intense that I have to leave the kitchen and walk into the bathroom. There, I look into the mirror, and see that I am myself.

My mother is everywhere in my kitchen. I have an old Sunbeam Mixmaster. It's not as useful as the newer machines which chop and grate and blend and shake. But I keep the Mixmaster in my kitchen because it is exactly the same model my mother had in her kitchen.

After my mother died, I took her rolling pin and her graters and sieves and poultry cutters and wooden spoons, and hung them in my kitchen. I use them every day. I stir onions with the yellow plastic serving spoon she used on her non-stick frying pan and I ladle soup into bowls with her green-handled ladle.

My younger daughter, who is a gifted cook, bakes my mother's klops in the very pan my mother cooked her klops in. This daughter used to pester my mother to let her taste the klops mixture raw. She became my mother's chief klops tester. The test was the salt: was it enough, or too little? She still remembers the taste of that raw klops mix. She was eleven when my mother died.

My daughter and I make my mother's chicken soup together. We put one kosher chicken (maybe they're better because they're blessed), one onion, one parsnip, two carrots, four sticks of celery, some parsley, and salt and pepper into a large saucepan of water. Sometimes we double the recipe. And we stand there, together, our hair pulled back, the loose strands of curls frizzing in the damp hot air. If it's winter, the windows steam up. We stand there, over the two simmering saucepans of chicken soup, and silently invoke my mother. It is a potent and unspoken ritual.

Occasionally, when we're cooking another of my mother's dishes, my daughter will correct the way I am slicing something. 'Nana never did it like that,' she'll say. And I wonder how she knows that.

She has been cooking since she was a small girl. She used to make breakfast on the weekends for her brother and sister. Toast and fried tomatoes and fruit salad and home-made muesli for fifty cents. Her brother and sister ate the breakfasts but failed to pay for them.

My younger daughter diligently kept an account of the money they owed her on a notice board. When she was twelve, she finally realised that they were never going to pay her. She took all the carefully written accounts off the board. She threw them away and wrote it off as a bad debt. 'You have to get the money up front,' she said to me.

I wasn't encouraged to cook at home. I was always supposed to be doing something more serious, like school-work or piano practice. So I had to grab my chance to cook whenever I could. And that was when my parents were not at home.

I used to assemble the oddest ingredients – things I thought my mother wouldn't miss. An old tube of almond paste, a few spoons of jam, half a cup of honey, the crumbs from the bottom of the matzoh packet, prune juice, pieces of chocolate and as much butter as I could neatly shear off all four sides of a block of butter.

This sounds like a promising mix. Potentially compatible ingredients. But my cooking techniques were very hit-and-miss. Most of my recipes missed their mark. My cakes never rose, my toffee refused to set. I wasn't daunted. I kept trying. Every time my parents went out, I rushed to the kitchen.

But I just didn't have what it takes to bake a cake. My cakes were woeful. Rubbery, round things with a spring in them; or the alternative, a slumped circle with a gluey, discoloured centre.

I never did catch on about cakes. The only cake I've managed to make well is a cheesecake, and I stopped baking cheesecake years ago. I had become obsessed with trying to get a cheesecake out of the oven without the top of the cake splitting. It's not easy. Sometimes I'd gingerly remove a perfect cheesecake, only to have a hairline crack appear by the time I put the cake down. So, I'd have to make another cake. This left me with an excess of cheesecake, a problem I handled by eating most of the surplus.

Although I clearly had no talent in the cake department, I developed an expertise in another area. By the time I was ten, I'd become quite a toffee expert. I used to add almonds and pieces of dried figs and dried apricots and sesame seeds and pumpkin seeds to my toffee, years before these items became fashionable. Most of the kids in Carlton had never eaten a pumpkin seed or a piece of fig, but my toffee became a hot ticket item at school fund-raising functions.

My parents never saw me cook anything. I could do a batch of a hundred toffees and have them cooled and set in their patty pans, and packed away in tins, before my parents returned from the pictures.

Sometimes I had a real emergency on my hands. My parents would come home early. The four or five times this happened I was in the middle of baking a cake. I didn't have much time. We lived in a tiny three-roomed cottage. It took half a minute to get from the front door to the kitchen.

I grabbed the half-baked cake out of the oven. Luckily I had the presence of mind to hold the baking dish with tea towels. I ran to the top of the steps that led to the backyard, and threw the cake over the next door neighbour's fence. I tried to aim for a tree, but the mixture twice landed on Mrs Dent's back steps. On one occasion, the baking dish flew over with the ingredients. Mrs Dent never mentioned any of the incidents to my mother, or to me. But she did offer to teach me how to bake a jam roll.

I'm not sure what my parents would have done if they'd caught me cooking. They wouldn't have been pleased, I'm sure. My mother would have thought I was in danger. Danger from the gas, danger from the heat, danger from the food. I think my mother thought that the less I had to do with food, the better for me it would be.

Another odd aspect of it all was that neither my mother or father ever commented on the obvious aromas that permeated the house after my episodes of culinary creativity.

I would have loved to cook with my mother. But I never asked her if I could. I knew she needed a lot of time alone. I knew there were parts of her life she could only deal with in solitude. I think that cooking Jewish food reminded my mother of her mother and her beloved father and her brothers and sisters. I think that the memories of growing up and being with her family, were possibly more painful than the memories of the horrors and brutalities she had witnessed and experienced.

She was a much-loved youngest child. The youngest of eight children, and the brightest. The only one to get into university, and one of the few Jewish girls to win a scholarship to go there. She had a dream of becoming a pediatrician, and her father believed vehemently that she would.

I think that the memory of growing up in Lodz, Poland, a country she loved despite the anti-semitism she grew up with, was overwhelming for her. She dismissed Poland loudly as a country she never wanted to return to. But in switching off all of the love and patriotism she felt for Poland, she almost eliminated the memory of her youth. It was as though she had had no life before her life of horror. And the life that she had had as a child and as a teenager, with the family that she loved so dearly, could only come back in small fragments. And only when she was undisturbed.

I envied kids who could cook at home. There was one friend I envied the most. Her parents owned a boarding house in Hawthorn. They had about twenty lodgers in the rambling, semi-dilapidated old Victorian mansion. Suzy had to cook the breakfasts in the boarding house on the weekends. I thought she was so lucky. At seven o'clock on Saturday and Sunday mornings she had to walk across the road from their house to the boarding house, often while it was still dark, to start preparing breakfast.

She had to set out plates and cups and knives and forks and spoons, fill milk and sugar containers, and put butter in small glass dishes. And then she started cooking. She had to toast slices and slices of bread, fry endless eggs, and in a separate frying pan, fry sausages.

When I stayed the night at Suzy's place, I helped her with the breakfasts. I was almost breathless with excitement toasting eight slices of bread at a time. And the thrill of making sure the sausages were ready at the same time as the eggs never left me. I cubed the butter and remembered to dip the knife in water, periodically. I arranged the toast triangles in the toast racks. I helped to fill the coffee urn. I was in heaven, I was so happy. I wasn't bothered by the semi-dissolute air of some of the boarders. I overlooked the seediness and loneliness of a lot of the lodgers. I was too busy cooking the food. I would have been happy to fry sausages and fill milk jugs all day.

My serving skills were less than they could have been. I sometimes spilled some milk or orange juice. But the men were nice enough not to complain. I think they noticed that I went to great pains to set the tables well. I folded the serviettes in the same way my mother did. I made sure the cutlery was placed evenly on either side of the plate, and that it was not crooked. I checked that each place setting was in line with the cutlery and plates on the opposite side of the table.

I was twelve or thirteen when I first helped Suzy in the boarding house. Suzy never quite understood my excitement, but she did know how much I loved it, and she often invited me over.

Working in a kitchen brings out the best and worst in you. It irons out lots of kinks and differences in a friendship. You can't be forced or formal or hesitant when you're working in a kitchen. Suzy and I became very good friends. We decided when we were fourteen, to get waitressing jobs for the summer.

Suzy could sew, so she made us each a sleeveless shift from some black cotton fabric that we bought from Job Warehouse, at the top of Bourke Street. I thought they were so *neat*. They weren't shapeless shifts. They were graceful A-lines. I walked around the house for hours in my shift, when it was first finished. And then we went into the city to look for jobs.

We were both employed by a different branch of Gibby's Coffee Houses. The menu at Gibby's was straightforward, and the kitchen system had been in place for years. The cafe was small. It had a quiet atmosphere. The waitresses wore black. The food was good and simple and the service was smooth and efficient.

But I just couldn't catch on. I couldn't work out how to carry more than one cup of coffee on a tray at a time. When I carried more, the coffee spilt and flooded the toasted crumpets, or drenched the boiled eggs. I was fired in the middle of my first day. I wasn't daunted. I smoothed my black shift back into its crisp A-line and walked to the Chat 'N' Chew in Swanston Street.

I said 'Gibby's' when they asked me where my previous waitressing experience had been. I wasn't lying. They were puzzled by how I'd managed at Gibby's when they saw that I could only carry a bowl of soup if it was half-empty. I lasted less time at the Chat 'N'

Chew than I did at Gibby's. I decided that serving food was not my forte.

At the next restaurant, I applied for a job in the kitchen. I was better in the kitchen. I chopped pounds of onions without dropping one, and I was quite good at shredding lettuce. I had to wear a huge white apron over my A-line shift and a green shower cap on my head, but I didn't mind. I was holding down a job and I was earning money.

It was quite a pleasant kitchen as far as restaurant kitchens go. The pace wasn't frantic. From one of the workbenches you could see through the restaurant and out into the street. I was proud of myself for managing the job well. In my lunch break on my third day, I got a pencil and some paper and calculated how much money I would earn that summer.

That afternoon, I looked up from what I was doing to see my best friend walking past the restaurant. I was so excited. I ran out of the kitchen and through the restaurant, calling her name. She was really surprised to see me. 'I've got a job,' I said to her. I was still holding the bunch of carrots I'd been about to peel, and wearing my green shower cap, when the manager came up to me in the street. He told me I was fired. I thought it was so unfair. 'But I saw my best friend,' I said. 'You'll be able to spend a lot of time with her,' he said.

I overlooked my lack of success in the restaurant business when I opened my own restaurant. It was called Lily's and was on Victoria Parade, East Melbourne, on the site that the Dallas Brooks Hall now occupies. I was twenty and working at *Go-Set*, the rock newspaper. I often worked late and noticed that there were very few places in Melbourne where you could get a meal after nine p.m. Treble Clef, in South Yarra, was always packed.

So, with one of my editors from *Go-Set*, and another minor partner, I opened my own restaurant. I knew nothing about restaurants. One of the first things I did was design the waitresses' outfits. They were based on my original A-line outfit, but were much shorter. We had no waitresses yet. In fact we didn't yet have a building. But I knew what the waitresses would be wearing. I also decided not to have the kitchen staff in green shower caps. They made everyone look so unattractive.

We found our building. We rented the basement of two terrace houses. We knocked out the dividing walls and made four large rooms and a kitchen. We painted the place, bought some basic second-hand kitchen equipment and put a hand-painted sign outside, at the top of the stairs, which said *Lily's*.

We hired a cook who put cordon bleu schnitzel on the menu and showed me how to reheat spaghetti. He was very young and this was his first job. He went on to become one of the most applauded chefs in Australia. We were lucky he was young. He had to work with people who had never worked in a restaurant before. We had given all the jobs to our friends, a motley assortment of young people.

Lily's was a wild success. Most of the rock stars of the day ate there: the Twilights, the Master's Apprentices, the Loved Ones, the Purple Hearts, Russell Morris, and my colleague Molly Meldrum, who was then still called Ian.

The restaurant was always busy. On the weekend, there were often long queues of people standing in Victoria Parade, waiting to get a table. By then I was doing the weekly television show 'Uptight'. I used to interview rock stars and review records. I mentioned the restaurant on air as frequently as I could. Tons of people came. The short A-line shifts were a great hit. The menu was what people wanted. And the restaurant remained open till four or five a.m.

Lily's had a great atmosphere. People loved being there. It was more successful than we could have imagined. And it was a disaster. We had no idea how to run a business. We took money out of the till, all the time. We didn't charge friends. We encouraged romance among the staff. It was truly a disaster.

When we ran out of food, I ran to my mother's. I once removed three chickens and two ducks from my mother's fridge while she was sleeping. I left her a note. There was more disarray than running out of food. When the staff got tired, they coated each other in gelati or squirted whipped cream around the kitchen.

Someone was always crying in the kitchen, or locking themselves in the laundry cupboard to weep. Everyone we knew seemed to have their nervous breakdown on the premises. Instead of supervising the staff, I spent a lot of my time advising my friends about their love lives. I'm not sure why they or I thought I was an expert.

The restaurant gradually came unstuck. Things broke down. Someone slashed some of the seats one night. I got married and had to pay attention to my own love life. Other late-night places opened. Sebastian's in Exhibition Street and Bertie's in Spring Street. Lily's wound down to a close.

I didn't cook at Lily's, but I loved being in the kitchen. I loved ordering the food in bulk. I loved all the equipment, and I loved watching the cooking.

When I was a kid, I was almost hypnotised by the man who decorated cakes in Myers. His piping tubes would fly across the surface of cakes, full of whipped cream or icing. And, almost out of nowhere, rows and rows of roses or violets, or notes of music or written greetings, would appear.

I have to stay away from the restaurant supplies stores on the Bowery in New York. If I go there, I turn into a maniac. I feel as though I can't live without an industrial grinder, a pizza oven, a couscousier and a dough blender. The last time I was there, I bought some round aluminium bowls. They are made for pizza dough to rise in. They are a beautiful shape and stack on top of each other. They're very cheap, about $3.50. I bought twenty. I store them in my laundry. Every now and then I go in and admire them.

I justified their purchase by serving salads in several of them at a large dinner party we had. 'You can't keep inviting thirty people to dinner just because you bought the pizza dough dishes,' my husband said.

I find it very nourishing to feed others. One of the sweetest memories I have of my children's childhoods is of them arriving home, one at a time, after school. The first question each of them asked when they stepped into the house was, 'What's for dinner?'

When the children were growing up we often had our friends and their friends eating with us. My kids would take their friends into the kitchen to look at the size of my saucepans. 'She always makes that much,' I heard my son say, nonchalantly, to a friend once. They were looking at two saucepans that each contained about one hundred servings of Napoli sauce.

The pleasure of cooking often reminds me of the pleasure I feel when I'm writing. There is a similar satisfaction and sense of peacefulness from assembling the different ingredients and putting them together. You need a clear head and an overview of where you are going when you put a dish together. And you need to be prepared. It's the same with a novel.

When everything is working in the kitchen, there is a musicality and a rhythm that reminds me of writing well. All the disparate elements slot in, under and over and beside each other, to form something new.

Cooking is a seduction of sorts. My younger daughter was always reluctant to eat at her friends' places. She would call home first to check that we weren't having one of her favourite dishes. And I know I have friends who overlook some of my lesser qualities because they love my food.

Cooking in bulk means that you have to shop in bulk. Going to the supermarket with my mother was a tense experience. She'd put one pound of butter in her trolley, move two feet, and return for another pound, and then another. The decisions about how much food was enough were exhausting. I am the same. It dements my husband. I have to sneak extra containers of laundry detergent or rolls of toilet paper into the trolley when we shop together. He wants to know why we need ten pounds of rice or four jars of wheat germ. I find it hard to come up with an answer.

In summer I buy plums and mangoes and apricots and pears in Chinatown. The produce is very cheap and always fresh. The shoppers, mostly Chinese women, are very fussy. They handle each plum or leek or piece of papaya. I can buy fifteen plums for a dollar or six large mangoes for five dollars. Chinatown is the most wonderful place to shop for fruit, vegetables and fish.

The signs on all the food there are in Chinese. I point to what I want. That's fine with the fruit and vegetables, but I've often ended up with fish I don't recognise. It has always been very good though.

I pickle and preserve the fruit and vegetables I buy

in Chinatown. I make chutneys and relishes and pickles and jams and jellies. I spend several nights a week in the summer stirring simmering cauldrons of rhubarb and onions and raisins, or pears and ginger, or tomatoes and chillies.

I stand over the pots and stir with my hair tied back, and my sleeves rolled up. Sometimes I am almost as damp as the chutneys and relishes I am cooking. Two or three hours of chopping has gone into each of the pots that I am stirring. I test the chutneys and relishes for texture and thickness. I rush between the fridge and the stove with cold plates to catch the setting points of the jams and jellies.

When everything is ready, I bring the sterilised jars out of the oven. I fill them and wipe them down with a hot cloth. Then I attach the labels. By the time I clean up, I'm exhausted. Each year I decide that I won't do it any more. I remember the way my back aches from bending over the chopping board, and the way it takes days to get the plum stains out of my nails, and the smell of fruit and vinegar out of our walls. And then I remember the jars. Rows and rows of them, their contents preserved for years. Ready for whenever we need them.

I know that there's no need to make any more. We still have dozens of jars in a dark, cool cupboard in the living room. But I have a need that feels inexplicable. When I am pickling and preserving, I am joined to the past. Joined to another time, another life; a life I was destined to live before Hitler intervened. I am in Lodz. I am joined to my mother. I am not just her Australian child. I am joined to a city and a time that was never mine.

I used to dream about Lodz. I dreamt about the tram tracks and the dark buildings before I ever saw them. When I salt the cabbage and chop the beetroot, I am in Lodz. I am with my father's mother, my grandmother (two words I've rarely put together), who each year carried her shredded cabbage into the cellar to pickle for the winter.

Some years I've managed to hold out until the last minute. Then I've rushed around almost frantically, getting the ingredients and finding the preserving pans, the ladles, the jars, the lids and the labels. And before I know it, I am back in front of those steaming vats, and I am happy.

I carry the beetroot and plums and onions and garlic and tomatoes that I buy, in a shopping trolley. My daughters call it the Embarrassing Trolley and will do anything to avoid any association with it. But I'm not embarrassed. I've wheeled the trolley down Fifth Avenue, and along West Broadway. I'm never embarrassed. I'm much less concerned about what I look like in New York. It's strange that in this sophisticated and glamorous city, I have the freedom to look terrible. I sometimes go to the corner store straight out of bed, with my hair awry and my brain at half-mast. I have shopped with my trolley in high heels and lipstick, and in a tracksuit. But I have to back track. I am not entirely unconcerned about what I look like: it is a chic, black, tracksuit.

I always take my trolley to Chinatown. I can just get it down the aisle in the chicken shop on Grand Street. The shop is housed in an old, brown, single-storey wooden building. The building is very out of character with the buildings around it. It looks as though it belongs in an old Western movie.

Inside, it looks as though it belongs in another country, in another age. Rows and rows of live chickens are crammed onto the wooden shelves. The place is dark and noisy, and it smells. You choose your own chicken, which is then slaughtered and plucked at the back of the store. The other customers, who are Chinese, all know what they are doing. They deftly pick up the chickens, and examine the chickens' bums. I wish I knew what they were looking for. When the chicken with the right bum comes along, they take it to the back of the store. I choose my chicken by size and ask someone, in sign language, to take it to the back of the store for me.

Chinatown always makes me happy. It is so robust and real. It is full of families, three and four generations shopping together, eating together, working together.

Eating in Chinatown is altogether wonderful. I doubt if you could find bad Chinese food in Chinatown. My favourite place is the Harmony Palace on Mott Street. I love to go there on Sundays for dim sum. Dim sum is yum cha. At the Harmony Palace they serve dim sum at breakfast and lunch, every day.

The Harmony Palace is a very large restaurant. Tough women wheeling steaming trolleys of food whiz by you at high speed. They shout indecipherable descriptions of the dishes as they pass. We just point to what we want. The food is so good. And it's so cheap. It's hard to leave before you're so bloated you feel ill.

New York has had an eat-out and take-out culture for such a long time. When New Yorkers entertain at home, the odds are that the meal will be catered. Or store-bought. In this city there is an inordinate amount of admiration attached to being able to cook.

What would be an ordinary dinner party in Melbourne is seen as something very special, if you cook your own food in New York. Having people to dinner was part of our life in Melbourne, and we continued living like that in New York. In Melbourne, friends would say that the meal was nice. In New York, the fact that I have cooked the meal is a lively topic of conversation at the table.

I love having people to dinner. I love seating the right people next to each other, the warm hum of people meeting and discovering each other. The noises of joy and curiosity and shyness and eagerness. The sounds of eating and the murmurs of contentment. I love the way the volume often escalates. Polite greetings and quiet interchanges at the beginning and, with a bit of luck, boisterous argument and raucous laughter at the end. I love people who eat well, too. Good eaters, I call them, and I invite them often.

When I have dinner parties, I am mimicking one of the

best parts of my childhood. My parents had people over almost every week. My parents' core group of friends, their 'company', as they called them, played cards together every Friday night, went to the movies or a dinner dance together on Saturday night, and had dinner together on Sunday night. They also celebrated each other's birthdays, children's birthdays, wedding anniversaries, children's bar mitzvahs, engagements and weddings. The company was composed of ten to twelve people. They holidayed together. They travelled together. Until I was quite old, I thought they were our relatives. I called several of them Aunty and Uncle.

They were all post-World War Two migrants. With the exception of a Russian couple, they were all from Poland. Most of them had been in labour camps or in hiding during the war. My parents were the only ones who had survived concentration camps. The politics and social upheavals in the group were always volatile, but when they got together no fractures were evident.

The card evenings were the best, but my mother hated them. She looked down on card players. She would busy herself ferrying bowls of chocolates and nuts and sweets around, and then she would bring out her book and read. Being a reader fetched my mother the respect that she wanted. She was accorded the position of intellectual within the group. If there was a question about history or science someone would say, 'Ask Rooshka', and my mother often had the answer.

The card players played poker and gin rummy. They

smoked and joked and exchanged gossip. Everyone appeared to be best friends. One happy family. Even my mother spoke affectionately to whomever it was that was her current nemesis, and she always had one.

This impromptu family felt like family to me. It took me years to work out that we weren't all related. The group fell apart in 1985, because of the same mixture of petty and serious grievances that part most people. I was stunned to see that such long friendships could dissolve. The bitterness that had been held in check for decades didn't diminish. It rose and caused enormous discord and discoloured everyone.

The company had all shared so much. Everyone knew everyone else's troubles. Troubles with their children, troubles with their spouses, and troubles with their work. They knew each other's histories, if sketchily, for most of them had the sort of history they didn't want to detail.

Even as a child I was hungry for news of their pasts. I picked up every small reference to the ghetto and to the camps. One woman had her hair torn out by the Gestapo and always wore a wig. Another couple had hidden in a three-foot-high underground bunker in Poland for two years. There were nine people in the bunker. At night one of them crept out and foraged for food. When the war was over, none of them could walk. Their muscles had atrophied in the small space. I used to look at this couples' legs, which looked normal again, in wonder.

The company shared momentous moments. I remember the day a photograph of my mother's father arrived. It was as though my grandfather himself had arrived. We had no photographs of my father's mother and father and brothers and sisters, or my mother's mother and father and brothers and sisters. Everything had been destroyed by the Nazis.

My mother spoke about her father, Israel Spindler, in idealised terms. He was a very sensitive man, she said. Highly intelligent. Poor, but always helping the poor. People came to him for advice, she said. She dismissed my father's parents, the wealthy Brajsztajns, as uncouth and stupid.

My mother almost went into a reverie when she talked about her father. He adored her, his youngest child. His baby. Beautiful and clever, she tutored other children to pay her way through her studies. She was bookish, like him. She adored him.

The day the photograph arrived was a day of huge excitement. I remember feeling sick with anticipation as my mother opened the envelope. The photograph had been found by a distant relative who lived somewhere in America. It had been sent to him from Poland, before the war. Somehow he tracked my mother down and wrote to her about the photograph. My mother took a small 4" by 3" photograph out of the envelope. And there he was.

My mother stood perfectly still for about ten minutes. She was so still I thought she had stopped breathing. I didn't want to interrupt her or intrude on whatever she was feeling, so I stood there, perfectly still too, two feet away from her. I hoped she wasn't going to cry. I was fifteen, and dreaded my mother crying.

When I looked at the photograph, I burst into tears. Israel Spindler had large, heavy-lidded wide eyes and high cheekbones. He had a fine aquiline nose and a sensitive and beautiful mouth. There was a delicacy and an unusual sensitivity in his expression. In Israel Spindler's eyes I could see my mother's eyes and my eyes. In the future, in a slightly different form, they would appear in my daughter. Israel Spindler's mouth and cheekbones would also turn up in my son. Suddenly we had a history.

We had the photograph enlarged and framed. A few years ago my son was looking at the photograph, which I now have in my living room. He groaned. 'Look at his hairline,' he said to me, pointing to Israel's receding hairline. My son clutched his forehead in despair. 'Men's hair genetically follows the pattern of their mother's family. I knew I was destined to go bald,' he groaned.

My mother talked less about her mother, although I picked up odd snippets. My mother's mother was a very good cook. She cooked for her children every night and she always took in strangers for the Friday night Shabat meal. In summer when the whole family went to Wisniowagora, about twenty five kilometres out of Lodz, Luba Spindler ran a restaurant for two weeks in the living room of the three-roomed house they rented.

I was named after Luba. Liebala is the diminutive form of her name. In Germany it became Lilijahne and in Australia, Lily. At the same time, in Australia, we made the switch from Brajsztajn to Brett.

At eleven a.m. my mother and her siblings would have to leave the rented house in Wisniowagora, and Luba would open the door and declare her restaurant open for lunch. She cooked goulash, blintzes, kreplach and chicken soup, in the heat of summer. For dessert she baked apple cake and cheesecake. The restaurant was always popular.

'She never made any money,' my father said to me. He ate there a few times. He would drive up from Lodz when he was wooing my mother. He knew he wanted to marry her from the time he met her. She was twelve, then.

My mother said that she sat outside and read a book while her mother ran her lunchtime restaurant in Wisniowagora. One of my mother's older sisters helped her mother in the kitchen.

The Spindler children were used to having other people in their house. On the high holy days, their small apartment was filled with Jews praying. These were the poor Jews who couldn't afford to pay for a seat in a synagogue. Israel Spindler led the prayers.

There was a lot of pressure on my mother to marry my father. Girls married very young in those days. His family was wealthy and he, with his good looks and Skoda sports car, was known to be a good catch.

But my mother resisted for years. Until she was seventeen and all of the Jewish families in Lodz were herded into the Lodz ghetto. Her father advised her to marry into the Brajsztajn family. He thought she would be better off in the ghetto with wealth to protect her. But she wasn't. No Jew was. Even the wealthy Jews were soon selling their diamonds for a few saccharine tablets or a bag of potato peels.

My mother and father were married in the ghetto on December 17th, 1939. He was crazy about her. He stayed crazy about her until the day she died on August 24th, 1986.

'I ate goulash in the restaurant, in Wisniowagora, and sometimes chicken soup with kneidlach,' my father told me. When I asked him why Luba Spindler didn't make any money, he said he didn't know. I was obviously following a family tradition with my restaurant. You open up, feed lots of people and make a loss. I hope that my younger daughter, whose dream it is to own her own restaurant, manages to break from this tradition. She knows her family history and is about to embark on a degree in restaurant business management. I have promised that I won't give her any advice.

I have been drawn to restaurants and cafes since I was a small girl. There was an Italian cafe close to us, in Nicholson Street, Carlton, always filled with men smoking and talking. You could almost smell the espresso from our house. I used to sit on the neighbour's fence across the road from the cafe and watch the men. They would shout and gesticulate at each other. They would slap each other on the back, or kiss each other with joy. They never stopped talking. I saw all of this through the thick haze of cigarette smoke that clouded the windows. My girlfriend's mother had told her never to go into that cafe, so I kept well away. But it looked very exciting.

I still like unpretentious, working-class restaurants and cafes. It gives me indigestion to have my chair pulled out and my pepper ground for me. All that forelock-tugging dulls my appetite. One of my favourite restaurants in New York is the Ukrainian East Village Home Restaurant on Second Avenue. The decor is 1960s, Eastern European and the waiters look jaundiced and angst-ridden.

I used to look angst-ridden myself when I was a folk-singer in a cafe, in Hawthorn, Melbourne. I was fifteen. I used to tell my mother I was staying at my friend Suzy's place for the night. I can't sing now and I couldn't sing then. Suzy was my singing partner. She sang in tune and I provided tuneless volume. We were paid in toasted crumpets. It was my first experience of cafe life.

I gave up folk singing, but kept my interest in cafes. I discovered Pelligrini's in Bourke Street and Leo's in Fitzroy Street. I thought I was so sophisticated drinking espressos on a stool at the bar in Pelligrini's. I didn't like the espresso much – I had to put half a container of sugar in each small espresso – but I loved the thought of an espresso. I was on my way to becoming a beatnik at the time. By the time I got to Genevieve's in Faraday Street, Carlton, I had dispensed with the sugar. I could take my espresso straight.

I used to have dinner with my son, when he was very small, at Genevieve's. He was good company, even then. He always had spaghetti al burro. He would pick every piece of parsley out of the dish first. He learnt to say 'no parsley' before he was two.

I have had many important moments of my life in cafes. I married the man I am now married to in a cafe. We were married in Tamani's in Toorak Road, South Yarra. We chose the cafe because we spent hours there, falling in love.

It was in a cafe that we decided to sell our Melbourne house and stay in New York. It was a traumatic decision. And I remember the agony of it each time I walk past that cafe, the Cupping Room, at the corner of Broome Street and West Broadway.

It was 1989. We had been in New York for three months when the Australian economy began to plummet. As did our income. We couldn't afford to stay in New York unless we sold our house in Melbourne. We made the decision over a cup of black coffee. We must have looked as distressed as we felt. Quite a few of the other customers were looking at us.

I was distracted from my distress by a woman who was having lunch with her still-single forty-ish son at

Cafe Dante, in MacDougal Street. She hooked me in with her first line.

'I told them at the Bridge club that I want a ban on people bringing photographs of their grandchildren to Bridge evenings,' she said to her son.

He grimaced. He clearly understood the subtext. 'I haven't met anyone who's exactly right for me,' he said.

'Why does she have to be exactly right?' his mother replied. 'What is so exactly right about you?' The son looked down at his cafe latte. 'I've met a young woman I think you should meet,' his mother said. 'She's clever, she reads interesting books and she's still on speaking terms with her mother.' She put her cappuccino down with a bang. I was so impressed. I wanted to follow her home. If I was going to have to stay in New York, maybe we could be friends.

DEATH

SOME MORNINGS I WAKE UP to a terrible feeling of impending doom. This anxiety is so thick that I feel sick seconds after I have opened my eyes. Sometimes I wake up like this for days at a time. It can take me hours to shake off the last shards of fear, and sometimes I feel shaky all day.

This has happened to me, on and off, for years. Just when I think it has gone and finally I can wake up feeling fine, it comes back to me. It is as though an errant part of me insists on a limit to the peacefulness and happiness I have struggled for.

I am so grateful when I wake up and feel normal. Normally sleepy, normally tired or normally refreshed.

I am so relieved not to wake up to a sickening pit of peril. The peril is associated with death. I can feel the death. I check myself. I'm breathing. I wake my husband. He's breathing. Later in the day, I call my children. I try to sound casual, as though this is just a routine call. As though I am not calling to confirm that they are still in one piece. Still with us.

Most mornings, I run through a list of possible fatalities. Illnesses that could afflict us, accidents that could occur. I check a checklist of tests and immunisations and check-ups we should undergo in order to forestall as much of anything ominous as we can. By the time I have poured through all of this I am exhausted.

I grew up with death. The dead were all around me. They were palpable. They felt more alive to me than the living. The dead were my mother's mother and father, her four brothers and three sisters. Her nephews and nieces and uncles, aunts and cousins and brother and sisters-in-law. The dead were my father's mother and father, his three brothers and one sister. His nephews and nieces and uncles, aunts, cousins and brother and sisters-in-law.

There were so many dead. They crowded the small room we lived in in Brunswick. They moved with us when we moved into our cottage in Nicholson Street, Carlton. And they stayed with us, and joined us on our upwardly mobile journey to a house my father built in St Kilda, when I was thirteen.

I remember wondering if they preferred the salt air

of St Kilda, or whether they missed Carlton and the Yiddish conversations you could hear in the street. I thought the dead relatives were alive. I thought they were real. And I knew they were unreal. I thought they were present. And I knew they were gone. I thought my mother spoke to them. And I knew she was talking to herself.

I felt bad for being alive when they had to be dead. I knew they would have preferred life. I would have swapped my life with them. I knew they deserved it more than I did. For they were good. They had done nothing to deserve their fate. And I was bad. I had done nothing to deserve my life. I stole, I forged signatures, I shoplifted. It was clear to me that I was not grateful for the gift of life that had been given to me. I was greedy. I was out looking for more. By any means I could find.

I felt separated from the dead by my bad behaviour. And I felt joined to them by genes and destiny. I felt they shared my heart, lungs and arteries. I had to live for them. A life worthy of all of them. It was a huge, overwhelming and impossible task. I felt my failure acutely.

I carried the dead, with their strange names – Luba, Israel, Szymek, Abramek, Jacob, Felek, Bluma, Esther, Hanka, Dvoira, Riven, Tadek, Shimek, Edek – with me all the time.

If I fell and hurt myself, I knew it wasn't worse than anything that Tadek or Felek would have experienced.

If someone was mean to me, the meanness paled next to the cruelty that Riven or Abramek would have endured. If I felt lonely, my loneliness was insignificant next to the loneliness of the dead. If I felt miserable, it was miniscule next to their misery. If I felt sad, my sadness was dwarfed by their anguish.

So I battened down all of my hurt and bewilderment and anger and sadness. I was a relentlessly cheerful child. I laughed a lot and I made others laugh. I was too busy to be frightened and too frightened to be angry. I laughed with such force I petrified all of my tears. I couldn't cry for decades.

Of course the whole course came apart when I went off course. I nearly came apart. I came down with every anxiety symptom on record. I couldn't laugh for years after the symptoms started.

I was beginning my own suffering. My own conscious suffering. I was about to join the dead in a half-life that would take me years to emerge from. I was frightened of everything. Frightened to walk, frightened to drive. Frightened to talk loudly, frightened to sneeze and frightened to cry. I was half-alive. I had finally given in. The price for being alive had become too high. It was a price I had inflicted on myself.

My suffering and my struggle were just small offshoots, little ripples, tiny after-shocks of the massive horror that Tadek, Moniek, Fela, Hanka, Jacob, Rooshka, Luba, Israel, and all of the other Jews had to endure. In a way I was comfortable in my distress.

Finally I was suffering. I was anchored to the dead, now, even more firmly.

My mother couldn't feel anchored enough. She couldn't get close enough to her beloved Israel and Luba and Szymek, Abramek, Jacob, Felek, Bluma, Hanka and Esther. And she couldn't get away.

She couldn't go to enough funerals. She went to the funerals of close friends and the funerals of acquaintances. She was trying to make up for all the dead she had not been able to bury. The dead who were thrown into pits and bulldozed into the earth, the dead who were gassed and then burned, whose ashes choked the Vistula River.

My mother didn't know how two of her sisters and her brothers had died. She didn't know where they had died. She didn't know how her father had died. She had seen her mother and her niece walking hand in hand to the gas chambers in Auschwitz. But what happened to their bodies was something she was never sure of.

Burial is regarded by Jews as a basic duty to be performed for all, including criminals, suicides and enemies. After death the body is washed and watched until it is placed in the earth. Burial takes place quickly and is conducted with simplicity. My mother knew that nobody washed the bodies of her mother and father and brothers and sisters. She knew that no one watched over them. She wasn't sure how they were placed in the earth. So she made sure that she was there to bury those who needed burying. When my mother went to a funeral, she was burying her mother and father and her nephews and nieces. She was burying everyone she had loved.

My mother couldn't, despite her lack of belief in God, shake off a belief that at the end of time there would be a resurrection of the dead. Those who had lived a pious life would be resurrected. The bodies of the dead would rise from their graves. But what about those who had no graves? Those who had not been buried in consecrated soil? Those who had not had psalms read over their bodies? Those for whom no one had said Kaddish, the prayer for the dead? Would they be left behind? Locked out of the eternal life in the world to come? She couldn't bring herself to ask anyone those questions. Particularly a rabbi. Her faith in God and in religion had been too trampled for her to show any interest in the subject. She had to appear indifferent. So she worried, alone, about the future of all of her dead. What would happen to them? Who would look after them?

I understood some of what she mused about when she was alone. I knew the dead were still in trouble. I wanted to be able to help. I wished I could have rescued them before they were murdered. I wished I could rescue them now. It was the beginning of a life-long series of fantasies about being a saviour that I would have.

I would sit at the back of the classroom while my German teacher at University High School, Miss Kleer-koper, conjugated the verb *to be*. As Miss Kleerkoper recited *ich bin du bist, er ist*, I was pulling a man and a woman out of a burning wreckage on the highway, with no regard for my own safety.

As the number 15 train rattled along Swanston Street on my way home from school, I was saving babies and teenagers and grown men. I was saving them on street corners and on expressways. I was saving them in swimming pools and on the top of mountains. In real life I had a fear of heights and I wasn't a very good swimmer. But I kept on saving.

Sometimes the saving got exhausting. I had bloodied and cut people scattered everywhere. I bandaged limbs and administered the Holger-Nielsen method of resuscitation. I changed to mouth to mouth resuscitation when that was introduced. I was nothing if not up to date with the latest in rescue techniques.

I carried out these rescues when people were talking to me, or while I was walking or shopping. The rescues even interrupted my reading. In the middle of a book I would find I had detoured off the page and on to my own story. Inevitably there was an emergency and I was saving someone's life.

In real life I know I'd be hopeless in an emergency. I appear to think with my feet rather than on my feet. I saw this quite clearly when the hairdryer I was drying my hair with in the bathroom recently started to smoke. Thick, black fumes curled out of the nozzle. After the initial shock I galvanised myself and went into action. I knew I had to disconnect the hairdryer. I quickly pulled the plug out of the wall. I felt pleased with the speed of my own response until I noticed that the hairdryer was on fire. I panicked and dropped it into the basin. Unfortunately, I had unplugged the wrong appliance and thrown the still plugged-in and switched-on hairdryer into a wet bathroom basin. Luckily, nothing more dangerous occurred than my own loss of faith in my ability to think clearly under stress.

I wished the fantasies would leave me. In my twenties I tried to replace them with what-if-I-won-the-lottery fantasies. In the middle of working out what car or clothes to buy with half a million dollars, I'd veer off and find myself donating the half a million to a family who had endured years of bad luck and who were on the verge of homelessness and starvation.

In my thirties I tried switching to sexual fantasies. It was a time of sexual liberation, with wife-swapping parties in every neighbourhood and sexual preferences extremely fluid. I had had so few sexual fantasies in my real life that I felt inadequate. But every sexual fantasy or reverie I began ended up as an act of rescue.

Sometime in my early forties I lost my need to save people. It showed in my friendships and in my fantasies. It is quite a relief not to have to leap into burning cars or wade through flood waters any more.

The state of shock associated with emergencies is a pale imitation of the shock of death. My mother used to turn to the death notices in the *Jewish News* as soon as it arrived on Thursdays. She would gasp at each name and shake her head, as though she knew the dead person. Every week I used to think that someone we knew must have died. Until I realised that my mother gasped and sighed at every one of the obituaries. I guess it was her familiarity with the death rather than the deceased that accounted for those gasps and the way she shook her head.

When she did hear news of the death of someone she knew, she was strangely electrified and awkward. She received the information with intensity and volatility. As though death was a dangerous yet revered relative, and she was not quite sure what to do with him. Physically she looked odd at the news of death. All contorted and crooked. As though she was carrying holy hot coals. She didn't want to hold them and she couldn't put them down.

When a friend of my father's died, my mother told me that she didn't want to tell my father until after he had had his dinner. We were all eating at my parents' place that night. My husband, the three kids and me. My mother reminded us all to say nothing until after dinner. When my father came home, my mother was noticeably subdued. My father asked her, several times, what was wrong and she said 'nothing' so vehemently that he looked worried.

We made small talk as my mother dished out the food. My father started to tell us about something funny that had happened to him that day at work. Everyone laughed at my father's story except my mother. 'Mr

Pincus won't be laughing anymore,' my mother said. My father, who had a mouthful of snapper and snapper bones in his mouth, nearly choked. As my father guessed at Mr Pincus's fate, a large bone nearly lodged itself in my father's throat. My mother had wanted to wait for the best possible time to tell my father the news of Mr Pincus, and she had chosen the worst possible time. I could see, however, that she had had very little choice in the matter.

My father's sense of timing and decorum where death is concerned is also awry. My father and I walked into a delicatessen in Acland Street, St Kilda one Sunday morning. We were going to buy some smoked salmon. Solomon Lew, the Melbourne businessman, was there buying some food. My father hadn't seen Solomon, who was by now one of Australia's leading businessmen, since he was a young boy. 'Hello Solly,' my father said. 'Remember me? Max Brett. I was there in the Flinders Street, when your father dropped dead on the stairs.' Solomon Lew looked astonished. 'He dropped dead on the stairs,' my father repeated. 'Straight on the stairs. I was standing there next to him. Remember?' My father looked at me. 'When Mr Lew dropped dead I was standing next to him,' he said to me. 'It was twenty years ago.' My father looked shocked, all over again, at the memory.

Solomon Lew looked as though he was coming out of the shock of this unexpected and emotional encounter in a delicatessen. He looked as though he was remembering my father. But not fast enough. 'You remember when your father died?' my father said. Solomon looked startled again. 'Of course I remember,' he said kindly. 'You were only a very young man,' my father said. 'A bit thinner than now.'

I couldn't bear it any longer. My father was veering from death and loss to weight and weight gain. I had to reign him in. 'We have to go now,' I said. 'We didn't buy the smoked salmon yet,' my father said. 'I think they have better smoked salmon next door,' I said. 'Your father was a very nice man,' my father shouted to Solly Lew, as we left the delicatessen.

'Why did you have to mention his weight?' I said to my father when we were out in the street.

'Why not?' he said.

'Because it's not a subject that most people want to discuss with strangers,' I said.

'I'm not a stranger to him,' my father said. 'I was there when his father dropped dead on the stairs.' My father paused and looked at me with annoyance. 'Anyway,' he said, 'I did only say the truth. He was very much thinner then. The truth is the truth.'

I have encountered this maxim of my father's before. I introduced him once to Mario di Pasquale and Mario Macaroni, the two young men who own Mario's in Brunswick Street and the Continental in Greville Street, Melbourne. 'It's easy to tell you two apart,' my father said, shaking the two Marios' hands. 'There's Mario the fat and Mario the thin.' Poor Mario the fat's face fell. I glared at my father. 'What's wrong?' my father said. 'The truth is the truth. He knows he is fat.' Mario looked even more miserable.

My father is a good man. He is always well-intentioned. And so far no one has held his reverence for the truth against him. Mario the fat and Mario the thin hosted a dinner for my father at the Continental, which was one of the highlights of his life.

My father has always been up-beat. Except for two periods of extreme depression, which seemed to appear suddenly and then disappear with the same rapidity, my father has been good-natured and good-humoured. He gets his pessimism and his anxiety out of the way at the beginning of any encounter, and then he can relax and enjoy himself.

I hadn't seen my father for nine months when I arrived in Australia for a book tour. We met for lunch at Scheherezade in Acland Street. As we sat down my father said, 'Well, I wonder when will be the next time we will have such a lunch.' 'Tomorrow,' I said. But I knew he was referring to the decreasing frequency of our lunches, now that we lived in different countries. I started to feel sad. But my father had already cheered up and was ordering herring, chopped liver and schnitzel.

My father flew to Brisbane to join me on one leg of the book tour. He arrived at the hotel and kissed me hello. 'I'm so happy to see you,' I said.

'I'll be going home the day after tomorrow,' he replied. After that he was free to enjoy himself. And he did. He came to the book launch and signings and readings. We went to the movies. We ate at the hotel three nights in a row. At the buffet, the two of us were out of control. After the first buffet we both felt ill. My father needed Alka Seltzer. 'I am all right,' he said. 'I shouldn't have gone to the McDonalds.'

'You went to McDonalds before dinner?' I said.

'Yes,' he said. 'I didn't have a hamburger or a thick shake for such a long time and the McDonalds make very good ones.' When he flew back to Melbourne, we both wept.

When my father meets me at airports, he mostly greets me with news of death. 'Izack Pilzer did die,' he says to me. Or 'Malka Friedman, remember her from Carlton?' he says. 'She is dead. Dropped dead at a game of cards.' He tells me this news before he has said hello.

In the car, on the way to the city from Tullamarine, he fills me in on the rest of the deaths. When he has finished he sighs. 'I know more people in the cemetery than out of the cemetery,' he says. This sometimes leads to a discussion of the condition of my mother's grave and my father's suspicion that the man who is paid to keep the grave clean and tidy doesn't give the job his full attention.

The problem with the upkeep and maintenance of the grave pales next to my father's difficulty in cultivating a pot plant to sit on the tombstone. He can't get any of the plants he has bought to grow. He's tried several varieties of fail-proof plants. They have all died. In honour of my visit this year he bought a new rubber plant from Coles.

I sometimes feel overwhelmed by my father's potted news of all the deaths. Especially as I'm always jet-lagged. But I know my father has to log and catalogue them. And I have to listen.

Most of us are not keen to hear about death. Death and illness are, I think, seen as contagious. I heard Olivia Newton-John talking on television about a friend she had bumped into in a store. The friend was shopping with her daughter. When Olivia's friend saw her, she pulled her daughter away from Olivia and drew her close to her side, as though Olivia's mastectomised breast might beckon to their breasts.

When Olivia talked about the incident she still looked hurt, and I remembered a young Olivia, in her University High School uniform. All large eyes and skinny legs. And laughing. We all seemed to do a lot of laughing then. Including my friend Suzy, who also went to Uni High. Suzy's husband died, leaving her with two small children, when Suzy was thirty. From the day she was widowed, all the other kindergarten mothers avoided her. At the time, I thought it was because Suzy was young and attractive and suddenly single. But now I think she was stained by death.

My darling husband nursed his first wife through her breast cancer. They were on the verge of separating when she was diagnosed. He fed her, bathed her, clothed her and drove her to her doctors' appointments for two years. He was thirty when she became ill.

Everyone avoided them. He was thirty-two when he buried her. Quite a few people came to the funeral.

The first funeral I went to was my mother's funeral. I was ten days short of my fortieth birthday. I couldn't stop crying at the funeral. And then I couldn't cry again for years.

I hadn't prayed much in my life. When the rabbi said that my mother had gone on to join her loved ones, I prayed that he was right. I badly wanted to imagine my mother reunited with her beloved father and mother and brothers and sisters. I wished I was a believer. I envied those who were.

I hardly remember turning forty. All I can remember is the numbness and disbelief that my beautiful mother, who seemed so strong, so suntanned, so healthy and so powerfully present, was dead.

When I started to cry for my mother, years after her death, I couldn't stop. I cried everywhere. And everything set me off. Puccini arias, slushy love songs, show tunes, old standards. One day 'Three Coins In The Fountain' came over the airwaves when I was in a cab. My mother used to hum this around the house. I had to change direction and go home.

Despite the omnipresence of death in our lives, no one I loved had died until my mother died. I still sometimes cry when I talk about her. Maybe I always will.

I will always hang on to her clothes. I have several of her dresses in my cupboard. When I look at them, I see her. One of the dresses is a bright red sleeveless dress with diamante straps. She used to look stunning in that dress. I wish one of us could wear it. It's miles too small for me or for my tall daughters.

I also have my mother's shoes and her handbags. Some of the shoes are still imprinted with the shape of her feet. I thought my younger daughter might wear them one day, but her feet grew almost as big as mine. A size nine. My mother was a size seven.

I keep the broad, black chiffon scarf that the rabbi cut on the day of my mother's funeral. I was wearing it around my shoulders. The mourners' garments are cut, symbolically, on the left side, close to the heart. It was a wrenching moment. And I can't part with the scarf.

Parting and saying goodbye are not things I am good at. When I left my younger daughter at college on her first day, I blew goodbye kisses to her all the way down the hallway. Several students at the academically rigorous women's college looked on in amazement.

One of the purposes for going away to a residential college, something a large number of American students do, is to leave home. To have a gentle separation. It is a declaration of independence. Halfway between home and the real world.

I wrote to my younger daughter every day for the first six months she was in college. I wanted us both to feel as though she had never left. My younger daughter found the leaving hard, too. At the end of the first week she was exhausted. 'We spent the whole week bonding,' she said to me on the phone. 'We had bonding activities day and night. I've bonded with every freshman twenty times. I've bonded with my dorm. I've bonded with people I share a birthday with, I've bonded with people shorter than me and people taller than me. I'm all bonded out.'

The first month was the hardest for her. Luckily she had a wonderful roommate. 'Alex and I are the only ones who miss our mothers,' she wept to me one night.

This poor younger daughter of mine has inherited my inability to say goodbye. Her brother visited her at her college, Bryn Mawr, for the weekend. On Sunday afternoon she began dreading the farewell. She walked him to the local train station. He was on his way to see a friend in Washington D.C. My son and daughter chatted in the station for half an hour.

When the train arrived, the departure felt too abrupt to her, so she hopped on to the train and went into Philadelphia with him. After three cups of coffee in Philadelphia, he persuaded her that he really had to leave. She began weeping, and was still weeping when she got back to college and called me. 'I miss him,' she said to me. 'And all my missing has got muddled up. I started missing you, and I started missing Nana.' As soon as she mentioned her nana, my mother, I started weeping too.

My emotions have always been a bit volatile. If indeed it is possible to be a bit volatile. More often than not, I see things as worse than they are. I manage to see the most ordinary occurrences as potential fatalities. Bites, bumps, bruises. Colds and flus.

Last summer on Shelter Island, my younger daughter was bitten by a tick. The ticks from deer, in this part of the world, can carry Lyme Disease. Lyme Disease can be disastrous. Or, in the more moderate words of a pamphlet produced on the subject, Lyme Disease, if untreated, can progress to more serious stages.

The pamphlet does state that if treated with antibiotics, in time, the disease is preventable. But I rushed straight past that sentence to the string of symptoms of the disease in its later stages. Symptoms that involved the joints, the heart and the central nervous system.

I read the advice under 'Tick Removal'. I was so anxious I had to read the two paragraphs three times before I began to comprehend them. If you are bitten by a tick, you remove the tick with tweezers. The important thing is to make sure that you remove the tick's head, which can require some manoeuvering as these ticks have barbed mouths which they sink into your skin.

This procedure would be unnerving enough on a large insect. But these ticks are the size of a pin head. How are you supposed to discern their heads? I made a note to buy a pair of heavily magnified reading glasses at the beginning of summer.

The pamphlet suggests that you save the tick in a jar of alcohol, labelled with the date, the body location of the bite and the place where you acquired the tick. I posted the pamphlet up on the kitchen wall. It made me nervous every time I passed it. We examined ourselves for ticks at the end of every day, however, and the summer passed uneventfully, in tick terms, until the day before we were due to return to Manhattan.

We were having lunch in the garden. It was a perfect day. Blue skies, sunshine, a slight breeze and a temperature of eighty degrees. We had been kayaking in the morning in the waters around the Mashomak Reserve. We had kayaked beside egrets and cormorants and geese. It had been blissful. Halfway through the lunch my daughter looked at her leg and said, 'I've got a tick on my leg.' I went to pieces. I didn't want the girls to see my panic. 'I'll get the tweezers,' I said, casually, and ran into the house. My husband followed me in. 'You'll have to remove it,' I said to him. I knew I'd be hopeless. I was already so tense.

The pamphlet said not to squeeze the tick's body, and to tug the tick gently and repeatedly until it released its hold. I could hardly see the tick, let alone work out how to tug it gently without squeezing its body or decapitating it. And my anxiety was blurring my vision further. I was so distressed that I knew I might have removed half of my daughter's leg in order not to leave the tick's head in there. My husband removed the tick easily. We looked at it through the glasses. It was whole. It had not been beheaded.

At the doctor's surgery they were unnervingly casual. 'You won't need the tick,' the nurse said, looking at the neatly labelled glass jar I was holding. I did feel a bit absurd. The only jar I could find had held three pounds of olives. The tick was a speck at the bottom of this large jar.

'Why won't I need the tick?' I said.

'We don't test ticks,' she said.

'You don't test ticks?' I said.

'There's no point,' she said. 'Not all ticks carry Lyme Disease and not all people get infected when they are bitten. If your daughter comes up with any symptoms in the next two to six weeks, we'll test her. If she tests positive we'll prescribe antibiotics.'

'You mean we just have to wait?' I said.

'Yes,' she said.

'Is there anywhere I can get this tick tested?' I said, holding up my olive jar.

'You could call the State Board of Health,' she said. 'But there's no point.'

It took my husband quite a while to persuade me that it was not a good idea to start tracking down a tick-testing laboratory. I also had to restrain myself from calling my daughter every day to see if she had developed any symptoms.

My fears, which I always hope have moderated and subsided, seem to spring out of me and escalate themselves alarmingly. I'm fearful of diseases, fearful of accidents, fearful of death.

But I love cemeteries. I love cemeteries with a joy

and an exuberance and enthusiasm that could appear morbid. I don't think it is. 'The only good thing about dying,' I once said to my husband, 'is getting to live in a cemetery.'

'You wouldn't be living,' he said. My husband is not usually a wet blanket, but I think he thought he should put a damper on this particular line of thought.

There is an awe-inspiring cemetery between the Williamsburg Bridge and the Long Island Expressway in New York. You get the best view of the cemetery from the Bronx-Queens Expressway. The Manhattan skyline is in the background – the Empire State Building, the Chrysler Building, the World Trade Center Towers, the midtown offices, the uptown apartment buildings. And in the foreground, mimicking and echoing the skyscrapers, are the tall, thin, narrow headstones and squat tombstones.

It is a wonderful metaphor. And a reminder. All of us here are just a few minutes, a few years, a few decades away from all of us, there. I love seeing that cemetery. I find it uplifting. I see it as a sign post. It says make the most of the minutes, years, decades.

The only funeral I have been to in New York was a funeral held in a large cemetery in Long Island. We knew a few of the mourners and were standing at the back of the crowd. As the rabbi recited the prayers, the man standing next to me in the solemn gathering started whispering to a young woman. 'I got the tests back,' he said. 'The sperm count was twenty-five million sperm per cubic centimetre.' He looked pretty pleased with himself. 'They were well-shaped sperm, too,' he said. I decided that the funeral must be making him nervous and he needed to re-affirm his own life.

Mostly people are not very talkative in cemeteries. On the whole, cemeteries are peaceful places. I always feel peaceful in a cemetery. Strangely soothed. As though all danger has been removed. I'm not sure exactly what the dangers are that I find so daunting. I do know that they seem ever-present. Although, in the last few years, I have managed to make their presence less.

I try to ward off danger by constantly repeating, 'Be careful.' I say it like a mantra. I'm not discerning about when I use the mantra. I say 'Be careful' indiscriminately. I say it when one of the children catches a train or goes out at night. I say it when my husband goes for a walk. Once I said 'Be careful' to him as he was about to go to the bathroom. 'You want to come in with me?' he said.

I inherited this admonition from my mother. She said it all the time. My son, when he was two, was standing in the middle of the living room when my mother arrived. 'Be careful!' she shouted at him. He got a fright and fell over.

I chose my best friend because she shared my anxieties. I knew this when I met her. We were thirteen. Quite a few years ago, her young daughter inadvertently locked herself in the boot of an old Cadillac we owned.

It was a large boot and she wasn't frightened. While I looked for the keys, my best friend shouted, 'Don't panic! Don't panic!'

When my friend Mimi Bochco had to have an operation for an aneurism that was growing dangerously large, I knew that her life really was in danger. Mimi was philosophical about the operation. She wasn't too frightened. She quoted me the success rates and they were reassuring. Mimi knew her doctor well. He was supposed to be one of the best in his field. I trust Mimi's choice of doctors. She has always had doctors as friends. Like many Jews, she feels more comfortable with a doctor in the vicinity. She and her husband, Win, often vacation with one of their doctor friends. I think it's a great idea.

But it was a big operation, and I was nervous. I love Mimi. For many reasons, not the least of which is I can complain to her and she listens. I spoke to Mimi the night before the operation. Just as I was saying goodbye to her, some strange impulse made me interrupt myself. 'I'm going to go to synagogue and pray for you,' I said to Mimi. 'When they wheel you into the operating theatre, I'll be in a synagogue praying for you.'

I found it hard to believe what I'd said. I hadn't been in a synagogue for years. Mimi was surprised too. We share the same ambivalence about religion. But she was touched. 'It can't hurt, darling,' she said.

I don't know where my desire to go to synagogue came from, but it was still there when I woke up in the morning. I thought I'd go to the Village Temple in Twelfth Street. I'd often walked past it. It looked small and welcoming. It was a cold, windy day, and I caught a cab to the synagogue. The synagogue appeared to be closed. I rang a buzzer at the front door. A woman's voice came through the intercom.

'Yes,' she said.

'Could I come into the synagogue and pray?' I said.

'No,' she said, 'The sanctuary is being cleaned.'

'When will it be finished?' I said.

'In two hours,' she said.

Two hours would be too late. I felt upset. I couldn't believe that having made the big decision to go to synagogue and pray, the cleanliness of the sanctuary was now thwarting my prayers. I remembered that there was another synagogue a few streets up. I pulled my scarf around my head and walked up Fifth Avenue.

The Young Israel Temple of Fifth Avenue didn't look too welcoming. The glass in the windows was covered with grime and dust. A sign pasted on the front door of the Temple said, 'The New York Sanitation Department will inspect the sidewalk in front of this building every day this week between ten a.m. and two p.m.'

I felt disturbed at the thought of the Temple's lawlessness. Maybe the sanitation violation had been perpetrated by someone else. Other people sometimes dump rubbish in front of the building we live in, in SoHo, and it is our building that gets fined.

I pressed the buzzer of the synagogue. A door opened. I stepped in. I was now standing in a small space the size of a closet. Another locked door was in front of me. I don't like small spaces. I pressed another buzzer. An indecipherable, loud crackle came through the intercom. I could faintly hear a voice at the back of the static. I couldn't understand a word the voice was saying.

'Hello!' I shouted, several times. Finally I made out a male voice. It was saying, 'Who do you want to speak to?'

'No one!' I shouted. 'I want to pray for a friend.'

'Who do you want to speak to?' he said again.

'No one!' I shouted, again. 'I want to pray for a friend in hospital.' By now I was red-faced and in a sweat. I was wildly over-dressed for this small space. I started to pull my scarf off so that I could unbutton my coat. I was trying to stave off an imminent flood of full-scale claustrophobia. 'I want to pray for a friend in hospital!' I shouted as loudly as I could, again.

'You can't come in,' the voice said. 'The man who has the keys is out. Come back at one o'clock.'

I almost started crying. One o'clock would be too late. Mimi would be over her operation. I decided to go home and think about my options. I was busting to have a piss, anyway, and New York is notoriously inhospitable to bladders. There are no public toilets, although I'm not sure you'd want to use them if they did exist.

I caught a cab down Fifth Avenue. I was feeling quite dazed by my inability to get into a synagogue.

As though I'd been shut out of something fundamental. I noticed that the cab driver was driving very slowly. Oh well, I thought, it's better than getting a lunatic driver who races and squeezes past every car on the road.

A few minutes later, the speed of the cab felt excessively slow. I looked at the driver. He was asleep. I shouted at him, and he rolled into another car at exactly that moment. It was quite a gentle bump. No one was hurt. A young man who was passing by opened the cab door for me, and I got out.

'Are you all right?' he said.

'I'm all right,' I said. I must not have looked all right. He looked concerned. 'I've just had a bad morning,' I said, 'I was trying to get to God.'

'I don't think a New York cab is the way,' he said. I walked the rest of the way home.

At home, I rang up the Village Temple. A woman answered the phone. 'Would it be possible to come to the synagogue at eleven o'clock and pray?' I said. 'No,' the woman said, 'the custodian won't be there.'

'But I came this morning and someone told me the sanctuary was being cleaned,' I said to her.

'It was,' she said. I took a deep breath. 'Is there any time between when the cleaning finishes and before the custodian leaves, that I could come in and pray?' I asked.

'Three o'clock,' she said.

'That'll be after my friend's operation, and I need to pray before the operation,' I said.

I think I must have sounded pathetic, because the woman suddenly gave an exasperated sigh and said, 'Be here in fifteen minutes.'

'I'll be there,' I said.

I have always found it hard to go to synagogue. When I was growing up we never went to synagogue. I knew I was Jewish. We had been punished profoundly for being Jewish. I knew we had been murdered in the millions because we were Jewish. I was in no doubt that I was Jewish. But I knew nothing about Judaism other than it seemed to kill you. This thought kept me well away from synagogues on those few occasions when, as a teenager, I thought I might turn to God.

My father was irritated by people of God. Jewish people of God. Not by their belief. By their dress. It drove him mad that they drew attention to themselves by their black hats and beards and long black coats. My father knew only too well what happened to Jews who drew attention to themselves. Sometimes when I was in the car with him, he would speed up if he saw a Hasidic Jew. 'What's the matter with you?' he would shout at some poor Jew crossing Hawthorn Road, all decked out in black, in one-hundred-degree-heat. 'You are in Australia, not Poland,' he would shout. And he would put his foot on the accelerator and make out as though he was going to run them down. 'Didn't you learn anything from what happened in the past?' he would sometimes shout at a fleeing Jew.

I felt sorry for the Orthodox Jews. I couldn't under-stand my father's fury. I was too young to understand. Too young to see how desperately, and unsuccessfully, my parents tried to blend in with the average Australian. My mother was always learning new English words. When I was young, she wouldn't say anything at all, in English, if she was not sure of exactly how to say it. And she was scath-ing about her friend, Pola, who pointed to a piece of meat in the butcher's shop and said, 'Cut me in half please.'

My father used his colloquial Australian liberally. He loved 'Give me a tenner', and 'Okey dokey'. When any-thing broke down − an appliance, a car, a piece of furniture − my father pronounced it 'Gone bong'. It took me years to get him to switch to 'Gone bung'.

My father felt very comfortable in Australia, and so did my mother. There were enough Jews for them to have a few friends. And not enough Jews to attract trouble. Enough Jews to attract trouble was not many Jews, for my parents. They belonged to no Jewish organisations or clubs. They didn't eat at the few Jewish restaurants that were in Melbourne. They never went to Jewish concerts or other Jewish cultural functions. They had no need to mix with too many other Jews. It was only when I was older that I saw how actively they avoided being surrounded by Jews.

My father came to Israel with us a few years after my mother died. He didn't really want to come. He didn't really want to do anything after my mother died. But, finally, he agreed to come with us.

It was my husband's and my children's first visit to Israel. My father seemed in jubilant spirits on the plane. He had joked with the El Al officials about not needing to be searched as he was only an old Jew returning to the promised land. He loved the food on El Al and kept leaning back to show me how good whatever he was eating from his tray was. On landing in Israel, he joked with the customs and immigrations people. He seemed to be very happy.

Two days later, he looked terrible. He had caught a slight cold. But he was not a man who went to pieces over a cold. 'I'm not well,' he said. He said it enough times for me to take him to a doctor who spoke Yiddish. I thought the Yiddish would reassure him. The doctor examined my father thoroughly and said that my father was fine. My father didn't believe him.

The next morning he told me he hadn't been able to eat the herring they had given him in the hotel for breakfast. 'If I can't eat herring, something is wrong with me,' he said.

He continued to look miserable. That night he showed me his watch. I wasn't sure what I was supposed to be looking at. The watch was on his wrist like it always was. My father pulled at the metal watch band. 'Look at how loose it is,' he said to me, in a panicked voice. 'I'm losing weight.'

'I don't think so, dad,' I said. I tried to explain to him that you'd have to have lost most of your body weight in order for your wrists to be thinner, but he wouldn't listen. 'I'm losing a lot of weight,' he said. He was really annoyed with me because I couldn't see the weight loss.

The next morning he was convinced he was dying. 'I have to go home,' he said. 'I don't want to be buried in Israel. I want to die in my own bed.' I tried to persuade him to stay. The children tried to persuade him to stay. But he was adamant. He wanted to die in his own bed. He told me he loved me and that I had been a very good daughter as I put him on an Olympic Airways flight to Melbourne.

He had to make an overnight stop in Athens. I told him I would call him at his hotel. 'They gave me a limousine from the plane to the hotel,' my father said when I called him. I knew he was fine when he started detailing the lunch he had just eaten. 'This hotel is very good,' he said. 'I like the Greek people.'

He sounded so happy I was startled. And then it hit me. Israel had too many Jews. My father knew what happened when you were in the middle of too many Jews. You died. In Israel he had been convinced he was dying. 'I think I'm already much better,' he said to me from Athens.

'I don't think my father narrowly avoided being buried in Israel,' I said to my husband.

Most of Melbourne's Jews when they die, are buried in one of the two Jewish cemeteries in Melbourne. The Carlton cemetery or the Springvale cemetery. My mother is buried in the Springvale cemetery, and even though it is so far away from where she grew up, and blanketed in summer by the bright, strident Australian light, so different from the muted light of Lodz, it feels like home. To me.

When I walk among the graves, I recognise so many names. People I grew up with in Carlton, names from the *Jewish News*, names of other people's parents. I feel my mother is back in the middle of a Jewish community. She is no longer out of place and out of kilter. She is resting next to people who speak her language and understand her culture. Some of those she is buried beside have shared her horror.

I wish she wasn't dead. I have wished it many times. But wishing doesn't seem to change anything. So I comfort myself with the thought that here, in Springvale, Victoria, my mother is finally at peace among her own people.

The last time I visited my mother's grave I went with my father. We took my elderly aunt with us. This aunt is a real aunt. The widow of my father's brother, the brother who migrated to Australia before the war. My aunt was formidable when I was young, and nothing has changed. Old age hasn't tamed her. For her outing to the cemetery she wore a black Chanel suit, black stiletto heels with sheer black stockings. She wouldn't accept any help getting out of the car, or walking along some of the unmade paths in the cemetery.

This aunt has turned out to be a person to be

admired. The same verve and drive that had her in lurid pink hotpants and white high heels in the 1960s enables her now, in her late eighties, to cook a three-course meal for ten people with no help. She has always had highly polished nails and a sharp tongue. At the cemetery, I notice that her nails are painted a deep purple, which reflects the blue in the black Chanel.

'Black is always elegant,' she says to me. I think she's referring to her suit, and nod in agreement. I don't want to talk, I want to think about my mother. 'Black is always elegant,' my aunt says again. I realise she is talking about the headstones. 'You can make a mistake with other colours. Even grey. A light grey stone can look like a stone from the street,' she says, 'an ordinary stone, even if it's marble.'

I hope that she'll quieten down when we get to her husband's grave. 'My God!' my aunt shrieks. 'Look what Helcha's husband made for her. Branches what someone threw away, he put on her grave. It looks like rubbish. Doesn't it look like rubbish? Who puts a thing like that on a grave?'

My aunt is talking about an abstract sculpture made out of small and large branches that sits, a bit uneasily, on a flat grey marble tombstone. 'He made it for her,' my father says. 'That's worse,' says my aunt. 'At least if you bought such a piece of rubbish you could think that somebody else meant for it to be beautiful.'

I find my aunt's bitchiness reassuring. I was worried that she might go to pieces at her husband's grave. 'I'm very happy I chose black,' she says at his grave. 'Black looks elegant, wouldn't you agree?' I agree with her. My father and I stand together, slightly behind my aunty. I hope she isn't going to go to pieces now. I start to think about my uncle, when my aunty turns around. 'Okay that's enough,' she says. She has been at the grave for less than thirty seconds.

We walk towards my mother's grave. I feel a bit trembly. It has been a year since I was last here. I remember the funeral. Bits and pieces of that day float in and out of my head.

'Oy oy oy, Moniek, look!' my aunt shouts at my father. 'Mrs Rosen is buried next to Mrs Berg.'

'So what?' says my father.

'So what?' says my aunt. 'Are you an idiot? Mrs Rosen had an affair her whole life with Mr Berg.'

'What, are you crazy?' my father says.

'Of course I am not crazy,' says my aunt. 'Only an idiot could live in Melbourne and not know that Mrs Rosen had a big affair with Mr Berg.'

'Then I am an idiot,' my father says.

'You are an idiot,' says my aunt. 'What would Mr Rosen say if he could see this?'

'He wouldn't say anything because there was nothing to say,' said my father.

'There was something to say,' my aunt says.

'Well he can't say it,' says my father. 'He is dead.'

I can't believe I'm in the middle of this. In the middle of the cemetery listening to my father argue with my aunty. I decide to distract her. We are approaching my mother's grave. 'I think black marble definitely looks best,' I say to her. She takes the bait. 'It's very elegant,' she says. 'Even the dark grey with the flecks in it doesn't look so good.' My aunty proceeds to dissect and evaluate every shade of marble on the market. I can't cry for my mother. I can't think about my mother. We go home.

My best friend, the one I met when I was thirteen, always seems to have a good time when she visits her father's grave. They make a day trip out of it. They take a picnic lunch. She and her daughter and her mother. First they clean the grave, trim anything that needs trimming, and polish the headstone. Then they sit down to their lunch.

Her mother is a fabulous cook. When we were young I used to love to eat at my best friend's place. For a start, her mother let me eat anything I wanted to eat. And the food was spectacular. My favourite dish was the baked pirogen filled with bacon and onion. I'd smell the dough rising hours before they were baked. I didn't know the filling was bacon, then. I only knew the pirogen were delicious. Her mother would also make exotic pickled appetisers, beautifully roasted meats, fresh breads and pâtés. And real coffee. And cake. She baked the most delicious butter-soaked cakes and gave me huge slices. My best friend goes to the cemetery to visit her father's grave five or six times a year. I always want a detailed description of what they eat there.

Remembering the dead does have its joyful

moments. But it is often painful, and never easy, and sometimes odd. On the eighth anniversary of my mother's death, I found myself singing 'God Save the Queen'. 'God save our gracious Queen, God save the Queen', I sang to myself over and over again. Other lines would pop into my head, out of order and back to front. 'May she be victorious, may she be glorious, long may she reign', I sang.

I started to feel demented. It is not a particularly melodic anthem and the lyrics are less than inspiring, especially when you have jumbled them. Anyway, why should I be singing about the Queen? I'm not all that interested in her.

I tried hard to stop. I thought about my mother and how proud of her grandchildren she would be. She only knew them as children and I think she would have liked them as adults. In the middle of feeling weepy about my mother, I found I had gone back to 'God Save the Queen'. A rousing rendition of it.

I tried humming something else. Something catchy. 'Uptown Girl'. I used to exercise to 'Uptown Girl', and then spend the rest of the day trying to get it out of my head. I tried 'Uptown Girl'. But it wouldn't stick. Billy Joel clearly couldn't compete with the Queen. 'God Save the Queen', I kept singing. By mid-afternoon, a few more lines were coming back to me. 'God save our gracious Queen, long live our noble Queen, God save the Queen'.

There were roadworks on Sixth Avenue. The pneumatic drill seemed to be in sync with the anthem. 'Long may she reign over us, happy and glorious', the drill and I sang in tandem. By the end of the day, I'd remembered the right words, in the right order, I think. 'God save our gracious Queen/Long live our noble Queen/God save the Queen/Send her victorious/Happy and glorious/Long to reign over us/God save the Queen'. I was still humming 'God Save the Queen' when I fell asleep that night.

When my mother died, the rabbi said that at least my mother had died surrounded by people who loved her, something no one else in her family had had the luxury of doing. At first I thought it was strange to use the word luxury in a situation as diminishing and bare and skeletal as death. Then the rabbi's words began to comfort me.

He was right. My mother went to her death surrounded and enveloped by love. The love for her was palpable. I was sure she could feel it, even when it was becoming obvious that she could feel less and less. I thought she could feel the love for her when she was barely breathing, barely there. And I hoped that the love would carry her, peacefully, out of this world.

My mother was haunted by the knowledge that her mother and father and brothers and sisters had died alone. Died without their loved ones. She guessed that they were either shot, burned alive or gassed and then burned, or left to die on a pile of corpses, or buried alive in a mountain of dead. But she knew they were alone.

The *New York Times* recently ran an article about

the Hebrew Free Burial Association on Staten Island, New York. The association buries Jews who can't afford a private plot and have no one to bury them.

That day the association's rabbi was burying an eighty-six-year-old woman who had never married and was too poor to be buried in the family's plot in New Jersey. A bedridden ninety-three-year-old sister was her only surviving relative. The *New York Times* reported the rabbi as saying his prayers to no one in particular.

The Hebrew Free Burial Association buried four hundred indigent Jews last year. Indigent Jews. It's hard for me to think of Jews as indigent. I want to make a joke of it. I want to turn indigent into indigestion. I want to say Jews suffer from indigestion not indigency.

I can't bear to think of Jews dying alone. I can't bear to think of anyone dying alone. And being buried alone. No one should be buried with no one to mourn them.

In New York there are dogs who have large groups of mourners at their funerals. There are dogs who are buried in satin-lined caskets. The dogs are laid out in a slumber room and a service is held for the departed dog. The deceased dog can be driven to the pet cemetery in a limousine.

Sometimes our final resting places are not so final. When the Missouri River washed through the Mid-West of America in the floods of 1993, it caused devastation. In Hardin, Missouri, a small farming town, the river demolished houses, barns, the Church, and, in a wild sweep, the flood waters washed away the cemetery. The river left a crater fifty feet deep where the cemetery used to be. Nine hundred caskets and vaults and headstones were swept away. Some were found, floating, miles away; others landed wedged in trees, or on the railroad tracks, or in fields in other towns. Others were never found. The remains of generations of whole families vanished. For many people in Hardin it was as though their loved ones had died all over again.

The loss of a cemetery is a massive loss. Cemeteries are archives. Archives of who we are, who we belong to, and who we used to be. Some people are starting to create artificial archives. There is a story in this week's *Village Voice* about Kazimierz, the old Jewish quarter in Cracow, Poland. Kazimierz's forty thousand Jewish inhabitants were marched out of their homes and murdered over fifty years ago. There has hardly been a Jew in the place since.

But recently there has been a renaissance in Kazimierz. Five Jewish cafes have opened, a Jewish history museum is housed in what used to be a synagogue, and there is a Jewish hotel and a Jewish bookstore-travel agency. These Jewish businesses are owned and operated by non-Jews. A Jewish renaissance without any Jews. Most of the businesses opened up during the small boom in tourism brought about by the movie *Schindler's List*.

As well as tours of Auschwitz, the travel agency offers tours of the sites used in *Schindler's List*. Like the site of the Plaszow concentration camp. The site of the

Plaszow concentration camp on the tour, however, is the site of Steven Spielberg's Plaszow. The real one is just an empty field. In this mini Jewish theme park, German tourists eat Jewish food made and served by Poles. The *Village Voice* says: 'It's a make-believe culture spawned by Spielberg's make-believe Holocaust – simulated Jewish life in a place of overwhelming Jewish death.'

When I was researching an aspect of Jewish death for my last novel, *Just Like That*, I asked for some material about above-ground burial from the sanctuary of Abraham and Sarah in New Jersey. Since then they haven't left me alone.

The most recent communication says that since they last spoke to me about above-ground burial, thousands of people have chosen this affordable, dignified alternative.

They ask me if I am putting off the decision even though I probably realise that above-ground burial is a beautiful, lasting tribute. They remind me that the mausoleums are heated in winter and air-conditioned in summer.

They tell me to act now when I am in the full bloom of life and there is no rush. And if I act before October 1, I can avoid the price increase and reserve a choice location at the current price. They say that chances are I'd prefer not to think about it, but the fact is that right now is the best time. The letter ends by asking me, 'Why wait to go shopping on the worst day of your life?' These letters are getting depressing. They make me feel morbid as soon as I see the envelope.

Some people think I am morbid. I see the expression of horror on their faces when they look at the books in my study. Volume after volume of books on the Holocaust. Titles like *The Abandonment of the Jews*, *Roads to Extinction*, *Facing the Holocaust*, *Hitler's Death Camps*, *Auschwitz and the Allies*, *Who's Who in Nazi Germany*. Rows and rows of disturbing titles. They don't disturb me. I have found it comforting to collect a comprehensive library of Holocaust publications. I have been reading these books for years. I think I've been trying to find some clarity and order in a very unwieldy and incomprehensible subject. I feel that if I read as much as I can, then maybe one day I will fully comprehend what happened, or more importantly, how it was allowed to happen. It could be a futile search. I buy more and more books as they are published, only to find the details of the horrors become worse, and the explanations for them become more oblique.

Much of what I read is extremely disturbing, but I manage to face even the most gruesome details. I remind myself that I am not experiencing this grim history, I am merely reading about it. Sometimes reading about it is strangely soothing. Somehow immersing myself in the heart-breaking suffering of the lives of so many good and courageous people puts my own life in perspective.

It's hard to complain about your hair, or an annoying neighbour, when you read about lines of Jews shot for a sudden, whimsical scientific experiment on eye-balls. Boxes and boxes of eyeballs were shipped all over Germany while the Jews who had owned the eyeballs were left in piles until their bodies could be disposed of.

Facing these details, becoming more knowledgeable about the subject, leaves me less fearful. Most of my fear comes, I think, from knowing, from the time I was a small child, that there was infinite evil in the world, and it came from ordinary human beings. How could you tell, I used to wonder, who was good, and who was bad?

When I was in my thirties I began to be afraid. Afraid of many things. One of the things I was afraid of was the dark. I wanted everything to be brightly lit. As though it would be easier to detect evil if it was illuminated.

I am still not crazy about the dark. We visited some friends who have a house in Buck's County, Pennsylvania. This was in the days when nature was still strange to me. The days before I discovered walking and weight-lifting.

I hated Buck's County. Everything was green. Oppressively green. There was so much green. It was the sort of green that makes me feel full of chlorophyll and dread. It was so green that sheep in fields had a green tinge and black and white cows looked brown.

I wanted to go home as soon as we arrived. 'Why would they have a house here?' I said to my husband.

'Because they love it,' he said. I pretended I loved it.

'Isn't it beautiful here?' my host said. I nodded enthusiastically.

'It's so peaceful,' her husband said.

At night I got no peace. The noise was alarming. I could hear bats and owls and frogs. 'I can hear worms squirming,' I said to my husband.

'You'll fall asleep soon,' he said. 'Just relax.'

'What's that noise?' I said to him a few minutes later, as a dreadful wail went through the night.

'It's a deer,' my husband said.

'I think he's crying or grinding his teeth,' I said.

I lay there trying to sleep. I was sure I could hear worms turning in the earth. There were so many strange sounds. I thought I could hear bats flapping. Then I realised I didn't know if bats flapped. I knew that there were some male bats who could double as wet nurses. They could lactate. These Dayak bats, found in the forests of Malaysia, have milk-rich breasts, although they are definitely male and their testes are full of normal sperm. I knew this, but I didn't know if bats flapped.

At three a.m. I woke my husband. 'I can hear weevils and ants and gnats,' I said.

'Read a book,' he said.

At six a.m. I woke him again. 'I've got to go home,' I said. I rang my elder daughter in New York. 'What a night,' I said. 'Ring me up here at nine a.m. and say a relative has unexpectedly arrived from Australia. Say he's only in town for the day and we have to go straight back.'

In the car on the way home I felt a bit embarrassed about our abrupt departure. And about my fearfulness. I turned to Judaism for help. 'Ancient and modern Jews generally thought that evil spirits were more dangerous at night,' I said to my husband.

'Really?' he said. He sounded surprised. I know so little about Judaism. 'With the rising of the sun, the evil spirits' powers wane or disappear,' I said.

We passed a cemetery. Aligning myself with religion restored some of my dignity. I tried again. 'Jews think that demons follow the dead and hover around graves,' I said to my husband. 'That's why you wash your hands after a funeral. It's because you've been in close proximity to unclean demons.' He was impressed by this. He knows so much about Judaism, but he didn't know that.

We were almost at the New Jersey Turnpike. We had left all that green behind. We were half an hour from Manhattan. 'I feel much better,' I said.

These days, the mornings that I wake up in fear are much fewer than they used to be. I woke up recently with a need to learn how to dance. It wasn't as sudden as it sounds. Learning to dance properly has been on my mind for a few years. I am so uncomfortable and so self-conscious whenever I have to dance. I don't know what to do on the dance floor. Whatever it is that is supposed to come naturally to you when you hear dance music, doesn't come to me.

I never dance with anyone other than my husband.

I look away if other people look as though they're going to ask me to dance. My husband is a great dancer. He won a dance marathon in Sydney when he was sixteen. I cling to him as we dance, and try not to let go.

I have wished I could dance with freedom and grace. I have wished I could just be a mediocre dancer, any sort of dancer. I've had years of smiling, stiffly, on the dance floor. Years of trying to imitate gay abandon.

The morning that I woke up with a pressing need to learn to dance, I looked up dance teachers in the Yellow Pages. I rang up the Fred Astaire Downtown Dance Studio. I booked us in for a trial lesson.

As soon as I arrived at the Fred Astaire Downtown Dance Studio, I wanted to leave. Fred Astaire was nowhere in sight. The dance floor looked too big, and the lighting wasn't right. It was very bright. There was a slightly second-hand air about everything. The cuban heels of a male dance instructor were worn and the back of his trousers had shiny patches. Several pieces of calico, draped across the ceiling to create an atmosphere, were sagging.

I met our instructor in the bathroom. She was brushing her teeth, vigorously. When she finished she sprayed her mouth with breath-freshener. She was a short, muscular woman with an astonishingly compli-cated hair style. She wore a white, frilled, multi-layered dress which matched her hair in complexity. She didn't introduce herself to me in the bathroom. And I kept a polite distance.

We introduced ourselves on the dance-floor. 'Which dances would you like to learn?' she said. 'Rumba, Samba, Waltz, Tango, Foxtrot, Quickstep, Box Step?'

'All of those,' I said.

We started the class. My husband had agreed to accompany me. She showed us some rudimentary steps. I watched her carefully. 'Quick, quick slow,' she was saying, as she danced. She partnered me on the dance floor. 'Quick, quick slow' she said. 'Quick, quick slow.'

She was very short. Even in her high heels she only came up to my chest. I felt very big, but she held me firmly. 'Quick, quick slow. Quick, quick slow,' she said. I started to catch on. 'Quick, quick slow,' I said to myself. 'Quick, quick slow.' I wasn't too bad at this. 'Quick, quick slow.'

I danced with my husband. He tried to talk to me. 'Can't talk,' I said. 'Quick, quick slow. Quick, quick slow.' We danced from one end of the dance floor to the other, 'quick, quick slow.'

I danced with the instructor again. It felt like fun now. 'Quick, quick slow,' I said. I asked the instructor a question and lost my footing. It was obvious that I would never be able to talk and dance. I concentrated again. 'Quick, quick slow.' As long as I kept repeating this, I was fine. 'Quick, quick slow, quick, quick slow.'

By the end of the first lesson I'd been taught the rudiments of the tango, the swing step and the box step.

I loved it. I was ready to part with any amount of money to get better at this. We booked a series of lessons.

Outside on the street again, I felt high. Someone had drawn a hopscotch grid on Eighth Street. I'd never played hopscotch. I didn't even know if I could hop. I did a couple of hops. I could hop. I hopped my way through the grid. I hopscotched backwards and forwards. I felt like a kid. I wanted to skip all the way home.

LOVE

'HIS WAIST HAS GOT TO be bigger than your waist,' my friend says to me. She is shaking her head. She doesn't want to meet the man I was planning to introduce her to.

He is a very nice man. He's about her age, thirty-three or thirty-four. And he's a gynaecologist. Clearly, neither my recommendation nor his medical degree can make up for his lack of height and his slight frame.

I tell her that his father is the chairman of a cosmetics empire. She shakes her head again. 'I'm not interested in that,' she says. Then I remember that her father is the chairman of an airline. Obviously, chairmen's children are a dime a dozen in New York.

Luckily, the gynaecologist doesn't know we are discussing his anatomy. He is talking to someone on the other side of the room. I open my mouth to suggest she could at least meet him. She cuts me off. 'He can be shorter than you,' she says. 'But his waist has to be bigger than your waist.'

I've never heard of this rule before. I go home and measure my waist. I hold the tape measure firmly. My waist is twenty-seven and a half inches. I pull the tape measure in a bit. My waist is twenty-seven inches. I breathe in and pull some more. I feel sick. My waist is twenty-six inches.

I go into my husband's studio, where he is painting a large canvas sixteen feet long and ten feet high. The colour and light coming from the painting is startling. It is a triptych. Each panel is a different colour. One is ochre, one orange, one red. But they are the ochre, orange and red of the desert – the Mojave desert, where we went last year.

Across each panel are small, black, potent and insistent markings. These markings are underpinned by textured lines. The lines look like surgical scars or stretched skin – the skin of the earth, or human skin. The ruptures have been sutured. They anchor the painting. They suggest an underlying pain, a counterpoint to the almost transcendental wash of joy over the canvas.

I have been standing at the back of the studio, looking at the painting for a few minutes. I look at my husband. He is covered with paint, and dancing to Bob

Dylan. My husband is in love with Bob Dylan. I would have written several fewer books than I have if my husband hadn't been in love with him.

Sometimes, when I'm working and I'd rather not face what I'm writing about, or I've had a late night and can't think straight, I decide to take a break and walk into my husband's studio to see what he is doing. More often than not Bob Dylan is on in the studio. After two minutes, I go back to my study. Bob Dylan's voice gives me a headache.

I shout to my husband, over Bob Dylan, singing 'If you got to go, go now', 'Can I measure your waist?' I wave my tape measure in the air. My husband doesn't look disturbed. Nothing I do seems to surprise him. Luckily, he is very good natured. He puts down his paint brush and walks over to me. He lets me lift his paint-soaked T-shirt, and measure his waist. His waist is thirty-six inches. My husband doesn't seem very interested in this measurement. 'My waist's been thirty-six inches for years,' he says as he walks back to his painting.

His waist is thirty-six inches. I ponder this piece of information. I have such trouble with my own size. I feel different-sized on different days. Some days I feel very big and other days I feel thin. I am neither very big nor thin. What am I? I am smaller-waisted than my husband. Twelve or thirteen years ago, my waist could well have been bigger than my husband's. Fortunately, neither of us was aware of the waist criterion for love, at the time.

The young woman who enlightened me about the waist ratio, in relationships, also told me that her mother starved herself when she was going out with her father. Before they were married, she never ate when she was with him. I can see how her daughter could think there was a link between size and romance.

She is a bright young woman. I like her a lot. She wants to get married. She wants to be in love. She is looking for someone special. Someone not too ordinary; someone a bit wild, but not too wild. Someone she can take home to her parents.

She is not alone in her prescription for a partner. Today everyone seems to have prerequisites for love. There are physical, geographical, chronological, political and cultural requirements. People know what they want. They want a short or tall person, with blue or brown eyes, a smoker or a non-smoker. They want a runner or a swimmer or a reader or a cross-country skier. A Christian, a Muslim, a Jew. They want big shoulders or a big bust or slender hips or a muscular physique. What happened to falling in love?

It seems to me that falling in love is now as finely calibrated as writing a resumé, applying for a job, or passing an exam. There is no room for chance any more. There is no room for the unexpected, no room for the unpredictable. And the notion of destiny disappeared decades ago. The requirements for love seem as regimented as a bus or train schedule.

There is also, now, the issue of readiness. My

generation never questioned whether they were ready for anything, which did have its drawbacks. Today everyone knows whether they are ready for a relationship or not. In New York, it seems they are not, mostly. Men in their forties talk about dating and girlfriends and whether they are ready for a commitment. They think they have plenty of time.

Then there is the matter of timing. It appears it is never the right time. 'I want to be in love,' a male friend said to me, 'but this is not the right time.' As though there is ever a right time for most of the most fundamental things in life. As though falling in love could be as carefully calculated as a mathematical equation.

My father fell in love with my mother when he was nineteen and she was twelve. He was from a wealthy family and a bit of a playboy. Her family was poor. She was a scholarly, quiet girl. But she was beautiful. Everyone commented on her beauty. She didn't think about it much. She was too busy studying, and tutoring other students after school, to bring in some extra money.

My father was smitten with her. He bought her a watch. Watches were an expensive item in those days. My mother refused to accept his gift. My father threatened to throw it on to the tram tracks which ran through Lodz. My mother was horrified. She took the watch.

He pursued her, relentlessly. Hitler aided him. When the war broke out, her plans to study medicine were aborted. All of Poland's Jews were herded into ghettos. My mother married my father. She was seventeen.

They spent the first five years of their married life in the Lodz Ghetto, living in fear and terror, with disease, starvation and death all around them. In the cattle wagon that took them to Auschwitz, my father told my mother, over and over again, how much he loved her. Two minutes before they were separated, on their arrival in Auschwitz, my father gripped my mother's hand and said he would always love her.

It was nearly one and a half years before they were to see each other again. One and a half years of horror. A horror more horrifying than most of us could imagine.

My mother and father emerged from this horror to find out that everyone they had loved had died. Neither of them knew if the other was alive.

I knew that it had taken my parents six months, after the war, to find each other. I had sketchy images of Europe after the war – images of chaos and mess; images of absent documents and no money; images of soldiers patrolling a paralysed transportation system; images of powerlessness, homelessness and aloneness.

When I was about thirteen, I made up a story about how my parents found each other. I told the story for years. I didn't know I had made it up until I was in my thirties.

In my story, my mother, travelling alone on the back of coal wagons, criss-crossed Europe looking for my father. She slept in fields and on roadsides. Whenever she saw members of the Polish army – my father had been in the Polish army before the war – or some fellow Jews, she would ask them if they knew Moniek Brajsztajn.

She travelled like this for six months. One day she was in a railway station. She asked a young Polish sergeant if he knew my father. 'Yes,' the Polish sergeant replied, 'he's on that train.' He pointed to a train that was pulling out of the station. My mother, almost incoherent with hysteria, explained the situation to the sergeant. He commandeered a truck and drove with her, at high speed, to the next station. My mother boarded the train and walked from one carriage to another. In the last carriage, she saw my father, and fainted.

That story always brought tears to people's eyes. I cried myself. I made the story up from bits and pieces of conversation: idle conversation and angry conversation. Bits and pieces of secrets. Secrets my mother revealed and secrets she tried to hide, and small fragments of the past that slipped out of her.

I didn't have enough information to make a coherent story, so I made it up. The truth of how my mother and father met, after the war, was as compelling as the story I invented.

My mother did travel all over Europe, on the back of local wagons, looking for my father. She did sleep in fields and on the roadside. She finally found my father in Czechoslovakia, where he had been hospitalised for two months with fluid on the brain.

He was out of hospital and recuperating when she

found him. He had thought that she was dead. He knew his mother and father were dead. He knew his sister and two brothers were dead. He was sure my mother was dead. He had started going out with a woman he had known in Lodz. He never forgave himself for taking this woman out. And, I think, perhaps my mother never forgave him.

When I was a girl, my father would come home from working in the factory and give my mother an affectionate slap on her bottom. 'My beautiful Rooshka,' he would say. She always tried to shrug him off, as though she were annoyed or irritated by the gesture, but I always knew that someone who had slept on coal wagons and on roadsides, looking for him, must really love him.

He was crazy about her. He stayed crazy about her until the day she died. And then he almost died of grief. My father's love for my mother was palpable, twenty-four hours a day. He looked at her, adoringly, first thing in the morning, and made a beeline for her when he came home from work every night.

There is a Jewish saying. 'Three things can't be hidden: coughing, poverty and love.' My father so obviously loved my mother. He was mad about her. He was madly in love.

Why do we call it *madly in love*? Is it because the reason we love one person over another, or over all others, is irrational? I often think my husband's love for me is irrational. He could have chosen someone more placid, more evenly-keeled, someone less anxious, less tense. He overlooks so much that is difficult about me. It has to be irrational. I think there were more of these irrational feelings decades ago. I think people loved each other deeply and saw their lives as soldered together.

My parents had a group of married friends who, it seemed to me, really loved each other. There were no questions about whether Shoolak or Marilla were really suited or whether Regina and Edek had married hastily. Matters of commitment and readiness and the right time didn't seem to be stumbling blocks. People fell in love, got married and stayed married. They didn't wonder if they had made the right choice. They didn't voice doubt about a loss of freedom, an erosion of individuality or a diminution of independence.

Co-dependence and interdependence weren't terms anyone was familiar with. 'My own space' meant, 'Move over on the sofa.' Options were more limited. Happiness wasn't dissected. Am I happy? or, am I as happy as I should be? weren't questions that were dwelt on. The idea of examining one's state of being hadn't arrived. My generation began this spate of questioning ourselves, and it has had its disadvantages.

We had requirements and expectations. We had television and magazines to tell us if what we were experiencing was the best we could be experiencing. We asked ourselves, were we as liberated as we could be? As enlightened and unencumbered as we could be? Were we sensitive lovers? Did we have vaginal or clitoral orgasms? Could we find our G-spot? There were so many questions. There were so many things to be concerned about.

We were supposed to be the generation that avoided the mistakes of our parents. We knew each other intimately, before we got married. We married later in life. We made more enlightened choices about our marriage partners. And our marriages dissolved in record numbers.

One of the most passionate loves I have witnessed, outside my parents' love for each other, was the love between Topcha and Herschel. Unlike some of my parents' other friends, they were not very well off. Herschel worked as a tailor all of his life. They lived in a two-roomed apartment in East Melbourne. They were both short and round. Herschel was dark and Topcha was blonde. She called him Ma Herschel, my Herschel. And he called her Ma Topcha, my Topcha.

They were always together, always holding hands and looking at each other. They only had each other. They had no children. I never asked why. I loved being with Topcha and Herschel. They were so happy to be together. Their happiness spread and covered anyone in the vicinity.

I saw a lot of my parents' friends' marriages. Much more than I see of my own friends' marriages. My parents and their friends ate together at each other's homes, once or twice a week. They celebrated all family occasions together. Birthdays, anniversaries, barmitzvahs, engagements, weddings.

They also vacationed together. They all went to the same place, once or twice a year. They stayed in hotels or rented adjoining apartments. They had breakfast, lunch and dinner together. At night, they played cards, or walked on the beach, or went to a nightclub.

I have had very few breakfasts with my friends. I have hardly ever seen them dishevelled and creased with sleep. By the time my friends and I see each other, we are showered and polished and our hair is at just the right angle.

I haven't even been to the beach with most of the people I know well. We don't see each other in bathers. We don't see each other's strange swimming styles or peculiarly-shaped waists or shoulders.

When we are together, we are decked out in clothes that cover up most of us. Everything is orchestrated, if not elegant. Yet there is something wonderful about seeing each other's imperfections. It is a relief to me to not have to pretend that I am as seamless as I can appear, dressed in my most flattering clothes. It is a relief to be able to display the scars and marks and bruises.

For all of its freedom, for all of its access to abundant jobs, abundant advice and abundant choice, my generation has turned out to be as stitched up and separated by super-ficialities as any generation before us. We are more mobile, more affluent and more distanced from each other.

'We never do anything ordinary with our friends,' I wailed to my husband, one night. He is used to my wails.

'We eat out with friends, we have friends over here for meals, we go to the theatre. We do lots of things with friends,' he said.

'They're not ordinary, everyday things,' I said, the wail still in my voice. 'We don't wash dishes with our friends,' I said.

'You hate washing dishes,' he said. But he knew what I meant.

My mother's friends often washed dishes together. Sometimes some of the men helped out, but it was mostly the women who washed the dishes. Any lack of harmony disappeared in the kitchen. They talked as they scraped, washed and dried in perfect synchronism. There was a palpable intimacy in the activity. A palpable happiness. It has been years since I washed any dishes with a friend. Or chopped onions, or sliced bread.

My generation don't touch each other much, either. With a bit of luck, we touch our own husbands and wives, but we never touch each other's husbands and wives.

My parents and their friends touched each other. They could put an arm around each other easily, or link arms. It wasn't taboo to touch someone else's partner. Physical familiarity was natural.

My parents' friends had all tangoed and waltzed and cha cha'd and rumba'd with each other. Dancing was a large part of their social life. Everyone's husband danced with everyone else's wife. There were no favourites. Couples didn't pair off. This arrangement was unspoken.

It meant that no one was left out. The not-so-good dancers were asked to dance as often as the best dancers.

Other things went on on the dance floor. Small fissures, or frissons of misunderstanding, could be cleared up quietly. Compliments could be delivered, confidences imparted.

Dancing together gave my parents and their friends the opportunity to know each other away from the rest of the group. You can know a lot about a person from having to move in time to music with them.

My parents' friends danced at cabarets and supper clubs. They often went to dinner dances. Whatever happened to dinner dances? No one I know has been to a dinner dance in decades.

There's a bookstore in 19th Street which I have heard holds dinner dances. It is called Bookfriends. They sell second-hand books and serve breakfast, lunch and dinner. You can just browse, or browse and eat, or browse, eat *and* dance. I call Bookfriends and ask them if their dinner dances are still on. A woman tells me they are, and that currently on Tuesday nights you can dance to Jordan Sandke and the Sunset Serenaders. I make a booking for next Tuesday night.

I am a bit preoccupied with dancing at the moment. I am halfway through a ballroom dancing course at the Fred Astaire Downtown Dance Studio. My husband, who is a good dancer, is taking the course with me. It was the same price for one of us as it was for the two of us. I persuaded him that it wouldn't do me that much good to become adept at dancing with my short, female dance instructor. I may turn out, I said, to be able to dance well only with women half my size. My husband agreed to accompany me.

I made him buy a pair of dancing shoes, and I bought a pair myself. I went uptown to a store that specialises in dancing shoes. I wanted to buy all of them. I wanted the tap shoes, the ballet shoes and the ballroom dancing shoes. It was really hard to resist the gold lurex T-bars with the cuban heel, and the silver glitter pair on six-inch stilettos. I settled for a boring black pair with sensible heels, a comfortable toe-box, and suede soles.

Next month we are going to the dinner dance at the Rainbow Room. I have wanted to go to the Rainbow Room for years. Friends of ours are taking us as a wedding anniversary present. Our wedding anniversary was two months ago, but I didn't feel I was ready, at the time, for the Rainbow Room. I wanted to be a better dancer when I stepped out onto the dance floor of the Rainbow Room.

Dancing hasn't come naturally to me. I want to lead and not follow. I start laughing when I lose my way. My tango is not bad, but I am still clumsy with my underarm turns in the foxtrot. And it would be good not to have to count time to the music.

I envy those people who learnt to dance at school. Everyone I know who went to a private school, is a reasonable ballroom dancer. They didn't have dancing lessons at Uni High.

I do, however, feel less self-conscious on the dance floor since joining the Fred Astaire Downtown Dance Studio. I had spent decades wearing a light-hearted expression while I pitched myself stiffly around the dance floor. I used to feel as though everyone were looking at me. I told this to a friend who said she, too, felt observed when she was dancing, and when she was parking the car. I felt thankful that I was an unself-conscious car parker.

My kids are unself-conscious dancers. Maybe all kids are, today. Maybe today's less regimented dance steps don't give rise to the same tension. The atmosphere on the dance floor seems to be less fraught. Men don't have to muster up the courage to ask for a dance. And young women no longer have to pass muster at dances. You don't have to wait for someone to ask you to dance. You can dance on your own, or with a friend of either sex.

When my son was four, a mother at St John's Kindergarten in Toorak, Melbourne, asked me if I would be interested in taking him to ballet classes. The Australian Ballet was short of males, she said, and my son had good calves.

I thought my son was clever. I thought he had a beautiful mouth, gorgeous eyes and great hair, but I'd never noticed his calves. I was pleased that he had good calves, but decided against helping out the Australian Ballet. 'I think us Bretts are not genetically pre-disposed towards dancing,' I said to the St John's mother. Later on, I realised that I was the only Brett with that predisposition.

Having children has meant that there are more of us Bretts. We were so diminished in number. Hundreds of us were murdered. I wanted there to be more Bretts. I felt so outnumbered when I was young. Outnumbered by dead Bretts. Outnumbered by normal Australian families. Families with grandparents, aunts, uncles, cousins.

If there were more of us, I thought, my every move wouldn't be so momentous. Every step I made was weighted with those who could no longer step on their own. They travelled alongside me. Out of step and out of breath. It was a rough ride.

Having children eased the burden I carried as my parents' child. My children turned out to be capable of doing many of the things I couldn't. For a start, they adored my mother and father. They had other attributes and abilities that nourished my parents. They performed well at school. They got university degrees.

'They're wildly over-educated,' I said to my father, recently, and he laughed.

'Maybe that's because no one told them to study,' he said to me. And I wondered if he was letting me off the hook for my own squandered education.

My children were a symbol of survival, for my parents, in a way that I never managed to be. They made my parents happy. The happiness was a pure happiness. The happiness of grandparents and their grandchildren, a happiness that is unadulterated by the twists and turns that exist in all parent and child relationships.

I am so grateful that I had my children. Grateful for whatever unconscious needs I was responding to when I suddenly decided, at twenty-two, that I wanted to have children. It was one of my better blind moves.

I've watched couples, today, try to calculate and calibrate the possibilities and probabilities of parenthood. Is this the right time to have children, they ask each other, over and over again. And, of course, it is never the right time. Children can't be plotted and slotted into a well-oiled, smoothly-running schedule. They are disruptive and unpredictable. What is most unpredictable, is how much you love them.

This is incomprehensible to those who don't have children. 'Four of my friends have had children,' my son said to me a couple of years ago, 'and they've all gone nuts. Their places are filled with baby junk, and all they talk about is the baby. What happens to their brains?' It's a good question.

My generation was the last generation to have children, unquestioningly. You got married and you had children. It seems so naive now. But the future seemed uncomplicated. We didn't know about the complexities of relationships. Dysfunctional families and family dynamics were phrases that were decades away from familiarity. Even divorce was an unfamiliar word. We didn't have to face unemployment or a competitive job market. Even ambition was uncool. We were so laid back. A lot of us were laid right out when things changed.

I tried so hard to be a good parent. I wanted to be a perfect parent. And I was young enough to think that that was possible. I didn't want to make the mistakes my parents made. I thought that if you put enough thought into parenting you could prevent all mistakes and mis-demeanours. I thought that if I tried hard enough, I could eliminate all errors and oversight. My poor children are the recipients of all of this earnestness and intensity.

I have loved my children with a passion that has probably constricted and restricted them. It is just as well they no longer live at home. My younger daughter told me recently that she could hear me blowing kisses into her answering machine at college, from the next dorm.

I have gone overboard about many things in my life. I have loved my friends with a love that has been as intense and tempestuous as any love. I have a string of past and present friends with whom I feel interwoven. I haven't seen some of them for years, and I still feel that connection.

My friend Mimi Bochco, who I call Mimala, has equally intense friendships. I am reassured, when I talk to her, that the volatility and scope of friendship doesn't falter or diminish with age.

She is still, in her seventies or eighties, as entangled and embattled with some of her friends as she is entwined and enlaced with others. One day her friend

R. had really annoyed her. 'Fuck her,' Mimi said to me, after telling me what R. had done. 'Fuck her,' Mimi said, again. 'No, that's too good for her. Shit on her.' This sounds even more emphatic in Mimi's thick Lithuanian accent.

When I look back, I have loved a lot of people. I have loved my analysts. Love for an analyst is often a reworking of a love for a parent. I have turned my analysts into irritated mothers and blunt fathers. And I have turned my analysts into perfect parents. I created, with one analyst, the strict parent I needed, and, with another analyst, the calm parent I never had.

The common link is the love I have felt for all three of my analysts. I thought I really was in love with my first analyst. And, in some way, I think he thought he was in love with me. This was not a good thing for either of us.

I loved and feared my second analyst. I turned her into the strictest mother. I felt so safe in the confines of this strictness that I managed to begin emerging without my armour.

I learned how difficult it was for me to feel my deep attachment to my mother, through my last analyst. I found it almost unbearable to feel the attachment I felt to this analyst. She was Jewish, very smart, and, like my mother, very good-looking. I put all sorts of obstacles in the way of the closeness I was frightened of feeling. I complained about money and my lack of it for months, if not years. I focused on everything except how I felt about her.

My equivocation and ambivalence made me feel fifteen again. I left home at eighteen because I couldn't bear my attachment to my mother. She was so easy to be attached to. She was so beautiful, so seductive. Her skin, her figure, her eyes, her hair. She wore silk and lace underwear, and Chanel No. 5 perfume.

Under this elegant exterior was an undercurrent of anxiety, anger, bitterness, agony and anguish. My mother did the normal things that other mothers did – she cooked meals, cleaned the house, shopped, and made school lunches – but there was an edge to everything.

I was always looking at her, trying to decipher what was going on. When I came home from school, I never knew what to expect. Would she be disturbed? Would she be angry with me? Would she be quiet?

My mother would open the door, to me, after school, and I would know that something was wrong. I thought it was something to do with me. I thought she must finally have found all the chocolate wrappers I had stuffed in the bottom of my wardrobe, or discovered that I had wagged school or forged a note explaining a previous absence. I used to feel so nervous, I braced myself by eating before I arrived home. Sweets, ice-cream, whole meals. And armed with a solid interior, I could come home.

Now I understand many of the reasons for her volatility. I have been unpredictable and explosive, with a fraction of the reasons she had for being that way. My mother had no one to help her sort out this welter of feelings. I have had the huge advantage of having help in understanding much of what seemed out of control in my life. But she had no help. No one to help her understand that what she had experienced had altered her forever. She was always trying to live a normal life, without ever being allowed to voice the turmoil and the mayhem that was left in her; the guilt and the grief and the shock and the horror that never went away. My mother was forever trying to keep the past at a distance, but the past was always part of her present.

I was torn between never wanting to leave my mother, and wanting to get away from her. Feeling I would die if I didn't get away. When I was very young, I wanted to be at my mother's side all the time. Later, in my teens, and until I was in my early thirties, I was mostly conscious of my need to get away from her. I couldn't bear to feel the intensity of my love for my mother. When I began to feel it, I almost came unstuck. For, with the feeling of love for her, came a flood of feelings I had suppressed for years. My own anguish at her anguish.

My own agony at all the loss she had lived through, and all the rest of the mess. The barbaric behaviour she had witnessed, the beatings she had experienced, the rape, the disease, the hunger. I almost unravelled with grief. I lay on my analyst's couch in Melbourne and wept for every one of the fifty minutes of my session. Session after session, month after month. I couldn't speak. I, who have always found words a consolation, couldn't find any words to console me.

It was the beginning of a reconciliation with my mother. My mother and I had never separated, physically. I saw her several times a week and talked to her on the phone every day, but there was a distance between us. It was a distance of resentment. Small resentments and large resentments grew into a tangible barrier between us. We went through all the motions of being a close mother and daughter, but there was much that was missing.

Part of my heart was shut off. The part of my heart that loved my mother so deeply it felt dangerous, had closed up. When it opened, I was overwhelmed by love for her. And I overwhelmed her. She didn't know what was happening. I visited her frequently. I talked to her in a new way. I looked happy, happy to be with her. I bought her beautiful flowers and clothes. I wanted to buy her the universe.

She never mentioned the change in me. She never asked what had happened to provoke the change. And I didn't feel the need to explain. I was so happy to be with her, and she was happy to be with me. It was so easy. I wish I'd done it years earlier. I wish I'd had more of those happy years with my mother. But easy things are often very hard to learn, and I wasn't a particularly fast learner.

I have had many happy years with my father. The happiest memories of my childhood are to do with him.

I used to feel bad about that, and sometimes still do; as though I were being disloyal to my mother.

My father used to take me out on the weekends. When I was small, he took me to the zoo. I can still remember riding around Melbourne Zoo on the back of one of the elephants. I used to sit up there, high above everyone else, waving my ribbon of tickets in the air. I was out of the house, away from Nicholson Street, Carlton, away from so much that frightened me. I was in another universe. I used to love the loping rhythm of the elephant; how high off the ground I was. The world seemed much quieter at that altitude. I liked to sit right at the back, so I could smell the elephant and watch him flick his tail. Sometimes I would touch his thick, grey hide. I rode round and round and round. I had more rides than any other child. It seemed as though I didn't have to get off, for hours. My father used to buy me the tickets for the elephant ride, and then he would sit on a bench under a tree, and read his book. When my tickets ran out, I would go back to him and we would go home.

My father also took me to Luna Park and, when I was slightly older, to the old Tivoli Theatre in Bourke Street. I used to feel I was at the epicentre of sophistication and glamour at The Tivoli. My father bought chocolates and lollies before the show. We always had front row seats. I would walk into the theatre, nearly hyperventilating with excitement. The second I inhaled that heady scent of all theatres, that mixture of powder and make-up and perfume, I would become almost giddy. We would take our seats and eat. By the time the first act came on, I had usually finished all the chocolate, all the Fantales and all the scorched almonds.

My father used to laugh so hard at the jokes, that the comedians would play to him. He often laughed until he wept. If anyone on stage asked for a volunteer from the audience, my father would be up there in a flash. He was a side-kick for comedians, hypnotists, magicians, even a ventriloquist.

In between these performers were the dance numbers. Showgirls in fish-net stockings and high heels kicked up their legs, twirled around and did the splits. I thought they were the most beautiful girls I'd ever seen. During the dance numbers, the stage was lined with semi-nude showgirls. They wore enormously high, elaborate head-dresses. They looked almost imperious. Because they were bare-breasted, they could not, by law, move on the stage. So they stood perfectly still while the dancers danced around them.

My father and I never talked about the nude showgirls, and we never mentioned them to my mother. We also kept quiet about the strippers on the programs and about the chocolates we ate before the show and at intermission.

I used to dream of being a Tivoli dancer. But I was a chubby teenager with thick thighs, and I knew I'd never make the grade. One of the strip-tease artists, Margot, befriended me. I had taken a present to her, backstage. Three black china cats, all chained together. She seemed to really like the cats, and invited me to have coffee with her.

I ended up having coffee with Margot after school quite often. I think I was in love with her. I used to gaze adoringly at her over the coffee. So did her husband, Jackie Clancy. He later became a comedian on television. I knew, even at fourteen, that he was a complex and quite brilliant man. One of the things I loved most about Margot and Jackie was their love for each other. It seemed to me that they adored each other.

I have always been a sucker for love. I still am. I am an incurable matchmaker. My dismal matchmaking record doesn't seem to deter me. Matchmakers have had an honourable place in the Jewish community. They are seen as doing God's work. I have been an appalling failure at this ecclesiastical art form.

I have matchmaked people who hated each other instantly, and I have matchmaked people who took three years after they were married to begin to hate each other. I have introduced strangers; strangers to me and to each other. I have interfered with happily single people, and inferred that their happiness would be short-lived unless they met a certain person I had in mind for them.

I have thought about mixing love potions and I have tried out old myths. Gimpel's Hoor seemed very promising. According to the myth, Gimpel, an old Jew, swore by his method. You took a hair from one person, chopped it up and mixed it with some food to be eaten by another person. The person who ate the hair-laced food was guaranteed to fall in love with the owner of the hair. There was no money-back on this guarantee. I tried Gimpel's Hoor several times. According to the myth, the hair could come from any part of the body. I tried head hair, underarm hair and pubic hair. Nothing worked.

I tried matchmaking my father, recently. Matchmaking a parent is not something I would advise anyone else to attempt.

My father was on his own, living in Melbourne again. I knew he was lonely. I hated the thought of him being alone. I knew he would be a different person with someone to do things for, someone to share things with. I suggested that he join a Jewish social club, but he was irritated with me for that suggestion. 'I'm fine, just as I am,' he said. Except that he didn't sound fine. 'Every day is the same,' he said to me, each time I rang him. He was bored and lonely.

He started applying for jobs. He applied for a job as a cutter, something he did, in clothing factories, decades ago. He lied about his age. He said he was sixty-nine not seventy-nine. He had no success. Two people said they were impressed with him and would call back. But the jobs went to younger applicants.

I couldn't quite understand why he wouldn't consider volunteer work. He saw it as a sign, I think, of his worthlessness. A paying job, no matter how small the pay was, was a sign that he was still worthwhile, still had qualities and abilities that were valued. He pored through the *Age*, week after week, looking for jobs. The cutting jobs were few and far between and when they came up, he didn't get them.

I decided that a wife was the answer. I began to look around. I rang Jewish friends in Melbourne and asked if anyone knew a single woman I could introduce to my father. People seemed startled by this request. Even those with widowed mothers didn't seem eager to activate anything.

I contemplated advertising in the *Jewish News*. I asked my best friend if she would vet the replies. She said she would, but she was worried. She said she wasn't sure exactly what type of woman I was looking for.

'Somebody very nice,' I said.

'Great,' she said. 'They'll all be very nice, couldn't you be more specific?'

I began to think about the specifics. How old should she be? I asked my son what he thought.

'Someone younger than Grampa is a good idea,' he said. 'We don't want someone Grampa is going to have to look after straight away.' I thought this was a good idea, myself.

'What about seventy?' I said.

'What about sixty?' my son said.

'Sixty, that's only about a decade older than I am,' I said. 'That seems unseemly.'

'I don't think sixty would be unseemly,' my husband said. 'That's because he's not your father,' I said. I couldn't come up with anything more specific than someone nice. I couldn't even come up with an age range. We never ran the ad.

But I did hear about a woman. I heard about her from an acquaintance. She sounded just right, to me. B. was in her mid to late sixties. Not too old and not too young. And she lived just a few blocks from my father. She was smart, but not really an intellectual. She was sophisticated, but not too sophisticated. She was widowed, and she loved to travel. I had visions of my father and B. travelling to New York, to visit us. I had fantasies about B. and my father spending the Melbourne winter in Queensland.

I rang up B. myself, from New York. I explained the situation to her. Her friend had told her to expect my call. I liked the sound of her. She was articulate and bright. She was originally from England. She'd been in Australia for thirty years.

I told her a bit about my father. Or at least I meant to tell her a bit about my father. Instead I talked, nonstop, for over an hour about him. By the time I had finished there wasn't a man in the world who could have competed with my father in terms of kindness, patience, tolerance, affection, warmth, generosity and a sense of humour. B. said she couldn't wait to meet him. As luck would have it, I was going to Australia for a book tour. I arranged to call B. when I arrived in Melbourne, in two weeks' time.

'What does she look like?' my son asked, when I told him the news.

'How could I ask her what she looks like?' I said. 'It would have been rude.' And then I gave him a lecture about the lack of importance of looks, in romance. 'Looks are not important, in the scale of things,' I said.

'Oh, yeah,' he said. 'That's why you married two good-looking guys.'

'What will Grampa say?' my younger daughter said.

'I'm not sure,' I said. My father knew nothing of my plans. I knew he wouldn't approve. How to get him to meet B. was going to require some thought.

In the end, I asked him if he would agree to do something for me, without knowing exactly what it was. He was very suspicious. 'It just means giving me two or three hours of your time,' I said. 'No harm will come to you,' I said.

'Are you sure?' he said.

He was furious with me when he found out what he had agreed to. He tried to back out of the agreement. I wouldn't let him. 'Did you tell her I haven't got any money?' he said.

'I told her everything,' I said. He then listed off the sources of his income.

'Did you tell her that?' he said.

'I didn't go into the details,' I said, 'but she's got

the general picture.' He was still furious with me, two days later. 'How could you do this to me?' he said.

'I did it out of love for you,' I said. He snorted.

'I think we should go on this date with B. and my father,' I said to my husband.

'You and me?' he said.

'That is the we I was talking about,' I said.

'Why?' said my husband.

'I don't know,' I said. 'Just a gut feeling.'

My husband has gone along with my gut feelings in the past. Not all of them have turned out well. He agreed, reluctantly. My father was so relieved when I told him that my husband and I would be joining him and B. on their date. 'Thank you,' he said. He looked so grateful, I started to lose confidence in the whole thing.

I called B. to arrange a time to meet for dinner. It was Sunday. I suggested Thursday. 'Could we make it Thursday week?' she said. 'To tell you the truth, I have to go to the hairdresser. I haven't had a haircut for a while. And I have to buy some new shoes, too.'

'Don't go to a lot of trouble,' I said. 'My father is very casual. He's not a formal person.'

My father sounded much more casual when he learned about the week's respite. 'Maybe you should get your hair cut,' I said to him.

'All right, all right,' he said.

'And do you have a good pair of shoes?' I asked him.

'Of course I do,' he said. 'But I'm not going to go all dressed up. I'm going to go as I am, a plain man. I'll wear the trousers what I am usually wearing and my usual shoes.'

'You don't mean the trousers you wear every day,' I said.

'Yes,' he said. 'They're perfectly good.'

'They were perfectly good, ten years ago,' I said. 'Please wear your suit.'

'Maybe,' he said.

I called B. a couple of times, so she would feel more comfortable with me. I thought it would be reassuring. I really liked her. My husband spoke to her. He liked her, too. B. seemed perfect for my father, to me. She wasn't bothered by the fact that he wasn't a wealthy man. She loved all the stories I told her about him. 'B. is going to fit right into our family,' I said to my elder daughter, when she called from New York.

My father asked me four times if we could cancel the dinner. We had booked a table for four at a quiet, elegant restaurant near the city. We had arranged to meet at the restaurant at seven p.m. I had promised my father I would be there at six forty-five.

On the day of the dinner, my father called me at five p.m. He sounded panicked.

'Are you all right?' I said.

'I had a bit of trouble,' he said. 'It was your fault. You wanted me to wear a suit. So I took the suit to the dry-cleaners.'

'They didn't lose it, did they?' I said. I knew there was no time to find another suit.

'No,' my father said. 'As a matter of fact they did a very good job.'

'So what's wrong?' I said. I could feel my blood pressure rising as I prepared for the problem.

'What's wrong,' my father said, 'is that the zip of the trousers is broken. Would it be all right if I wear my grey trousers?'

'The ones you wear every day?' I said. 'No, it wouldn't be all right.'

'What about the blue trousers?' he said.

'The light blue trousers you wore in Florida? They'd look stupid,' I said, in a more terse tone than I intended. 'I don't know what we can do,' I said.

'It's quarter past five,' my father said. 'I'm going to jump in the car and see if I can catch the tailor in Alma Road.' He hung up, and I wondered how ludicrous his pale blue slacks would look with his charcoal grey suit jacket. Very ludicrous, I decided.

At six o'clock, my father called again. 'The tailor was already shut,' he said.

'Oh, no,' I said.

'Don't worry,' my father said. 'I fixed things up.'

'How?' I said.

'I sewed the zip up,' he said. 'I sewed it up while the trousers was on me. I did small, little stitches. You can't see anything.' My father has often left me speechless. I was almost speechless.

306

'What if you have to go to the toilet?' I said.

'I'll wait till I get home,' he said.

My father, who knows Melbourne very well, asked me again exactly where the restaurant was. I told him, again. 'How will I find you in the restaurant?' he said.

'It's not an enormous restaurant,' I said. 'You'll see me.'

'Where will you be sitting?' he said.

'I have no idea,' I said, 'but I promise I'll get there before you. I'll watch the door. I'll see you as soon as you arrive.' He sounded so nervous, I felt worried myself. 'Drive carefully,' I said to him.

'Wouldn't it be wonderful,' I said to my husband, 'if this turns out to be the perfect match.'

'We don't have to wait for very long to find out,' my husband said. 'They'll be here in ten minutes.' We were sitting at a table with a full view of the entrance to the restaurant. I didn't take my eyes off the front door. 'I can't believe he's arriving with his zip stitched up,' I said. 'I should have bought him a new suit.'

'He wouldn't have let you,' my husband said.

I was wondering whether I had enough time to duck to the bathroom, when my father arrived. I had to look twice. My father looked the most debonair I'd seen him look in years. So handsome. So dashing. So distinguished. He had a crisp white shirt on underneath his suit. And he was wearing a pale grey silk tie with flecks of darker grey and black. The shirt and tie looked perfect with the dark, tailored suit.

He saw us straight away.

'You look fabulous,' I said to him.

'Yeah, yeah,' he said.

'You've had a haircut, too,' I said.

'Yeah, I went to the barber,' he said. 'It's no big deal.' Underneath the dashing and quite radiant exterior, he looked nervous. It was the nervousness of a school-boy. A sort of sick-looking nervousness. 'I shouldn't have agreed to this,' he said. 'I shouldn't have let you talk me into it. You could talk anybody into anything.'

'The worst that can happen, Dad,' I said to him 'is that we'll have a nice meal together.' He stood up. For a minute I thought he was going to leave. 'Can you see my alterations?' he said. I didn't know what he was talking about; then I remembered the zip.

I didn't know what to do. You can hardly peer at your father's crotch in public. It's not something most people would want to do on the whole, anyway. 'It's too dark to see,' I said. He leaned towards me. I took a cursory look. 'You did a very good job,' I said.

'I thought so, myself,' he said. 'I didn't have black cotton, but I used a navy, and you can't see a thing.'

'Here she is, I think,' my husband said.

'Oy, oy, oy,' my father said. He looked pale. B. had told me she would be wearing an emerald green scarf. There was a woman wearing an emerald green scarf looking anxiously around the restaurant. 'Oy, oy, oy,' said my father. 'You go to meet her.' I got up and waved to B. She looked very relieved and walked towards us.

B. was not what I expected her to be. The emerald green scarf was tied in a large bow at the side of her neck. She was wearing a bright red dress which came to just above her knees. She had on large white patent leather shoes and black stockings. Her hair stuck out at very odd angles. It was quite wild, a sort of grunge-punk look. I wasn't sure that she had made it to the hairdresser's as she had planned to. I quite liked the eccentricity of her ensemble, the idiosyncracy of her dress sense. But the individuality of her outfit was lost on my father. He read it as odds and ends. 'She must be very poor,' he said to me in Yiddish, just before B. got to our table. 'Make sure you pay for the meal.'

My father looked paralysed. He stared fixedly at my husband. B. looked so nervous. I suggested we order. B. looked for her glasses. She couldn't find them. She had to empty out all the contents of her handbag in order to find the glasses. The table was covered in B's purse, her keys, her lipstick, her face powder, some odd scraps of paper and a bottle of pills. She kept apologising for not being able to find her glasses.

'You order for me,' my father said.

'What would you like?' I said.

'Anything,' he said.

I tried to find some common ground between them. 'Do you play cards?' I said to B.

'No,' she said, 'although I don't mind other people

playing cards.' Her nervousness was beginning to feel heart-breaking. My father seemed unable to look at B. 'I play cards,' he said to me.

'I don't play cards, myself,' I said to B. 'And my mother never played cards.'

The food we had ordered arrived. B. looked at her whole fried snapper with French fries and said, 'I haven't seen a meal as big as this in a long time.' Then she looked bothered, as though she may have inadvertently said something offensive. 'It's the most beautiful meal I've seen for a long time,' she said.

'My daughter eats at restaurants all the time,' my father said to me. 'Sometimes she takes her father.' I had ordered a rabbit stew. I don't like stews and I rarely eat rabbit. I tried to work out which part of the rabbit was on my plate. My head hurt.

My husband looked after B. He told her funny anec-dotes about New York, and odd bits of information about our lives. 'Do you speak Yiddish?' he asked B.

'No, I'm afraid I don't,' she said.

'I speak Yiddish,' my father said to me.

My father did try to speak to B., but in his nerv-ousness all of his English disappeared. He couldn't remember basic words, and none of what he said made sense. B. tried to understand, and I tried to translate. Just before the dessert arrived, we all gave up.

I talked to my father, and B. chatted to my husband. My father cheered up. 'This chocolate cake is really a very good chocolate cake. Nearly as good as the chocolate cake from Scheherezade,' he said.

'Scherezade hasn't got a chocolate cake,' I said. 'You mean Monarch.'

'Maybe I mean Monarch,' he said. He was starting to look like his old self.

By the end of the meal, B. was ready to marry my husband. 'He's a wonderful man,' she kept saying.

'He is wonderful,' I kept answering her.

'Where did you find her?' my father said to me, after we'd seen B. to her car.

'What do you mean?' I said. 'She's a very lovely woman.'

'But the way she looks,' he said. 'Who looks like that?'

'Just because she doesn't look like one of the coiffeured blondes of Caulfield doesn't mean she's strange,' I said.

'She's very strange,' he said. I felt furious with him.

'How can you judge someone on their appearance?' I said.

'You have to have something to look at,' he said.

'Well, who do you think you are?' I said. 'Cary Grant?'

I could hardly speak to my father for two days. The anger I felt was partly an anger on behalf of all women who are judged by their looks. I finally calmed down. 'My father needs someone who plays cards and speaks Yiddish,' I said to my husband. 'I guess we all respond to what is familiar to us,' I added.

I rang B. I told her my father thought she was wonderful, but he really wasn't ready to go into a relationship. She was very sweet. 'I had a wonderful evening,' she said. 'It's been a long time since I've been out to a restaurant that nice.' I felt sad.

My father, to his credit, called B. and told her that he enjoyed meeting her very much. He said he had really enjoyed the conversation and the evening, but he was settled into his life and didn't want to make any changes. B. said that if he was ever in the area he should drop in and see her. My father said he didn't go out much. I decided never again to interfere in the matter of love.

Jews fear interference with love. At Jewish weddings the groom breaks a glass, usually by stamping on it, at the end of the ceremony. The Kabbalistic explanation for this is that there are demons intent on disturbing the happiness of the new couple, and that by destroying a glass the evil spirits will be satisfied.

Another explanation, is that the noise of the glass breaking is a warning to man that he must temper life's joyous moments with sober thoughts. A reminder to the young couple to prepare for all of life's eventualities.

The Australian redback spider literally dies for love. These are the redback spiders whose female mates devour them during copulation. Some people think that this redback spider dies for sex, but I have preferred to think of it as dying for love. Recently a scientist at Cornell University demonstrated that those male redbacks who were eaten during copulation sired

proportionately more offspring than the partners the
female spider chose not to chew. Sex, the scientist from
Cornell said, helps to ensure the redback's paternity,
and apparently discourages the female from mating with
a rival redback. The *New York Times* ran a story on
the discovery. The headline read: 'For an Australian
Spider, Love Really is To Die For.'

In New York, they bandy love around. 'I love you,'
people you hardly know, say to you. 'I love you', 'I love
him', 'I love her'. New Yorkers are very loose with
love. I was talking on the phone to an Australian movie
producer who was interested in optioning one of my
books for a movie. I asked her a question, and then I
waited for an answer.

I waited and waited. I started to think we must have
been disconnected. I waited some more. Finally, I said,
'Hello, are you there?' She was there.

'I'm Australian,' she said. 'We don't speak unless we
have something to say. I'm thinking about your question.' It made me laugh. Clearly, by her standards, I was
an excessive, impatient New Yorker.

I may be. But I am a long way from being able to
say, 'I love you' to everyone. My friend Belinda Lus-
combe, who writes the People Page of *Time* magazine
in New York, was in the middle of her first day on the
job, when she got a phone call from Tony Curtis.
Belinda took the call with some trepidation. This was
her first major job in America. 'Hello,' she said.

'Belinda, I love your work,' Tony Curtis said.

THE WRITING LIFE

I'M NOT ONE OF THOSE writers who knew, from the time they were young, that they wanted to be a writer. I wanted to be slim.

That's the only ambition I can remember. I didn't make any plans about what to do with my life. I wasn't sure I was going to have a life. I couldn't think about the future. I thought people died in the future. My weight loss plans were to do with the present. That's why they were so radical. I needed to lose a lot of pounds in a short period of time.

When other kids at Uni High were deciding whether to do law or science or medicine, I was trying to calculate if it was possible to lose two stone in two weeks. Those two stone, and more, were going to stick with me for a long time, but I didn't know that then. So I sat and calculated and recalculated while my classmates graduated, made their career choices and began their lives.

I spent a couple of years pretending I was trying to get to university. I enrolled at Taylor's, a private coaching college in the city. At Taylor's they gave you sheets and sheets of notes on every subject. I stacked my neatly-labelled notes in colour-coordinated folders. I never read them.

My father tried to keep up his faith in me. 'You could be better than Perry Mason,' he would say. 'No one can win an argument with you.' His dream was for me to metamorphose into Raymond Burr. Perhaps a slimmer Raymond Burr. I would remain cool through the most trying and seemingly insoluble cases, and then, at the eleventh hour, I would come up with the evidence that won the case.

He was not altogether unjustified in seeing me in this role. I certainly appeared cool. Nothing perturbed me, or disturbed me. Not my endless failing of the final school year, not my lack of direction, not even my dismal diet record.

I was so calm, I was in a stupor. Until the day my mother said I had to get a job. I think it was my weight that finally wore her down. I'd spent days riding my bike around the small square of our backyard in an effort to counter weeks of Cherry Ripes or Kit Kats or Snack

Bars. My mother encouraged the exercise, but in the end was forced to face the fact that it appeared ineffective. My weight was escalating.

I was so peeved when she said I had to get a job. And shocked. I had thought losing weight would always take precedence over everything else.

I applied for a job with ICI. I had my interview in one of the upper floors of what was then the tallest building in Melbourne. I lied about my mathematical ability. I didn't get the job. I applied for a job with a French hair supply company and lied about my fluency in French. I didn't get that job. I applied for a job at *Go-Set*, the newly-established rock newspaper. They asked me no questions I had to lie about. I got the job. It never occurred to me to question whether I could write. Everyone at the newspaper assumed I could. And so did I.

I wrote my first article on my first day. I just sat down and wrote it. It was such good fun. The only question I asked was how to put the paper into the typewriter. I'd never used a typewriter before. It took me a while to get the hang of it, but once I did, I was hooked. I have been in love with the feel of a keyboard ever since.

I interviewed pop singers and pop groups and rock groups, then went back to the office and wrote up the stories. After a while, I started suggesting answers to the questions I was asking. I made these suggestions only to those rock stars I knew well. Several of them appreciated my suggestions. So I made up the questions and made up the answers. The stories were praised by my editors.

I went from being miserable Lily riding her bike around the garden, to Lily Brett of *Go-Set*. I hung out with everyone that everyone my age wanted to hang out with. I interviewed the coolest groups and musicians and I interviewed the pop stars. I spent my days with boys who drove hordes of girls wild.

But boys were not what was on my mind. Writing was. I wrote page after page of the newspaper. I never tired of writing. I came to work early in the morning and I left late at night.

My parents weren't any happier with me. They thought *Go-Set* wasn't a real job. People who had real jobs were lawyers or doctors. Journalism was not in their lexicon of real jobs.

But I was much happier. *Go-Set* bought me an electric typewriter about six months after I started. I was in a state of bliss. I would feel my happiness as soon as I pressed the 'on' switch, and the soft hum of the machine started up.

Go-Set was spectacularly successful. They publicised their writers. My photograph was on my articles and in the social pages of the newspaper. I became as well-known as some of the people I was writing about. I found some of the attention unnerving. Shop attendants asked for my autograph. I hated it. I would race through Myers at top speed if I wanted to buy something. Girls either giggled when they saw me, or were rude. 'She's fatter than she looks in photographs,' one young girl said to her friend as I walked briskly up Bourke Street.

The British airline BOAC offered *Go-Set* two round-the-world tickets in exchange for publicity. My editors asked me if I'd like to go overseas. I said yes. It was 1967. I was twenty. 'How long will you be away for?' my mother said to me. 'I don't know,' I said. 'Maybe six months.' She looked miserable. She always looked miserable, whenever I went away. I felt her love for me most intensely when I was departing. She cried whenever I left for anywhere. And I knew those tears were for me, not for any of the dead.

I wasn't sure exactly what I was supposed to do on this world tour, and Colin Beard, the photographer I was travelling with, was even less sure. When we arrived in Hong Kong, I was interviewed by a local radio station. The interviewer spoke to me in English and then repeated my answers in Chinese. I recognised the words Normie Rowe, Johnny Young, Marcia Jones and the Cookies and the Easybeats interspersed with lots of Chinese. Colin took photographs of me during the interview. Our *Go-Set*/BOAC world tour was underway.

Not realising how insignificant *Go-Set* and Australia were, was an advantage to me when I got to London. I set about organising interviews. I rang managers and publicists and record companies and said I was here to interview their stars. I think I got quite a few of my interviews simply because I expected to. My confident, assertive attitude took people by surprise. And so did my age.

I laughed and chatted and joked with managers and publicists who were decades older than I was. I didn't realise I should have been subservient. I didn't see the pop world as serious. I thought everyone understood that we weren't dealing with issues of life and death. I thought we were all enjoying ourselves.

I started six months of interview after interview. I sat in offices and hotel foyers and dressing rooms and dining rooms with Herman's Hermits, the Trogs, the Rolling Stones, the Who, Manfred Mann, Spencer Davis, the Hollies. With everyone who was anyone, really, except for the Beatles.

What I remember more clearly than the swivel of Mick Jagger's hips, more clearly than the intensity of Eric Burden and the Animals or the seriousness of the young Stevie Winwood, was my writing.

I have very clear memories of my typewriter. A beautiful black portable Olivetti. I remember writing my stories, in different rooms, in the different apartments I lived in. I remember balancing the typewriter on my knees sometimes, in bed at night and typing out the stories which were posted back to *Go-Set* each week.

I remember trying hard to start each story with an interesting sentence, and trying not to lose the essence of the different people I was writing about.

I do remember Jimi Hendrix, clearly. He had an electrifying sexuality about him. He bit into his guitar as though he were biting into another life. He swung it around his heart and in between his legs. He strummed and plucked it as though it was a lethal animal.

I sat in the front row of his first concert. His sexuality was so overpowering that I felt a bit frightened of him. A large number of the kids in rock bands then were English migrants. And here was this black man, ablaze. Off stage, he was very sweet, very courteous, and very smart. One of the nicest of all of the rock stars.

In many ways, the rock world was a world in which I felt alienated. Dominated, like most of the rest of the world, by males. Groups of boys who were in love with who they were. Groups of boys so bowled over by how great they were together. They were completely pre-occupied with each other, as though they weren't indi-viduals but part of one fabulous person. They looked at each other, admiringly, as they answered my questions. They stripped in front of me, in dressing rooms and bandied about names of possible groupies with abandon.

Sometimes I found a person behind the self-satisfac-tion, but it was rare. Actually, I was hardly there myself. I was a fat Jewish girl who wasn't at all sure of where she was. On the surface, I glittered. I had sequins glued to my cheekbones, and sometimes strands of them tied in my hair. In the dressing rooms and concert halls and recording studios, I was an outsider on the inside.

I felt as though I had come to a new world when I arrived in California for the Monterey Pop Festival. I was so excited. Everyone was carrying flowers, talking about love and peace. I thought I was witnessing a revolution.

There were drugs everywhere. People passed around joints. It would have been anti-social to say no. I puffed on the joints and I held my breath in the same way that I saw others do. People gave me pills. Perfect strangers said, 'Let me turn you on.' I was well-mannered. I always said, 'Thank you very much.' By the end of the festival, I had a large stash of those white LSD pills.

I sat in the front, near the stage, at the Festival. It seemed to me that the press and the performers were all in this front section together. At different times, I sat next to Janis Joplin and Mama Cass and Michelle Phillips.

I was drawn to Janis Joplin. She had a great sense of humour and an exuberance, and a lack of pretension. She was down to earth and kind and she had clearly experienced suffering. There was a tenderness and a vulnerability about her that made you want to look after her. She came off the stage to thunderous applause from the audience. 'Was I good? Was I okay?' she repeatedly asked those around her.

I remember her running off the stage. Her out-of-control hair, patched into place with assorted ribbons and combs, flying everywhere. She was great to talk to. She had ideas and opinions about everything. She argued passionately and laughed vigorously.

These were the days before celebrities and their personas were manufactured and every hint of personality was pasteurised and homogenised. The days when celebrities were individuals. Unlike today, where one rock star or actor sounds much like all the other rock stars or actors.

An inordinate number of the stars who performed at Monterey died young. Janis Joplin, Jimi Hendrix, Keith Moon, Mama Cass.

I liked Mama Cass. She seemed a nice person. She smiled readily, and always had a kind expression on her face. I felt sorry for her because she was so large. One day at the Festival, a young man asked me if I was Mama Cass.

I interviewed Brian Jones at Monterey, too. He couldn't put two words together. The blond, angelic-faced Rolling Stone was so out of it. I waited minutes after I asked each question, in the hope that something had registered. But nothing had. He looked at me, then stared into outer space. We were sitting side by side on a bench. Every now and then he tilted forward, and I thought he was going to fall off. Even though the interview was going nowhere, I stayed with him until his minder arrived. I was too worried to leave him alone. He seemed to me to have died well before his death.

I had an adult concern about this group of people who seemed, for different reasons, to be in peril. Yet at the same time, I was smoking pot and dropping acid. I crawled around Haight-Ashbery, in San Francisco, hallucinating unpleasantly for several days after Monterey. Luckily it didn't take me long to figure out that I didn't like drugs. Pot made me feel sick and the distortions and confusions of LSD frightened me.

Despite the number of words I wrote every week, I didn't feel as though I was a real journalist. I felt a fraud whenever I wrote it down as my occupation. Real journalists worked for real newspapers, like the *Age* and the *Herald*. Years later, I had trouble calling myself a poet. Even after I'd won prizes and published several books. It seemed pretentious to call myself a poet. So, years after I was no longer a journalist, I wrote 'journalist' in all forms requiring my occupation. I still feel a bit embarrassed when I say I'm a writer.

The right word was very important to my parents. They searched for the right word in many of their sentences, and were wildly impressed when I could come up with it. When they were lost for a word, I would try to find it. I became adept at producing multiple possibilities for an elusive word. The admiration I received for this ability inspired me to stretch my vocabulary to its limits.

Finding the right word was one of the few ways I could help my parents. I knew they needed help, and I knew it was more than help with their English. But helping them with more than that was beyond me, although I tried, in my fantasies. I used to imagine myself sewing the most beautiful clothes for my mother. Ball gowns, dresses, suits. My mother would put on the clothes that I'd made for her, and she would be so radiant and so happy. This fantasy continued until I was in my twenties or thirties.

I wanted to align myself with my parents in so many ways. I think this is a common desire in children of traumatised parents. As a child, and for a lot of my adult life, I tried to imagine the atrocities my parents had experienced. Children's imaginations are boundless. They often imagine things as worse than they actually are. But this was a situation which was impossible to imagine worse than it was. The snippets of information that I got from my parents about their past and all its horror were small and horribly potent. My mother and father told me these things with the blunt and awkward words of a new language. The phrases lacked all subtlety. The sentences were stilted, missing much of the detail, but the evil was intact. I found these bits and pieces of their lives terrifying.

My parents never spoke to me in their mother tongue, Polish. They spoke English and occasionally Yiddish. They reserved Polish for each other. I knew I wasn't getting the full extent of their expression. I knew I was getting a chopped and fractured understanding of their intention. I longed to speak to them properly. I toned down my own language. I spoke to them in simplified sentences. Simple sentences eliminate a lot of complex thought. I often thought that despite our intense attachment and connection to each other, we spent our lives perched on the surface of things.

All my life I have had a need to make myself

understood clearly. I have over-explained every explanation and over-done every apology. I can't make things clear enough. I used to end many of my sentences with 'Do you know what I mean?' It drove my husband mad. It took me a long time to stop myself.

I don't know why my mother insisted on speaking English to me. I don't know why she didn't speak Yiddish to me. When my children were small, I couldn't imagine speaking to them in French or German, or any other language I was clumsy in. The language of mothers and children is full of playful intimacies, the sort of intimacies that are unfamiliar in a foreign tongue.

Yiddish is such an affectionate language, full of diminutives, caresses and love. It is also a language of concern. In German or Italian or Spanish phrase books you find phrases like, 'How long does the train stop here?' and, 'I would like an omelette.' In Yiddish phrase books, you can learn how to say, 'My parents aren't well' and 'What's wrong with them?' and to answer, 'They have heartaches from their children'.

In 1947, a year before I arrived in Australia, the Australian government established a migrant Reception and Training Centre in Victoria called Bonegilla. Bonegilla was just about in the middle of nowhere. It was eight miles from Albury, the nearest town, and hundreds of miles from any urban centre. The Australian Immigration Department brought hundreds of thousands of immigrants to Bonegilla. Part of the purpose was to teach them English and acclimatise them to the Australian way of life. The government taught these mostly displaced people English by teaching them songs. It is hard not to laugh, or cry, at the thought of a bunch of displaced people, learning the lyrics 'Pack up your troubles in your old kit bag and smile, smile, smile.'

My parents and I were lucky. We didn't have to learn our English at Bonegilla. I'm not sure my father would ever have cottoned on to 'Roaming In The Gloaming'.

I spoke at a very young age. My mother swore that I could string sentences together, in German, when I was eighteen months old. As soon as we arrived in Australia, my parents wanted me to learn English. They encouraged me to play with the Australian girl next door. They thought that would be the best way for me to learn the language.

One day the girl's mother arrived at our place in a state of agitation. Her daughter, she said, was speaking strangely, and she would rather my parents didn't send me over to play any more. I hadn't picked up any English. The girl next door had started to speak German. My mother loved that story. For her, it was an example of how strong-willed I was.

In Germany, my mother had talked to me in German. It was my native tongue. I ditched it as soon as I could, and forgot that it was once my mother tongue. I didn't want to remember. I didn't want to speak German. I didn't want to *be* German. Because I was born in Germany, people have assumed I was German. I hate that assumption and I have tried to feel more moderately about it, but I have a visceral reaction to being seen as German. It makes me feel agitated and ill.

I studied German for years at Uni High. My mother was really pleased. She thought that it would make things safer for me should the Nazis ever arrive in Australia. The Nazis would see my eloquence in their mother tongue, which would make it harder for them to murder me, she thought. So I studied my German nouns and verbs and I recited Goethe and Schiller. I had no memory of ever being fluent in the language, but I often wondered why I knew how to say things we hadn't covered in class.

Then one year all of my German went out of my head. It was the same year many other things went out of my head. I was about eighteen. I couldn't recall the simplest German words or expressions. I couldn't believe I had buried all that German. I had studied French for the same number of years, and could make my way, albeit haltingly, around Paris. But all of my German was lost to me. It stayed lost for decades.

Six months ago I bought a German phrase book – *Schiesse: The Real German You were Never Taught at School.* I bought it for my elder daughter who has retained the German she learnt at school and university. I thought she would find it hilarious. I was reading phrases such as, *Mach mich nicht an* (Don't mess with me), *Mir ging der*

Arsch auf Grundeis (I was scared shitless) and *Dieser alter Grabbelheini hat schon wieder versucht mir unter den Rock zu fassen* (Can you believe it, that old letch was trying to get his hand under my skirt again). I was laughing and laughing.

I realised, with a shock, that I was laughing at the German. I was sitting alone in my room, laughing at how hilarious some of the German phrases and word orders were. I don't know what unlocked my German. Maybe some of my anger and fear have diminished. Maybe I don't have to associate the language so strongly with its people and their past.

Part of my need to write comes out of a need to document my parents' past. To let people know what happened to them, and to all the other Jews. There were so many terrible things that were allowed to happen. And they all happened because so many people agreed that the world could afford to lose a few of its Jews. Or all of its Jews. They agreed overtly and enthusiastically, or by their agreement to look away. Individuals agreed, governments agreed, politicians and diplomats agreed, religious leaders and communities agreed, welfare organisations agreed and newspapers and radio stations and newsreel companies agreed.

What they agreed to was a carefully orchestrated and systematically carried out plan in which the millions of Jews in Europe were gradually stripped of all their rights until they could barely survive. Then they were herded together, imprisoned and cut off from the outside world. In these isolated ghettos, the Jews were starved and terrorised and tortured, before being shipped off to concentration camps to be murdered.

These brief paragraphs neatly skip over all the horrendous details of human horror. And that's what I didn't want to do, in my writing; skip over the horror. When I wrote *The Auschwitz Poems*, I wanted the book to be read easily. I wanted people to pick it up in a bookshop, glance at the first page, and be halfway through the book before they knew they had begun. The poems are skinny, one or two-word lines. They look like skeletons or thin ghosts. You can read the whole book in thirty minutes. In later books, I interspersed the past and its horror with humour and love, as it is interspersed in my real life.

Being funny has always paid dividends for me. As a child, if I could make my mother laugh, it would make my day. It wasn't easy to get her to laugh. When I write something funny, I feel good. Sometimes I feel embarrassed at how hard I can laugh at something I have written. It seems so immodest. I noted what made my mother laugh and I would try several variations of similar themes to see if I could repeat my success.

I noted everything about my mother. The smallest change in her expression signified large things to me. I was trying to understand and to alleviate something I would never be able to comprehend – the enormity of her anguish. I noted every inflection in her voice and tried to interpret the subtlety missing in her English.

My mother couldn't answer personal questions. She couldn't afford to. She couldn't stop and think about what had happened to her and who she had lost. It was as though if she stopped to think, her thoughts might stop her permanently. So she busied herself. She cooked, she washed the dishes, she cleaned the floors and changed the bed linen, every day. While she was absorbed in this, she was all right. While she banged saucepans and scrubbed floors and hung sheets on the line, she was fine. But at night, when she was forced to be quiet, everything she had kept at bay came to her, and she often woke up screaming.

I knew that I couldn't ask my mother too many questions, but I was desperate to know what had happened, and desperate to know what was happening now. There were so many unsaid things in our house. Small explosive pockets dotted the air. Pockets of shame, degradation, bitterness, and guilt. They were secret pockets, never talked about. So many secrets. They seemed to spill out of cupboards and drawers. Nothing was what it seemed. They were not trying to be secretive. They were trying to protect me. My mother and father were trying to make new starts. So I listened for odd fragments of conversations, and tried to translate the quick Polish exchanges. I was on the look-out for glances or gestures that would reveal anything.

I still have a tendency to embroider everything with an elaborate interpretation. A simple event turns into a mass of possibilities, in my hands. It is just as well that there is an outlet for these sorts of machinations, in fiction. When I write, I can tie up loose ends and frayed edges and threads. I can order things. I can offer explanations, appease anxieties. I can make things make sense.

That's what putting the right words together does for me. It makes sense of a world that has often appeared senseless. When I order events, I restrain the random elements that cauterised my parents' lives.

My parents often told me that I couldn't trust anyone other than them. They knew what people were capable of. But when anyone offered them any kindness, they glowed. They were very quick to see the worst in people, but just as fast to see the best. I fought against the notion that most of the world was bad, and I think they did too. They were looking for goodness in people, despite themselves.

I continued that search, in my life and in my writing. Sometimes I want to make someone unredeemingly bad. I can manage to do it in my real life. I can be unforgiving and hateful. But in my writing, no matter how hard I try to prevent it, redeeming features seep through. I see kindness in unkind people, and compassion in the uncouth and uncomprehending. I have reconciliations between people I set out to separate. It seems to be out of my control.

All of my main female characters have been writers. A poet, a playwright, an obituary writer. I have an almost infantile belief in the power of words. The right words could change the world. The right words could move people.

I used to feel so happy when the other kids cried when I was telling my stories, as a kid. I was always making up stories. They were mostly stories of hardships. I remember looking at the kids' solemn expressions and occasional tears, and feeling an acute satisfaction. I was about eight.

I wanted to make people cry. I knew there was a lot to cry about. I wasn't yet clear about what it was, but I knew that in order to make people cry, I had to choose my words carefully.

I think the need to move people comes from growing up with the knowledge that very few people were moved by what happened to my parents and to all the other Jews. While Hitler was murdering Jew after Jew, American Jews were shopping in shopping centres and going to the movies. While hundreds of thousands, and then millions, of Jews were dying, America's quota for Jews went unfilled.

Britain also didn't want to admit too many Jews. There was a fear that allowing too many Jews into the country would create rampant anti-semitism. It was considered more reasonable to allow Jews to die than to risk what the then British Prime Minister, Neville Chamberlain, called the 'serious danger of arousing anti-semitic feelings in Great Britain'.

The British government also issued a White Paper in 1939, limiting Jewish immigration to Palestine to

75,000 people over the following five years. Australia and Canada were willing to take in some Jewish agricultural workers, but no professionals or merchants. Unfortunately, not a lot of Jews were agricultural workers.

Individuals, too, were nervous about the possibility of admitting Jews. In Britain and America protests were organised against the admission of Jewish doctors.

I didn't know these facts when I was small, but I knew the repercussion of these facts. I felt them in my bones. I inhaled them; I smelled them. I knew no one had cared.

I think one of the reasons funerals move me is that they are a sign of caring, a sign of being moved. I hate tepid funerals, the sort where slow speeches are given and everyone keeps a stiff upper lip. I feel winded if there are not overt expressions of grief. I want to rewrite the eulogies and the speeches. I want to reorder the words to allow people to weep. I have been overly emotional even when I haven't known the deceased very well. But then I am quietened by the sight of a hearse or a gathering of mourners.

Recently there was an item on the news about a funeral parlour in the Bronx which had burned down. Two firemen were hurt, the reporter said, but the five bodies that were stored there were unharmed. I was struck by the reporter's concern about the bodies being unharmed. I thought that death meant you were out of harm's way. I wondered, aloud, how the bodies had escaped harm. 'They were probably in the fridge,' my husband said.

This made me think about an article I had read, in the *New York Times*, about the contents of fridges. The researchers had found that people now had less food in their fridges, but more cold drinks. As a result, they were redesigning fridges to hold more cold drinks and less food. The article listed a series of odd things people kept in their fridges: batteries, jewellery, rolls of film, a writer's man-uscript. The writer was worried about a possible fire.

I had forgotten to worry about the possibility of fire. I have been writing this book by hand. I write all of my books by hand, but I usually type up each chapter before beginning the next one. This time, however, I had planned to type the whole book when I finished the last chapter. After I read the fridge article, I began storing the chapters in the fridge. My husband said it was going to be one of the few manuscripts to exude an aroma of pesto sauce and parmesan cheese.

I stopped keeping the manuscript in the fridge after a few weeks. The manuscript was getting damp. I was wrapping it in layers and layers of plastic, and nestling it in the vegetable crisper, but it still seemed a bit limp. So I bought a small fireproof safe. I ordered it over the phone, and hoped my husband wouldn't be home when it was delivered. He doesn't worry much. He doesn't worry about fires or accidents or the weather. He laughed when he saw me wrap and unwrap my chapters in the fridge.

My safe arrived. It was compact and unobtrusive, and guaranteed to protect its contents, in a flash fire of two thousand degrees fahrenheit, for thirty minutes. It provided up to five times the fire resistance of ordinary insulated metal boxes which incinerate their contents during a fire. I was glad I hadn't bought an insulated metal box.

I learnt some interesting things from the pamphlet that came with the safe. Sleep with the bedroom door closed, the pamphlet said. Stop, drop and roll if your clothes catch fire. The safe had a combination lock which I decided I would never master. Anyway, locked, my safe might look as though it contained jewellery. So I left it unlocked. I put all my chapters, plus notes for a novel, inside the new safe.

I felt pretty pleased with myself. I stuck a note saying 'Documents Only' on the top of the safe, to let burglars know they needn't bother with it. I'm not sure why I worry about burglars. The crime rate in New York keeps dropping and dropping.

I have often been asked if it is hard to write in New York. I say no, it's not hard to write in New York, it's hard to write. Hard to discipline yourself, to sit alone in a room, day after day. Hard not to make phone calls, not to stay up too late, not to be diverted from what you are writing by all the diversions in life.

It is easy to isolate yourself in New York. No one drops in unexpectedly. You don't often bump into friends in the street. Neighbours are friendly, but they don't linger. And everyone respects work. Work is almost like a religion in New York. No one expects you to put anything above work. Having work to do is a sufficient reason for declining any invitation from the most highbrow to the most casual.

In a way, it *is* easier to write in New York. As soon as you step out in the street, you are instantly connected to the world. I went out for a cup of coffee this morning. I had been working for a few hours and needed to clear my head. I walked three blocks to Gourmet Garage on the corner of Broome and Mercer Streets.

I bought a coffee and sat on a bench outside the store. A shabbily-dressed black man approached me. 'I'm not going to hurt you,' he said. 'I'm only asking you for help. I live in a cheap hotel and if I can't pay my rent by the end of the week, I'll be evicted.' He showed me his ID card. I'm not sure why he showed me the card, or why I checked out the photograph on the card. I gave him a dollar. 'Thank you for looking at me ma'am,' he said. 'And thank you for listening.' I felt bad. I hadn't wanted to look at him, and I hadn't wanted to listen. 'God bless you, ma'am,' he said.

I went back to my coffee. A middle-aged woman with a dog approached me. 'I've got to go inside the store,' she said. 'Would you mind taking care of my dog?' I looked bewildered, which she took as a sign of consent. She handed me the dog's leash. 'His name is Dexter,' she said. 'He's a very good dog.'

Dexter didn't seem to mind being left with a stranger. He looked quite happy sitting on the sidewalk, with his tongue hanging out. That is, until another dog came into view. Dexter, a large, black labrador, leapt all over the other dog. I tried being firm. 'Sit Dexter, sit,' I said. But Dexter wasn't taking any orders from me. I couldn't drink my coffee. I needed both of my hands to restrain Dexter. By the time Dexter's owner reappeared, Dexter had returned to sitting obediently at my feet. 'You're a good person,' the woman said to me.

Just as I was finishing my coffee, Sean Lennon, son of John Lennon and Yoko Ono, walked by. He had brightly coloured yellow and green streaks through his hair, and he looked eerily like his father. He was much chunkier than I expected him to be. I walked home. This outing, this coffee break, this brief entry into the outside world, had taken twenty minutes.

I find it hard to balance the part of me that is quite gregarious with the part that loves being on my own. I often emerge from months of writing with a feeling of loneliness. 'I haven't got any friends,' I moan to my husband, like a lacklustre teenager. But in New York everyone is always coming and going, so no one takes your absence as a personal affront. People are used to seeing each other intermittently.

And I know that no matter what time of day or night I surface from my work, there is always life outside. Bookshops that stay open until midnight. Cafes that serve coffee all night. Twenty-four-hour supermarkets and convenience stores. Restaurants that don't close until dawn and others that open at dawn.

A French writer who lives nearby sleeps during the day and works at night. He says when he is stuck for an idea at three a.m., he steps out for a spot of recreational shopping at the local supermarket. He says it's the best time to go there. He can study the specials in peace. There are no customers, no check-out queues.

New Yorkers are very respectful of writers. If you're a bit odd, or forgetful, or shy and awkward, they put it down to your creativity. 'You're so *creative*,' they say to me and my husband. I'd never thought of myself as a creative person before I came to New York.

The neighbours in the building I live in put everything about me down to the fact that I am a writer. 'You're so quiet,' one woman said to me, 'but then writers are quiet people.' I *am* quiet by New York standards. I wasn't sure whether most writers I knew were quiet. I thought about it and decided they were.

When I asked another neighbour a perfectly innocuous question about her pregnancy she said, 'Oh, that's the novelist in you. Always asking questions.' I wondered whether it was the novelist in me who asked people questions, or the curious person in me, and how I could distinguish between them.

I have always been curious, and somehow ashamed of it. As though it is unseemly, almost obscene. I want to know more about other people than most people want others to know. I want to see behind the showered and deodorised image we all present to each other.

I grew up scrutinised, and I scrutinise others. I take in such a lot of detail about people that it is no wonder I feel embarrassed. I don't try to do this, I just do it. I remember, forever, the expression, the phrase, the clothes, the gestures. It's absurd. Frightening to some people. I can quote something someone said to me years ago. I remember ridiculous things, like the dates of other people's holiday travels, and details of their mother's illness. If I could have put this ability to absorb and remember things to better use, I could have been a rocket scientist.

My poor husband has been the chief victim of my observations. I love watching him. I love knowing the choreography of his ablutions. How he washes his hair and dries his arms and legs. I like watching him dress and undress. I like watching him paint. I know the angles of his brushstrokes as he underpaints a canvas, and the movements he makes when he paints in the detail. I love watching him eat. I once told a friend that I could describe every movement my husband made with his mouth when he ate an olive. She looked at me with an expression of distaste on her face and said, 'You like knowing that?'

I have spent a lot of my life trying to know things. Trying to make the unfamiliar familiar, and the familiar more familiar. Being the child of people who were forced to step out of their lives makes you feel forever out of step. I have been lucky. I have had a lot of help in finding my footing.

I found this help almost inadvertently. I was twenty-five, and I had tried every weight loss remedy known to man, to no avail. Someone suggested psychotherapy. I had no idea what that was. I would have gone to any therapy at that time. My third hypnotist had just told me I was unhypnotisable.

I found an analyst for my psychotherapy. In seven years of psychotherapy I hardly mentioned my parents' past. I hardly mentioned *my* past. I wept about my present.

Seven years later, I began my first analysis. The first year of this analysis was full of shock and revelation. Every session uncovered something. I felt as though everything I had kept cloaked and closeted was pouring out of me.

I had a very strict analyst, which suited me. She called me Mrs Rankin for the entire five years of the analysis. In the sessions, I didn't call her by her name, and in the outside world I referred to her by her initials.

Within the confines of her strict, no-nonsense structure, I felt safe. Safe enough to feel terrible. Safe enough to face what felt like terrible revelations about myself. Safe enough to begin to understand what I had been covering up.

There has always been someone to advise me against analysis. From my mother and father who, in the early days, saw it as something shameful that reflected badly on them as parents. I tried to explain to them that this wasn't the case. I said to them, over and over again, that I was the same child, with or without an analyst, and they were the same parents. The need for an analyst didn't imply any fault on their part. But they never swallowed that line, and were angry with me for a long time.

Years later, my father has mellowed. He has allowed me my own struggles. Struggles which were obliterated and diminished by his and my mother's struggles. He has become philosophical about it. He doesn't understand the value of paying someone large amounts of money to lie on a couch and talk, but he can see that it has been valuable.

My doctor in Melbourne also advised me against seeing an analyst. 'I don't think you need that,' he said, weeks after I'd been rushed to him in a state of high anxiety. Other people said the same. Seeing a psychiatrist would make me sick. Psychiatrists were all mad. I would go mad. Everyone was adamant. I didn't need a psychiatrist or a psychologist or an analyst. These were well-meaning, kind people.

It made others angry. 'You just need to talk to a friend,' one friend snapped at me. It was a refrain I was to hear many times over the years. Everyone seemed threatened for a different reason. I am not sure why I persevered against all of that opposition. I must have been desperate.

Even today, in the age of therapy and counselling,

analysis still threatens people. It seems all sorts of therapy are okay, but analysis is still under suspicion. In the twenty-five years since I went to my first analyst for psychotherapy, no one has ever suggested to me that analysis is an admirable thing to do, a beneficial or courageous thing to do. I don't talk about analysis much, but when I do, it provokes an agitated response.

I have heard artists and writers say they would never enter analysis. They don't want to disturb their neuroses. They are convinced that their neuroses are a conduit to their imaginations, and are prepared to battle with alcoholism or marital problems, or whatever their symptoms might be. They see it as the price they must pay for their creativity, which fits in well with the public image of the tortured artist. It is a romanticised image, one I have never subscribed to.

I have no imagination when my head feels as though it is in a bucket of mud. My fears and anxieties fetter me. Acting irrationally doesn't free me. It ties me up and exhausts me. My world feels fuzzy enough. I need clarity and insight. Analysis has uncluttered me. Analysis has freed me to feel, in my life, what I previously could feel only in my writing. I am the bold person I write about. It has taken me years to grow into her.

I used to have a clarity in my writing that I didn't possess in my days. Now the two are less distant. It has been a struggle to come to this clarity. I can see the insights and understandings in my work that, once written down, eluded my daily life again for years.

The struggle is really apparent in the diary I kept of my first analysis. I don't know why I kept the diary. I used to carry it with me to my sessions, and then sit in the car, afterwards, and fill up page after page. As though if I wrote down what I was learning about myself, it would become less nebulous and stay with me.

I wrote out every detail I could remember, then I wrote summaries of some of the sessions in point form, like guide lines. But I would forget the points and forget the point of them.

I can't bear to look at those diaries now. They are filled with lists of things to aspire to. Lists of warning signs, things to look out for, things to ignore. They are full of declarations and despair. The same sentiments repeated endlessly.

The analysis diary that really distresses me is the one that covers my mother's illness and death. I was so frightened of losing my mother, I froze in the weeks before her death.

I didn't say what I could have said. What I have wished I had said, hundreds of times, in the years since. I wanted to tell her how much I loved her. I wanted her to know that she would always be inside my heart, always be a part of me. I wanted her to know that nothing would ever separate us. But she didn't want to know that she was dying. And I was frozen.

I have seen others in the same position. Absent, emotionally or physically. And I rush to reassure them that it is a lifetime of being joined that matters, not a few last-minute phrases. But the diary still bothers me.

I keep these diaries in a locked suitcase in my closet, as though they have to be contained under lock and key. I have always imbued pieces of paper, with words on them, with an exaggerated importance. I keep notes my children have written me, in my purse. I have drawers of letters from them, and letters and faxes from my father. I've got hundreds of messages my husband has left me. Small messages that say he's at the post office or gone to see an exhibition.

I have one piece of paper that is almost in tatters. The librarian at Glamorgan, the primary school my children went to in Melbourne, wrote my younger daughter a note which says that she will be fined unless she returns her library book by Thursday. Across the librarian's terse note, my daughter, who was a very shy, small girl, wrote, in her five-year-old handwriting, *Well fuck you*. I find it hard to throw any of these written words away.

I look at my father's faxes and his sweet handwriting, and the precise way he gets straight to the point, in his less than perfect English. He has a poetry in his lines and has always had. I can't bear to throw any of his letters out. In the last few letters, he asked me to correct his spelling. I didn't bother, and he was very annoyed. 'Where are the spelling corrections?' he faxed. I said that there were not many mistakes. He said could I please write out each mistake and the correction. So I did. But I was sad. I love the mistakes. *Sytuation, traying, realy, stil.* They make the words my father's and not anybody else's.

Over the last few years, I have become more casual about my pages. My letters and my work. I no longer have to tie elastic bands around chapters of a novel to stop them from taking off. I don't feverishly clip every page to another page as though the pages will get lost if they are not pinned and attached. The pages no longer represent the life in me. I have my own life.

Analysis has given me back my own life. The life I squashed because I felt guilty for having one. Guilty for feeling joy and excitement when there was so much death and so much suffering. I have been given this life back, slowly. It has returned to me in bits and pieces. Sometimes it has burst out of me, awkwardly and all over the place. I want to ride a bike and run and walk, all at once.

It feels heartbreaking to look back on what it took to get this life. I don't want to remember all the symptoms, all the sadness. I had almost a decade and a half of intermittent, unbearable anxiety symptoms. Agoraphobia, depression, panic attacks.

I can remember driving along Punt Road, swaying in and out of terrible anxiety. Covered in sweat, and with my heart pounding. I never wanted to stop the car. My fear was that I'd pull over and pass out. Then I'd be carted off to hospital. An anonymous, unconscious body. Patient number XYZ. I kept several identification documents in the car, so people would know I wasn't just a number.

This fantasy of being just another statistic was one

of the symptoms of my inability to separate my life from my parents' life. Particularly from my mother's life. Were we both in the Lodz Ghetto? Were we both in Auschwitz? I could describe the layout of the Lodz Ghetto. I knew the names of the streets and the boundaries. I could describe the three wooden foot bridges. I could describe the excrement removal wagon, drawn by Jewish women instead of horses. I was familiar with the Most Blessed Mary Church, where down and feathers confiscated from Jews were sorted and sent to Germany.

Was I there? No, but I might as well have been. I wished I had been. I wanted to join myself to my mother. My beautiful mother who had trouble joining herself to anybody, after the war.

To try and quell my anxiety, I took pills. Valium, mostly. Then I added Inderal, a beta blocker. I took enough Valium to knock someone else out, but I was still anxious. I swallowed Valium in cars, offices, airports and bathrooms, all around Australia. I became adept at slipping the tablets out of their foil-covered sachets, with no noise and little movement. I could, if I had to, swallow them without water. Although I almost choked in a theatre, once, when a Valium stuck in my gullet. I was trying to swallow the pill to lower my anxiety about being trapped in the theatre. After that, I avoided theatres for years. I still prefer an aisle seat in case I have to make a rapid exit.

It was hard to get enough Valium. I would try to look casual when I asked my doctor for more, but I felt like a thief, if not a hardened criminal, as I off-handedly asked for another prescription. I asked friends if they could get prescriptions from their GPs. People overlooked my requests. Nobody wanted to aid me, but no one wanted to confront me. I stashed my supply of Valium away in safe places. I was as secretive and subversive as a heroin addict. I never told anybody how much I took.

In the early eighties, the Melbourne psychiatrist Ainslie Meares asked me if I would write his biography. I had written a profile of him for *Pol* magazine.

Dr Meares was a tall, aristocratic, handsome man in his seventies. I had never been close to anyone that age. I had a reverence towards Ainslie that I never would have had if I'd had grandparents. I was thrilled at the idea of being close to him, and learning from him.

What I didn't know was that Ainslie Meares wanted an *autobiography*. It took me a while to notice that he was dismissing all of my questions, and feeding me with information that he wanted noted about himself. I couldn't argue with him. I was struck dumb in front of this tall, silver-haired man. I was stuck in the role of good grandchild. I started swallowing Valium before each of our interviews. As Ainslie Meares changed from a loving patriarchal figure, to a stern, agitated and domineering man, I swallowed more and more Valium.

Our roles were established by the size and position of the chairs Ainslie had arranged for us to sit in. He sat me in a low armchair in his office, while he sat, elevated by several inches, in an ornate upright chair. He faced the window and I faced him.

Armed with enough Valium, I disagreed with him, and attempted to ask questions of my own. It made him furious. This project was not progressing in the way he had planned. He started to go out of his way to hinder any initiative I might have. He made sure that I only spoke to those friends and acquaintances he wanted me to see. He asked other people not to agree to be interviewed by me. I was swallowing so much Valium in an effort to swallow my anger at Ainslie, that I frightened myself.

One day I told him that I could no longer continue with the biography. I must have seemed more malleable than I was because he appeared stunned by my decision.

One of Ainslie's chief complaints about me was that I was too analytical. But being analytical has saved me. Analysis has allowed me to feel that the world is a safer place. Safer, not safe. I no longer have to carry enough ID on me to identify a battalion. I no longer have the emergency kit I carried in my handbag for years. It contained Band-Aids, scissors, tweezers, needles and thread, a torch, antiseptic lotion, burn cream, headache pills, Lifesavers and lipstick.

I no longer have the list of phone numbers I needed to have on me at all times. I don't pack a parcel of food for every outing over twenty minutes. I haven't taken any drugs − Valium, Inderal, or anything else − for six or seven years. I'm reluctant to take a headache pill. I've kept the tortoise shell pill box I used to keep my pills in. I left one Valium in there. When I look at it, I remember all the other Valium and feel tearful. One day I'll throw it away.

I switched to Allen's Butter Menthols as an interim measure when I stopped swallowing Valium. The Butter Menthols seemed to calm me down. Their old advertisement, familiar from my childhood, was still on the side of the packet. *Butter soothes the throat. Menthol clears the head.* All of my handbags have old, sticky Butter Menthols in them.

Analysis is something that happens almost outside the real world. And yet the understanding and exchanges that take place inside small, mostly quietly-lit rooms, anchor you and connect you to the real world. Lying, almost motionless some days, on my analyst's couch, grounded me. When I moved off the couch, I really wanted to move.

I used to twist my fingers and wrench my wrists in some of my more painful analysis sessions. I moved on to contortions of another sort. Bench presses, dead-lifts and squats. It was as though all the hours of lying still, connected me to my desire for movement. I began to walk. To power walk. And I began to lift weights.

Some days I would grimace in pain as I lifted myself up from the couch. It always made me want to laugh. The pain that was twisting my expression, was not psychic pain, for a change. It was my pecs or my glutes.

I love it when my muscles ache as a result of a work-out. It is a relief to ache from a straightforward cause. No interpretation is needed for sore hamstrings or sore calves. In fact, it's a symptom of muscles having extended themselves, which is what you want when you lift weights.

I am so proud of my weight-lifting. I tell perfect strangers, who haven't asked, that I lift weights. There's not much they can say. Most people look polite. I love it, I say. The words burst out of me. I can no longer contain my excitement.

Sometimes when I'm writing, I find myself prodding my biceps or pecs, in an absent-minded rhythm. My muscles are solid evidence of the changes I have made. Sometimes when I'm submerged in the past, in my writing, I need that evidence to show me that I am no longer there.

Being in analysis and being a writer are each seen as unorthodox pursuits. In each case, whether it's from an analyst's couch or from behind a writer's desk, you are engaged in a lonely and solitary struggle to connect with a larger universe.

Writing and analysis are long-term options. Neither has instant rewards or gratification, although the pleasure of writing is pretty heady. Nothing occupies me as wholly as writing. I am completely immersed. Time passes and I am oblivious to it. My world has stood still. Safely ensconced and encapsulated between crisp pages of white paper. Two hours can feel like two minutes.

Sometimes I only move because I am stiff or need a piss. I have missed whole days holed up in my study. I have to ask others what the weather was like, or whether anything earth-shattering occurred in the world.

My writing is all mine. I need no one's help. I do it by myself. It is my private world and no one can encroach on it. This may be a more important aspect of writing, for me, because I'm female. Women have to share so many parts of their lives. It is rare for us to have a domain that is exclusively our own. I share all of my life with my husband and with my children. But when I write, I am on my own, with only my own references, my own feelings and my own interruptions.

Sometimes, when what I am writing seems too painful, I wish I had been a chef, or a restaurant owner or a caterer. I wonder if I would have had a more cheerful disposition if I'd spent my days choosing herbs and vegetables and cheeses. There's something uplifting about fresh produce. About markets, early in the morning. And something very satisfying about feeding people.

It is a fantasy that I've had for a long time. When I was very young, I longed to open a sandwich shop. I wanted to be able to butter enormous piles of sliced white bread. With butter from a large glass container. Butter that had been so softened it smeared the surface of the bread with one sweep of the flat palette knife they used to use in Australian delicatessens.

As a child I loved everything about sandwich

making. I loved the rectangular plastic containers of sliced tomatoes, sliced cucumbers, sliced beetroot, chopped egg and shredded lettuce. I loved the slices of ham and corned beef and cheese that sat, in squat stacks, on the work benches, waiting for the lunch-hour rush.

I could watch the women spread and fill and fold and wrap, for hours. They were so efficient. Each sandwich was sliced in perfect triangles and wrapped, symmetrically, in the square waxed sheets. I wanted my own supply of waxed paper and brown paper bags. I had ideas for sandwich fillings. I suggested to the woman in the delicatessen, on Nicholson Street, that maybe she could put horseradish on the corned beef. 'What's horse-radish?' she said.

I still enjoy making sandwiches. I enjoy inventing different fillings. Goat cheese and oil-cured olives. Aged cheddar and rhubarb chutney. Turkey breast, peach jam and pepper. Would I have been rich if I'd stuck to sandwiches or to cooking? Who knows? Horseradish and corned beef still sounds good to me.

It's a nice fantasy. But it is a fantasy. I can't imagine a life in which I didn't write. I think I am so lucky to be able to do something that gives me so much pleasure. And something that is so simple. Writing requires no expensive equipment, and it is portable. I carry a pen and a notebook wherever I go. I never have to be disconnected from my writing. I can remain as attached as I want to.

I am ending my six-year analysis as I end this book. It is my last analysis. I have emerged from it with a physicality I have never possessed. It is funny to think that all those hours I spent lying on a couch propelled me into physical activity. I can run. I can walk for miles. I am a reasonable swimmer. I am not the person I once was. For the first time in my life I have a strong sense of my own good fortune, as well as an understanding of the limits of my ability to tolerate this good fortune.

For someone who doesn't like change, I have made a lot of changes, and I am grateful to the analysis for allowing me to make those changes. Grateful to not have remained locked into routines, structures or locations. I am looking forward to civilian life, a life in which my days and months are not structured by the times and dates of my analysis sessions.

Part of me is afraid of this ending. I have always feared endings. And part of me is pleased. I see it as a beginning. I have dreams of bicycling through China and walking through Italy. I have contemplated cross-country skiing and even thought about rock climbing.

I often used to wonder what sort of life I would have had if Hitler hadn't intervened. Would I have been a Jewish-Polish Princess? My father's family were very wealthy. Would I have been less anxious? Not have had to endure years of anxiety symptoms? Would I have been less fearful? Confident of my place in the world?

Would I have been relaxed and cheerful and charming?
Who knows?

I'm not sure that I would have ended up a bicycling,
walking, potential rock-climbing, cross-country skier.
I'm very glad I have.

Lily Brett
Just Like That

'Brett's book is a joy'
ELLE

This is the story of Esther Zepler, modern woman. Happily
married wife of artist Sean, and mother of Zachary, Zelda and
Kate, she lives in a New York loft, enjoys long lunches with her
pregnant friend Sonia, and writes obituaries for a living. But
life is never smooth, especially for the daughter of Auschwitz
survivors, and her father Edek, communicating via fax and
phone from Australia, is an insistent reminder of who she is
and where she comes from.

'funny, moving, informative and instructive in a way that is
entirely its own. Reading it creates a similar effect as reading
Catch 22 the first time round'
CANBERRA TIMES

'You'll love the family, laugh at the jokes, cry (perhaps) at their
situation in life'
BRISBANE SUNDAY MAIL

'serves as a song of praise to the modern world in all its
pathos, bathos, silliness, tragedy and heroism'
AUSTRALIAN BOOK REVIEW

AVAILABLE FROM PAN MACMILLAN

Lily Brett
Mud in my Tears

I want to say
I love you
in a new way
with a new face

and I am caught with my words
poised in mid-air
hovering out of reach
over there.

Mud In My Tears is Lily Brett's sixth collection of poetry. Her
first book, *The Auschwitz Poems*, won the 1987 Victorian
Premier's Award for poetry.

In these moving and varied poems, Lily Brett explores her
roles as daughter, mother, wife and friend in a family full of
love but haunted by the war. In a language steeped in
memories, full of vivid images and dark humour, these poems
leave an enduring mark upon the reader.

PRAISE FOR LILY BRETT:

The Auschwitz Poems
'The poems are something quite amazing . . . intensely
wrought, artistically, yet pure and direct and real and
life-size'
Ted Hughes

DRAWINGS BY DAVID RANKIN

AVAILABLE FROM PAN MACMILLAN